IMAGES
of America

ROCK HALL

On the Cover: The Rock Hall Fire Company, pictured here shortly after its opening in the spring of 1928, was built for $6,000. The members of the fire company provided most of the labor. The firehouse was used from 1928 until 1950, when it was replaced. (Photograph courtesy of Kevin Hemstock and the *Kent County News*.)

IMAGES
of America

ROCK HALL

Robin Wood Kurowski,
Patricia Joan O. Horsey,
and R. Jerry Keiser

ARCADIA
PUBLISHING

ISBN 978-0-7385-5310-8

Published by Arcadia Publishing
Charleston SC, Chicago IL, Portsmouth NH, San Francisco CA

Printed in the United States of America

Library of Congress Catalog Card Number: 2007935141

For all general information contact Arcadia Publishing at:
Telephone 843-853-2070
Fax 843-853-0044
E-mail sales@arcadiapublishing.com
For customer service and orders:
Toll-Free 1-888-313-2665

Visit us on the Internet at www.arcadiapublishing.com

Contents

ACKNOWLEDGMENTS

The authors are indebted to many people for sharing information, family photographs, and personal collections to make this book possible. We also want to acknowledge the many who shared photographs but may not find them in this book. Space was limited, and many of the wonderful photographs had to be eliminated for this volume. These photographs may be used in a second volume, and we invite readers to submit additional photographs should we decide to do a second book.

Among those who contributed photographs and information that enabled this book to written are Vicky Anderson, Anna "Miss Rock Hall 2006" Ashley, Beverly "BeBe" Ashley, Danny Ashley, Joanne Ashley, Kathy Ashley, Orville and Janet Ashley, Anna "Miss Rock Hall 2007" Baker, Kay Barnes, H. Edward Beekman Jr., Steve Belcak, Bill and Mary Betts, Wayne and Nancy Brady, Becky "Queen of Rock Hall 1957" Hepron Brilz, Tracy Carter Brilz, Joyce Christian, Norris "Hick" Clark, Maria Ashley Coakley, Cliff "Sniff" Coleman, Madelyn Cornelius, Rose Elma Cornelius, Vernice Covany, Adam Cox, Harriet Creighton, Jerry Creighton, Cindy Crouch, Maddy Crouch, Bill and Louise Dannenberg, Heather Davidson, Helen DeFord, Joe Dickerson, Blanche Dlugoborski, Quentin and Ida Mae Dulin, Helen Durding, Debbie "Dinks" Edwards, Emory "Pie" Edwards, Donna Hubbard Edwards, Jennifer Edwards, John Daniel and Joanne Edwards, Danny and Rita Elburn, Jay and Miriam Elburn, Steve and Marilyn Figlin, Cathy Fisher, Ronnie and Robin Fithian, Jean Foreman, Naudain and Oneida Francis, Jeanie Geibel, Abby Glenn, Myra Glenn, Karl Gottesman, Bob and Alice "Inki" Greenwald, John Albert Groves, Tiffani Gagalski Hague, Jack Heffner, Bill and Pat Heinefield, Kevin Hemstock (editor, *Kent County News*), Ann Hennessy, Frank and Gail Hepbron, Dennis and Laura Herrmann, Judy Hickman, Herman Edward and Christy Hill, Jeff and Margaret Hill, Historical Society of Kent County, Cope Hubbard, Bobby Jacob, Dawn Jacobs, Jay Jacobs, Betty Jacobs, Albert "Buffalo" and Betty Ann Jacquette, Curtis Jacquette, Jack Jester, Sandy Joiner, Carolyn Jones, Gordon and Linda Kimble, Linda Kraus, Ed and Rosalie Kuechler, Rita Kulley, Ed Kurowski, Joe and Ellen Labuda, Clay Larrimore, Elmer and Ann Leary, Edgar Legg, Stephanie Loller, Dorothy McKenney, Anne Willson Grim McKown, Rose Marie Metcalf, Robin Myers, Pat Newman, Edward "Bunky" Nordhoff, Gregory Nordhoff, Mike and Anna Nordhoff, Rick and Dawn Nordhoff, Tim and Janet Nordhoff, George and Peggy Parsons, Edward "Pete" and Rose Ellen Reihl, Jimmy and Mary Reihl, Patsy Reihl, Jim and Joanne Rich, Pamela Cowart Rickman, the Rock Hall Museum, Mary Saner, Larry Simns, Diane Smith, Leroy and Charlotte Squares, Carl "Snowball" and Pam Stenger, Julie J. Stephens, Ernest "Tot" and Millie Strong, Jane Strong, Joan Strong, Mildred Strong, Aleah Sullivan, Alvin Suskin, Edna Marie Hubbard Sutton, Jane and Carroll Thompson, John and Denise Thompson, Ethel Toulson, John "T-Bird" Toulson, Burgess and Betty Tucker, Tom Tucker, Joe and Cecil Unruh, Bernadette Van Pelt, Nancy Walls, Bill and Debbie Weldon, Harry "Chucky" and Jan White, Jim "Crow" Wilson, Mary Sue and Art Willis, Jean Willson, Honey Wood, and Michael Wootton.

We'd also like acknowledge the following for their special support: Frank Ozman Smith, Carli Crew Smith, James Thomas Ozman Landon, Baker Fallon Horsey Landon, Kathryn Macey Smith, Jennifer Ashley Horsey, Lauren Nicholson Horsey, Alexia Grace Nadel, and Jacob and Evelyn Keiser.

INTRODUCTION

On July 24, 1608, Capt. John Smith and 12 of his men boarded a shallop and started on their second voyage of the summer up the Chesapeake Bay. Leaving Jamestown, the weather soon carried their boat past the Potomac River to the headwaters of the bay, where Captain Smith and his crew discovered the four tributary rivers that fed into the bay. Captain Smith entered one of those tributaries on what his men called the "Easterne Shore" of the bay. The tributary that Smith and his men entered is referred to as the Sassafras River today; however, in 1608, Captain Smith named it "Tockwough" after the Native Americans who lived in the towns on the banks of the river. After several good days of trading with the Native Americans, Captain Smith and his men sailed from Tockwough in northern Kent County and headed south. While sailing south, Captain Smith and his men skirted the Kent County coastline; its many inlets and tributaries have caused more than one sailor to remark on the similarities it shared with the Barbary Coast. Before heading west toward the other shore of the bay, Captain Smith and his shallop continued exploring these waterways and went as far south as present-day Swan Creek.

Swan Creek meanders slowly southward toward the Chesapeake Bay through the many granges of Kent County. As the creek reaches the bay, it engraves a natural harbor into the fertile soil of its banks. This harbor would soon draw fishermen who would use the harbor as a refuge from the bay in which they could safely fish. Soon after the arrival of the fisherman, and probably drawn by the tales they told of the tremendous hauls of rockfish, recently freed Irish indentured servants would be lured to the area by subsistence fishing and farming. It is from those referenced anecdotes of hauls of rockfish that Rock Hall would derive its name.

Rock Hall is a waterman's town, famous for its rockfish, oysters, and crabs and for the men who fished the waters of the bay for them. In addition to being a community famous for its relationship with the water, Rock Hall has played an important part in Kent County. In the early days, Capt. Thomas Harris practically built Rock Hall into a mercantile center for the southern part of Kent County. His ships would carry tobacco and grain from the surrounding areas to market by either using his freighters, which came right up to the farms, or by loading them at Rock Hall Wharf. Rock Hall Wharf was the mercantile center of the area, and most of the commercial activity in the area centered on Rock Hall and the wharf. It would remain that way until the railroad provided a more economical way to transport goods to market in the northeast.

Rock Hall would be the gateway to Kent County and the northeast. Several luminaries would traverse the county coming through Rock Hall, including George Washington, Thomas Jefferson, Benjamin Franklin, and James Madison, to name a few. In addition, an Eastern Shore Revolutionary War hero, Lt. Col. Tench Tilghman, carrying the news of Gen. Charles Cornwallis's capitulation at Yorktown, crossed the Chesapeake Bay by ferry, landing at Rock Hall. Tilghman then galloped north through Kent County toward the Congress in Philadelphia, thereby signaling the end of the Revolutionary War.

Over the years, Rock Hall continued to be a community that depended on the water and watermen for their way of life. However, tourism would become a larger part of Rock Hall's economy and history when Rock Hall was selected to be the host of the 1938 Fishing Fair. The Fishing Fair, with the Pennsylvania Railroad promising fishing trains and hundreds of anglers descending on the town, would forever make Rock Hall associated with great fishing, and along with that would come the tourists and boaters.

As Rock Hall celebrates 300 years, it is our hope that this book will be a small part of the celebration providing a glimpse into Rock Hall's rich cultural history. We realize it in no way covers the area and its progression through time, but perhaps for those who have spent their lives in the area, it will offer a pleasant reminder of days gone by. For those unfamiliar with the town, it will be received as an invitation for further investigation about this beautiful town on the Eastern Shore of Maryland.

The proceeds of this book go to the Rock Hall Museum and the Rock Hall Branch of the Kent County Public Library.

One

Our History and Institutions

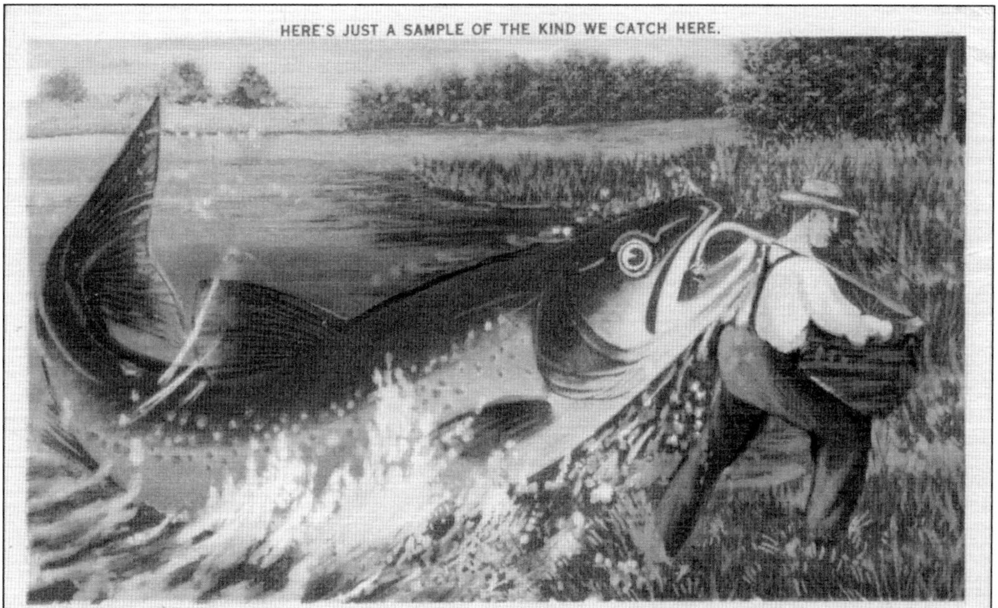

Famous for great fishing and trying to capitalize on the notoriety that followed the Fishing Fair of 1938, this "Greetings from Rock Hall" postcard portrays the town as a sportsman's destination during the early 20th century. (Courtesy of R. Jerry Keiser.)

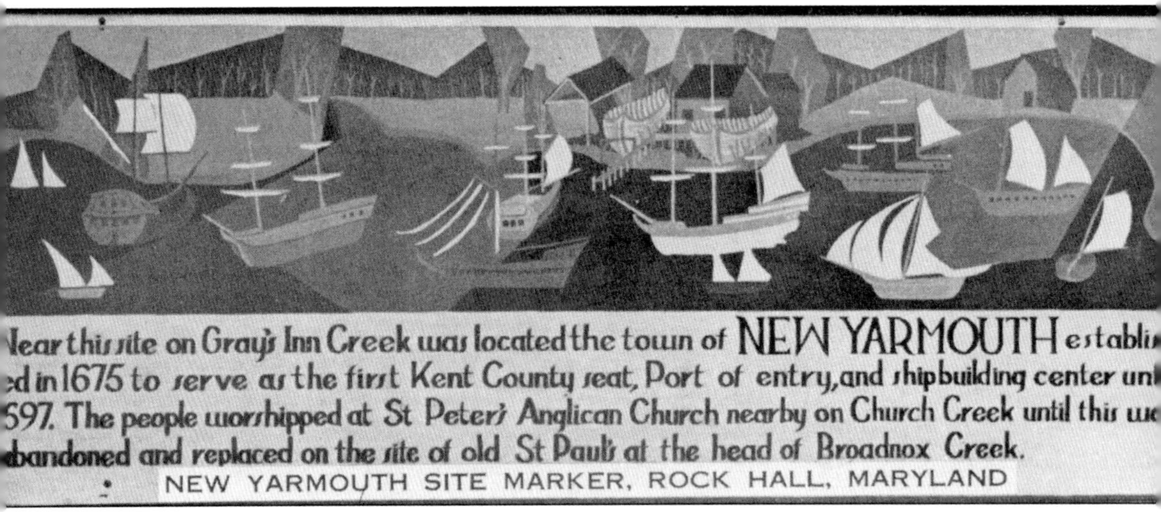

This site marker at Rock Hall, Maryland, celebrates New Yarmouth, a town that no longer exists. "Near this site on Gray's Inn Creek was located the town of New Yarmouth established in 1675 to serve as the first Kent County seat, Port of entry, and shipbuilding center until 1697. The people worshipped at St. Peter's Anglican Church nearby on Church Creek until this was abandoned and replaced on the site of Old St. Paul's at the head of Broadnox Creek." (Credit: Rock Hall Civic Association, Inc., Rock Hall, Maryland; by Picto Cards Kaeser and Blair, Cincinnati, Ohio, 7-58; courtesy of Anne Willson Grim McKown.)

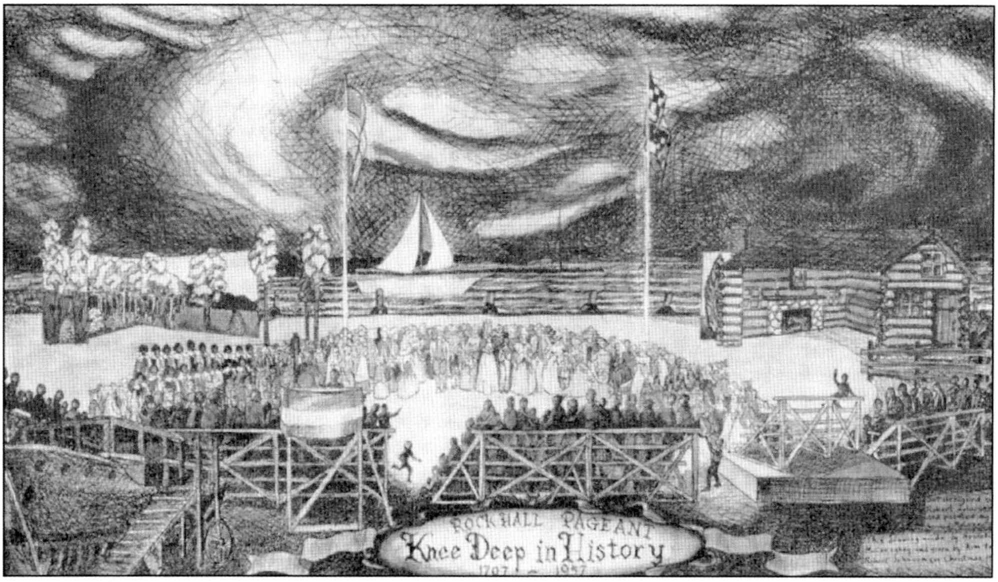

This sketch, *Knee Deep in History 1707–1957—Rock Hall Pageant*, depicts Washington landing at Rock Hall. The historical pageant *Knee Deep in History* was performed during the celebration of the 250th anniversary of the founding of Rock Hall, Maryland. (Drawing by Howard McConeghey; credit: Rock Hall Civic Association, Inc., Rock Hall, Maryland; by Picto Cards Kaeser and Blair, Cincinnati, Ohio, 7-58; courtesy of Anne Willson Grim McKown.)

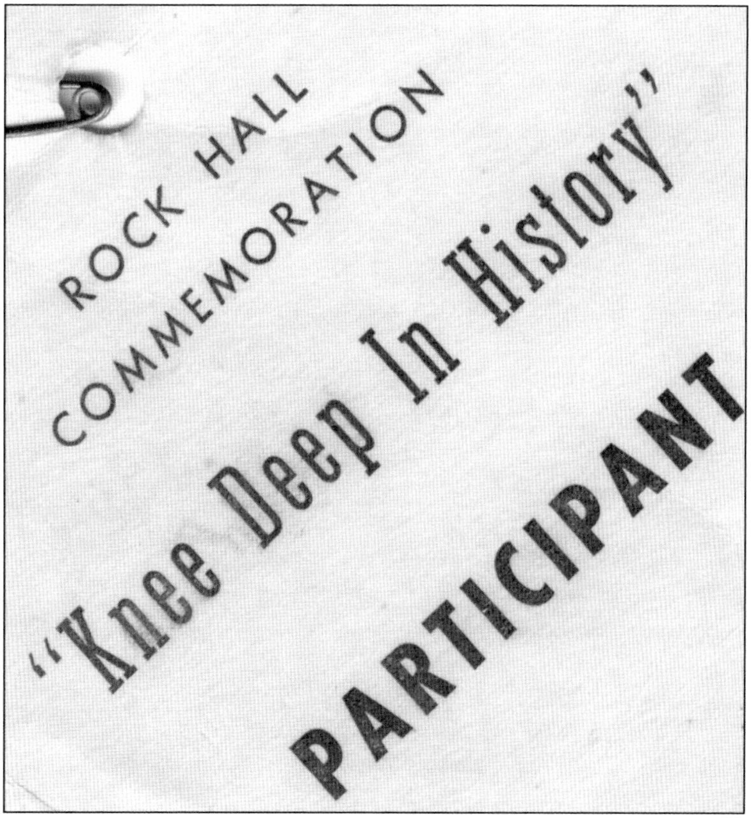

This tag was worn by the participants of the *Knee Deep in History* performance in 1957, which celebrated the 250th anniversary of the founding of Rock Hall. (Courtesy of Dorothy McKinney.)

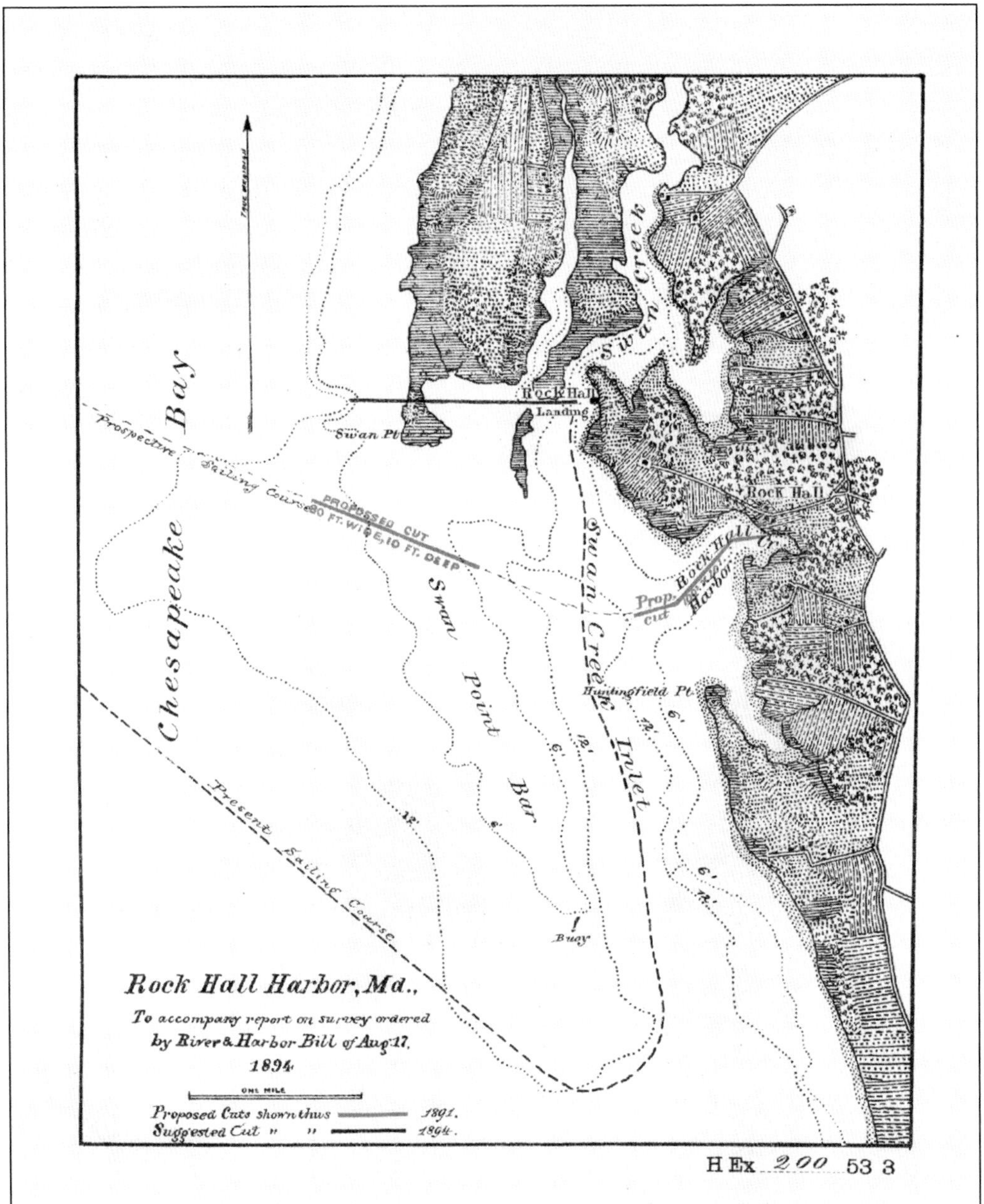

This map of Rock Hall Harbor accompanied a report ordered by the River and Harbor Act of August 17, 1894. The River and Harbor Act of 1894 authorized the secretary of the army to prescribe rules and regulations for the use, administration, and navigation of any canals and similar works of navigation owned, operated, or maintained by the United States. Rock Hall's harbor played an important roll in the early days of travel by boat. It has been said that George Washington, Tench Tilghman, Thomas Jefferson, and James Madison were among the notables who landed at the harbor during their journeys. (Courtesy of Steven Belcak and Adam Cox.)

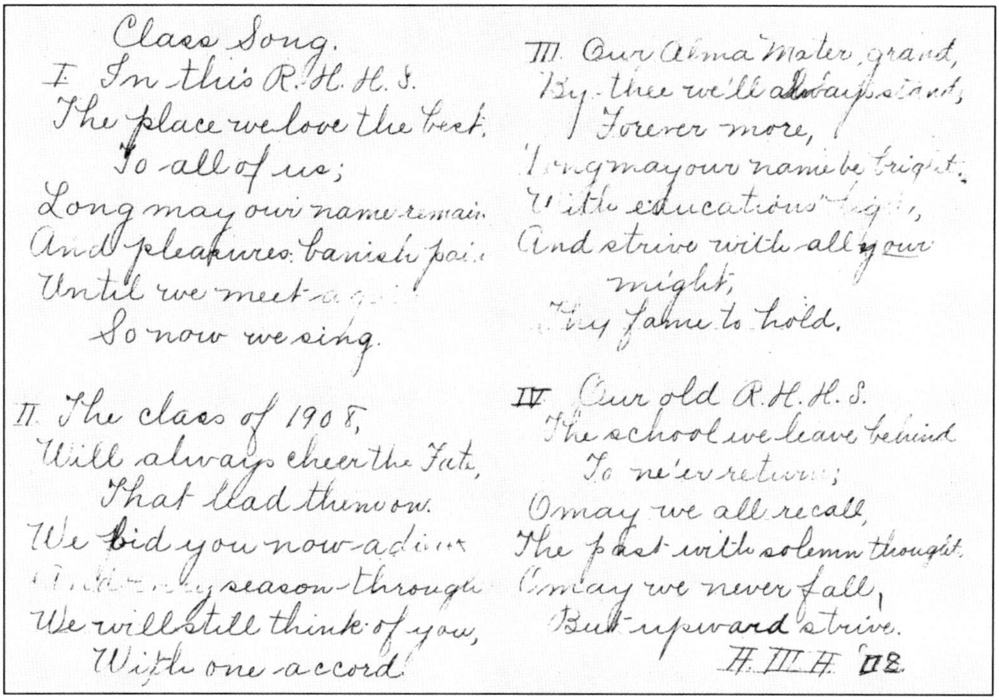

Class Song.

I. In this R.H.H.S.
The place we love the best;
To all of us;
Long may our name remain
And pleasures banish pain
Until we meet again
So now we sing.

II. The class of 1908,
Will always cheer the Fate,
That lead them on.
We bid you now adieu
And every season through
We will still think of you,
With one accord.

III. Our Alma Mater, grand,
By thee we'll always stand,
Forever more,
Long may our name be bright,
With education's light,
And strive with all your might;
Thy fame to hold.

IV. Our old R.H.H.S.
The school we leave behind
To ne'er return;
O may we all recall,
The past with solemn thought,
O may we never fall,
But upward strive.
R.H.H.S. '08.

Anna Mae Ayres Willson, a student in the class, signed this handwritten version of the Rock Hall class of 1908 class song. The first high school graduation exercises were held in a little schoolhouse at the Rock Hall crossroads in 1898. Walter Davis was the principal. The high school was eventually moved to a larger building in 1915. (Courtesy of Anne Willson Grim McKown.)

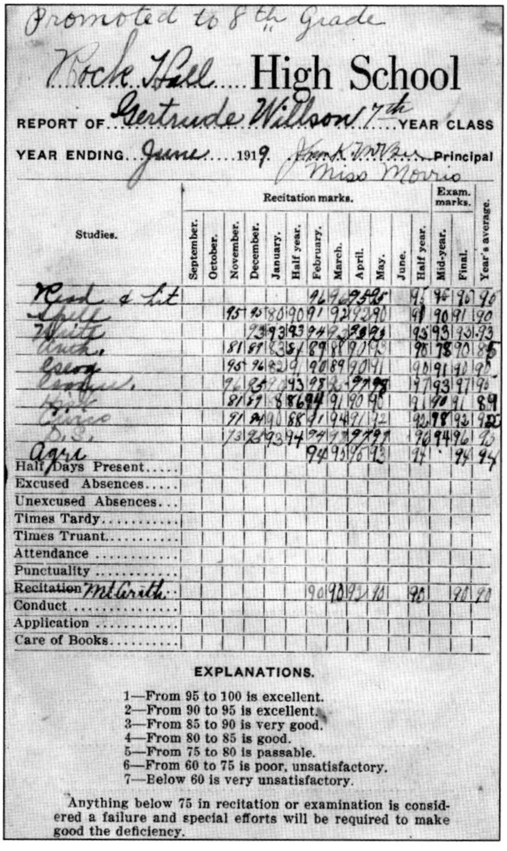

Promoted to 8th Grade

Rock Hall High School

REPORT OF Gertrude Willson 7th YEAR CLASS

YEAR ENDING June 1919. Frank T. McBee Principal

Miss Morris

Studies.	September.	October.	November.	December.	January.	Half year.	February.	March.	April.	May.	June.	Half year.	Exam. marks. Mid-year.	Final.	Year's average.
Read & Lit							96	96	95	95		95	96	90	90
Spell			95	95	80	90	91	92	92	90		91	90	91	90
Write				93	93	93	94	[illegible]	93	93		93	93	93	93
Arith.			81	89	83	85	89	88	90	93		90	78	90	85
Geog			95	96	82	91	90	89	90	91		90	91	90	90
Grammar			96	95	90	93	98	[illegible]	97	98		97	93	97	95
Hist			81	89	[illegible]	86	94	91	90	90		91	90	91	89
Civics			91	94	90	88	91	94	91	92		92	98	92	92
D.S.			73	93	93	94	94	[illegible]	97	97		96	94	96	95
Agri							94	95	96	93		94		94	94
Half Days Present															
Excused Absences															
Unexcused Absences															
Times Tardy															
Times Truant															
Attendance															
Punctuality															
Recitation McGrath							90	90	92	90		90		90	90
Conduct															
Application															
Care of Books															

EXPLANATIONS.

1—From 95 to 100 is excellent.
2—From 90 to 95 is excellent.
3—From 85 to 90 is very good.
4—From 80 to 85 is good.
5—From 75 to 80 is passable.
6—From 60 to 75 is poor, unsatisfactory.
7—Below 60 is very unsatisfactory.

Anything below 75 in recitation or examination is considered a failure and special efforts will be required to make good the deficiency.

Gertrude Willson's Rock Hall High School seventh-grade report card is dated June 1919. Mr. McBee was the principal. The early curriculum provided classes in typing, shorthand, French, and geometry, along with the required courses. The Rock Hall High School faculty included Miss Biddle, Miss Hadaway, Mr. Strang, Miss Fell, Miss Douglas, Mr. Guth, and Miss Morris in 1918. (Courtesy of Anne Willson Grim McKown.)

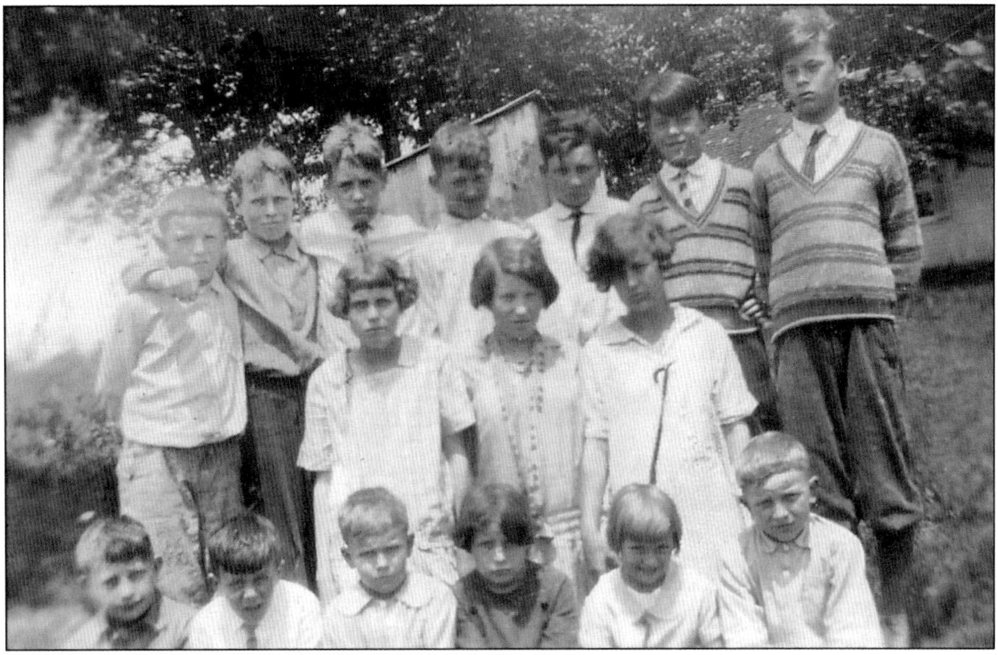

The Rock Hall High School class of 1926–1927 is pictured in this photograph from a private collection. Those who served as principals of both Rock Hall Elementary School and Rock Hall High School were Walter Davis, Mr. McBee, and W. A. P. Strang. The schools each had their own principals beginning with Bayard Ayres, who served as the principal at Rock Hall High School starting in the early 1940s. Lewis Davis and Robert Johnson followed Ayres as principal. (Courtesy of Anne Willson Grim McKown.)

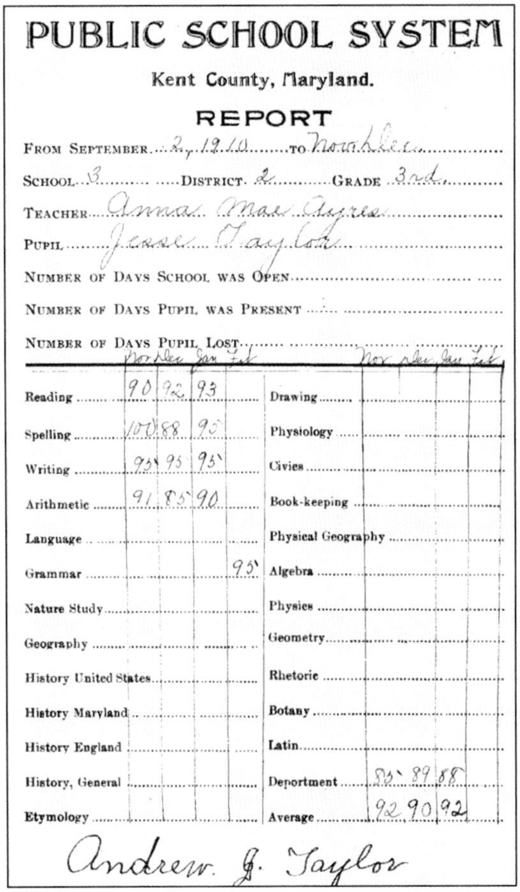

PUBLIC SCHOOL SYSTEM

Kent County, Maryland.

REPORT

FROM SEPTEMBER 2, 1910 TO Nov. Dec.

SCHOOL 3 DISTRICT 2 GRADE 3rd

TEACHER Anna Mae Ayres

PUPIL Jesse Taylor

NUMBER OF DAYS SCHOOL WAS OPEN

NUMBER OF DAYS PUPIL WAS PRESENT

NUMBER OF DAYS PUPIL LOST

	Nov	Dec	Jan	Feb		Nov	Dec	Jan	Feb
Reading	90	92	93		Drawing				
Spelling	100	88	95		Physiology				
Writing	95	95	95		Civics				
Arithmetic	91	85	90		Book-keeping				
Language					Physical Geography				
Grammar				95	Algebra				
Nature Study					Physics				
Geography					Geometry				
History United States					Rhetoric				
History Maryland					Botany				
History England					Latin				
History, General					Deportment	85	89	88	
Etymology					Average	92	90	92	

Andrew G. Taylor

Jesse Taylor's third-grade report card is pictured here. Anna Mae Ayres was the third-grade teacher at "School 3, District 2" in 1910. Twenty-five classes are listed on the report card. (Courtesy of Anne Willson Grim McKown.)

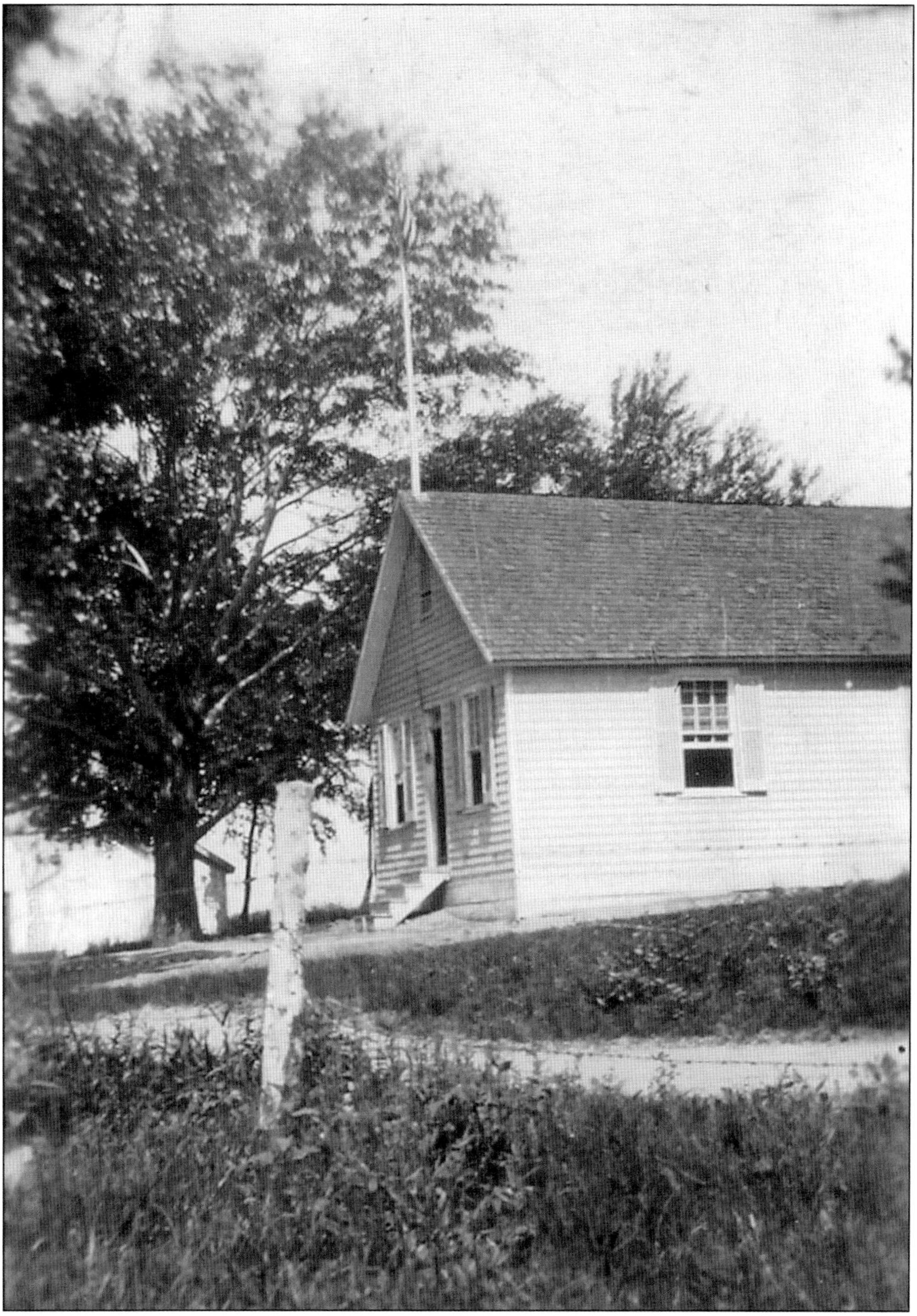

Swan Creek School was a one-room schoolhouse originally located near the small bridge close to Swan Creek Road near Rock Hall. It is reported that the schoolhouse was moved to Liberty Street and is at the Baptist church site. The school building was first purchased by the Daughters of America Lodge to be used as their meeting hall. (Courtesy of Ida Mae Dulin.)

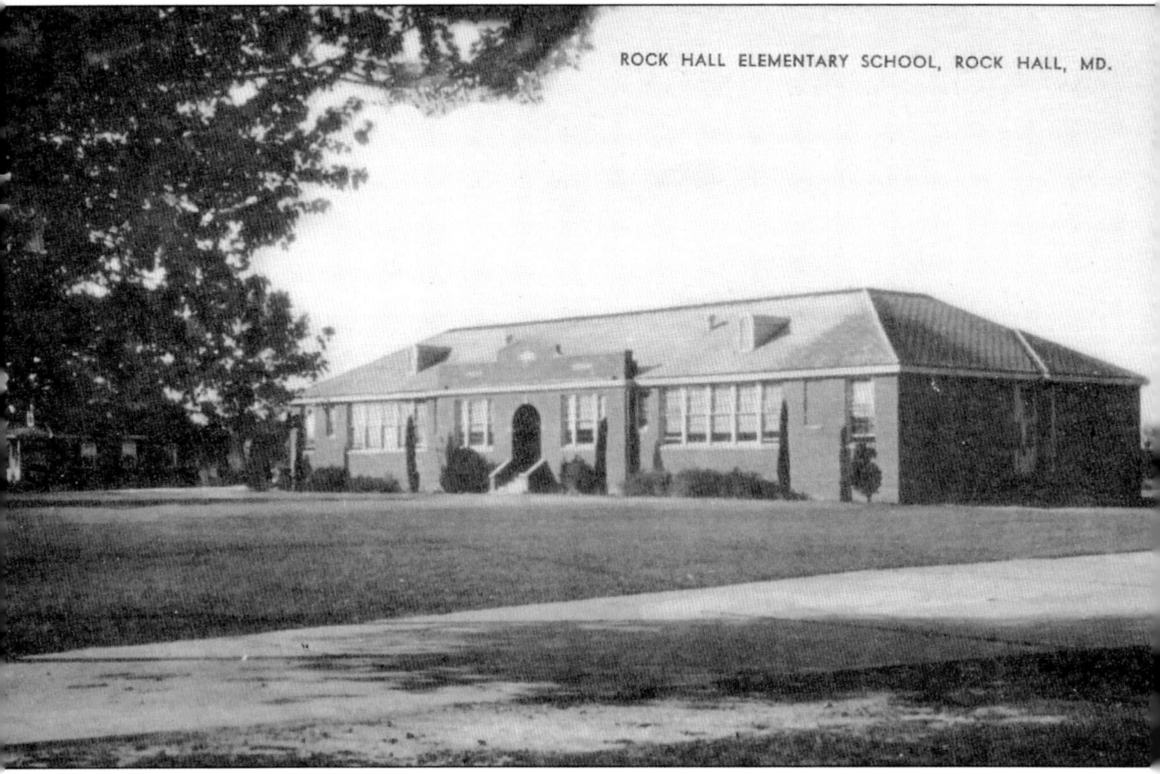

Rock Hall Elementary School was built on land purchased from Mr. and Mrs. Max Alexander in 1929 for $1,000. Children ate lunch in their homerooms until a kitchen and cafeteria were added. A hot-lunch program was started in 1947 with the help of the PTA, who donated $900, and parents and friends, who donated $500 worth of equipment. The cafeteria was first under the management of Eva Price and a helper, Agnes Stauffer. The building is now the Rock Hall Municipal Center and includes the Rock Hall Town Hall, Rock Hall Police Department, Rock Hall Museum, Townsend Medical Clinic, and Rock Hall Branch of the Kent County Public Library. (Courtesy of Dorothy McKinney, Ida Mae Dulin, and Madelyn Cornelius.)

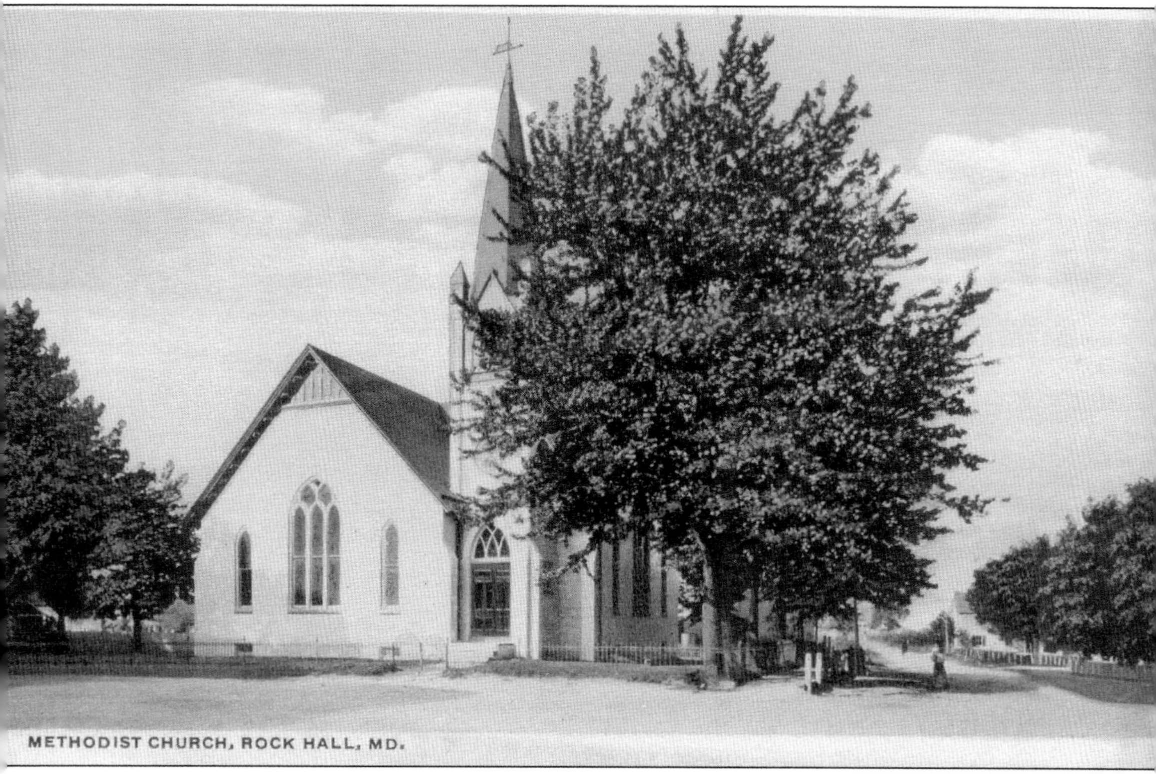

Rock Hall Methodist Church is located at the crossroads of Main and Sharp Streets in Rock Hall. The Methodists were the earliest religious body to settle in Rock Hall. Property was purchased in 1821 from Thomas Harris of Rock Hall for $20 by Charles Rigby, William Copper, William R. Durding, William Downey, Jacob Stevens, and John K. Ayres, who were elected trustees of the church and who were to oversee the building of a chapel with an adjoining cemetery. The church grew, and in 1854, a new, larger church was built in this same location and named Rock Hall Methodist Episcopal Church. The church burned in 1900, and the church that remains today was built. (Courtesy of Dorothy McKinney, Ida Mae Dulin, and Madelyn Cornelius.)

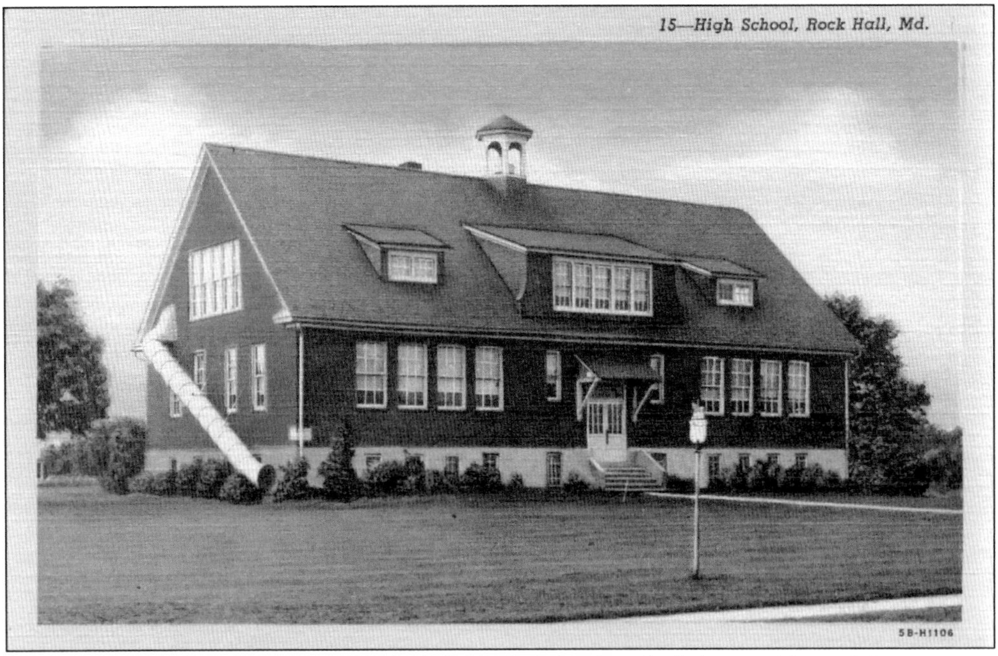

The extracurricular program at Rock Hall High School included assemblies, club programs, student government, publications, year-round sports, and dramatic and musical productions. This building is now Rock Hall Middle School. (Courtesy of Dorothy McKinney, Ida Mae Dulin, and Madelyn Cornelius.)

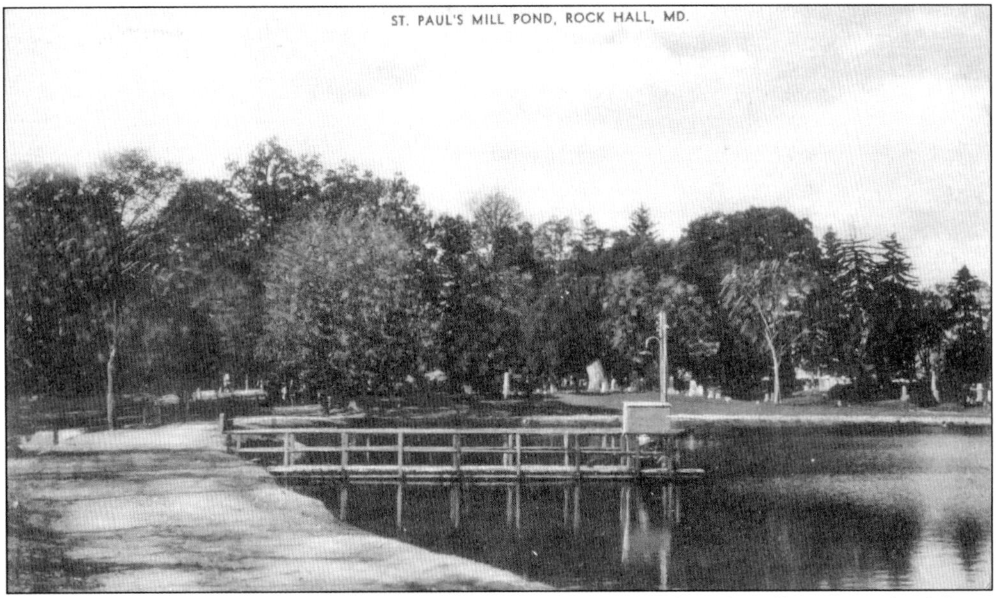

The St. Paul's Millpond near old St. Paul's Church, just outside of Rock Hall, is a popular fishing spot in the spring. Old St. Paul's Church Parish was established in 1693 and was one of the 30 parishes laid out in the Province of Maryland by an act of assembly in 1692. The earliest part of the present building was constructed in 1711. St. Paul's is the oldest Episcopal church in Maryland used continuously as a place of worship. The vestry house was built in 1766. (Courtesy of Patricia Joan O. Horsey.)

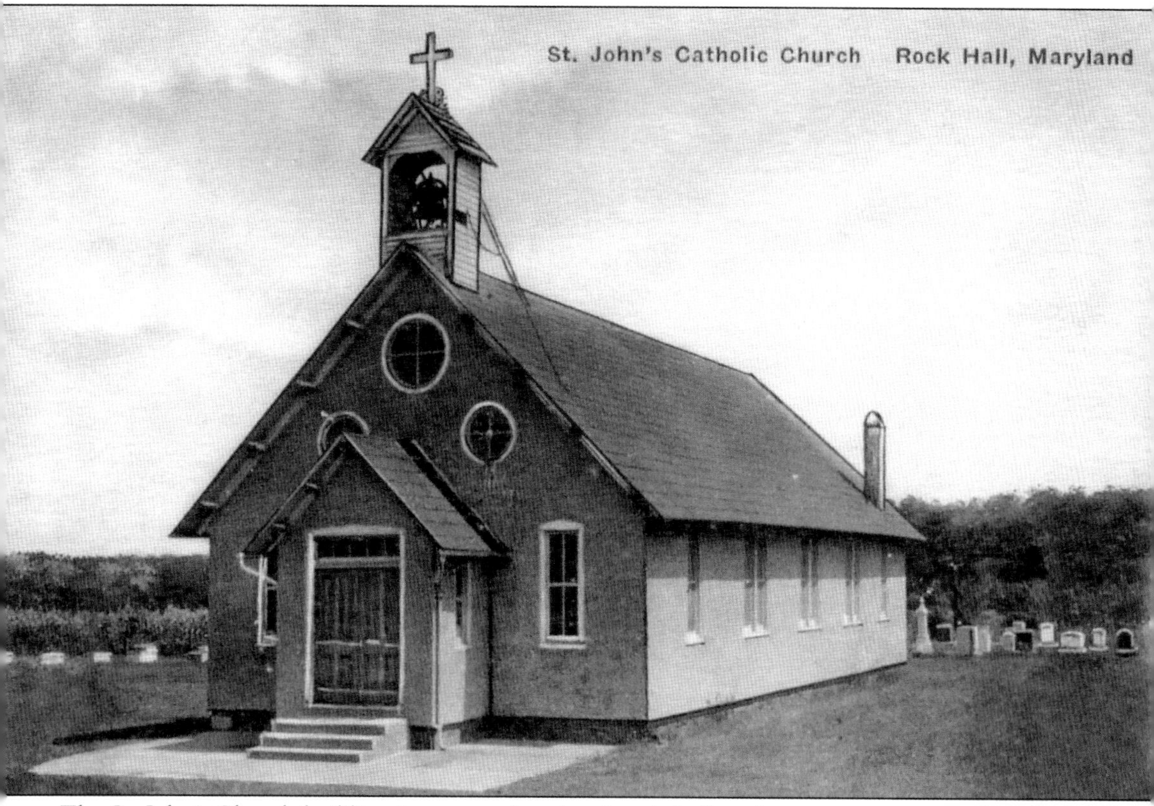

The St. John's Church building is now used as the church hall and sits next to a newer church building. In 1890, Fr. James A. Murphy led the effort that resulted in sufficient funds to build a Catholic church in Rock Hall. In 1892, Fr. George L. Ott provided the parish with the Catholic cemetery, where many pioneer Catholics are interred. (Courtesy of Judy Hickman.)

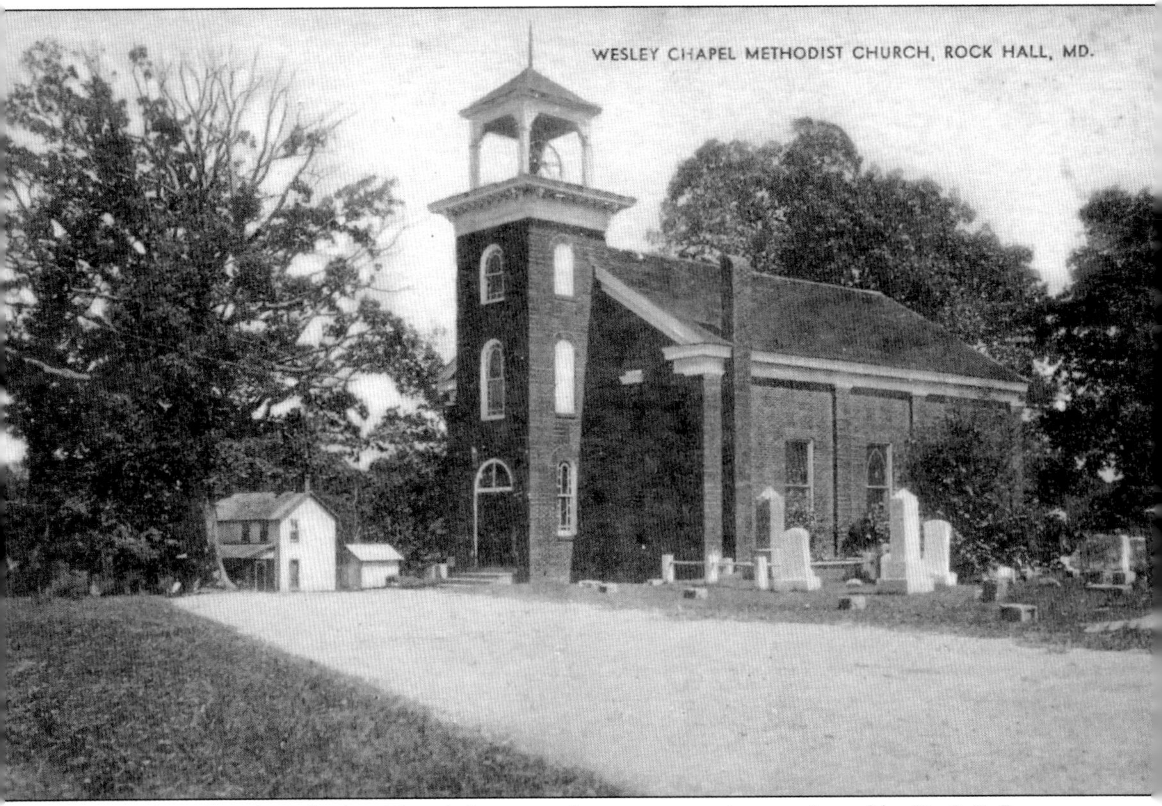

Wesley Chapel Methodist Church began with a camp meeting conducted by Dr. J. S. Reese on September 5, 1828, near Rock Hall. Originally, a committee of seven men was named to locate a place for a new house of worship and schoolhouse. In 1830, the present location was selected by a group of trustees, including James Eagleson, John Urie, Hiriam Jones, William Copper, Charles Rigby, Daniel Collines, Dr. Jacob Fisher, Thomas Adkinson, Thomas Bryan, Joseph Downey, Nathan Hatcherson, Gen. P. Reed, P. M. Rood, Michael Miller, and Henry M. Hyland. Wesley Chapel has been holding a popular annual fish fry in the summer for many years. (Courtesy of Judy Hickman.)

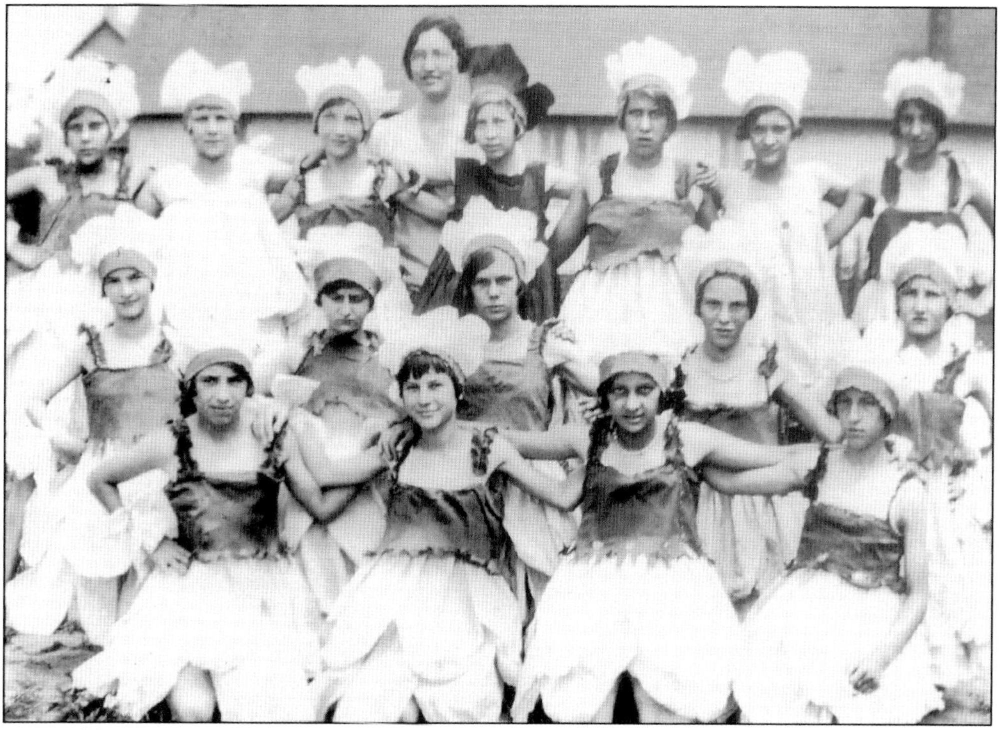

Pictured here are Rock Hall Elementary School fifth-, sixth-, and seventh-grade students on May Day in 1929. Hilda Hill was the teacher. (Courtesy of Patsy S. Reihl.)

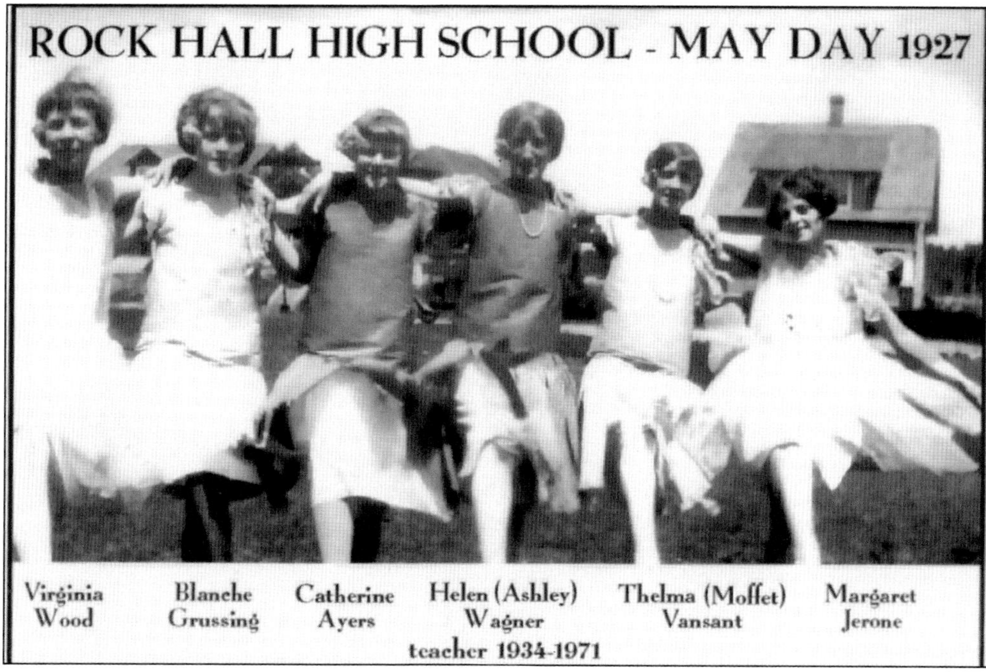

This photograph was taken at the Rock Hall May Day in 1927. Pictured are, from left to right, Virginia Wood, Blanche Grussing, Catherine Ayers, Helen (Ashley) Wagner (teacher from 1934 to 1971), Thelma (Moffett) Vansant, and Margaret Jerone. (Courtesy of Patsy S. Reihl.)

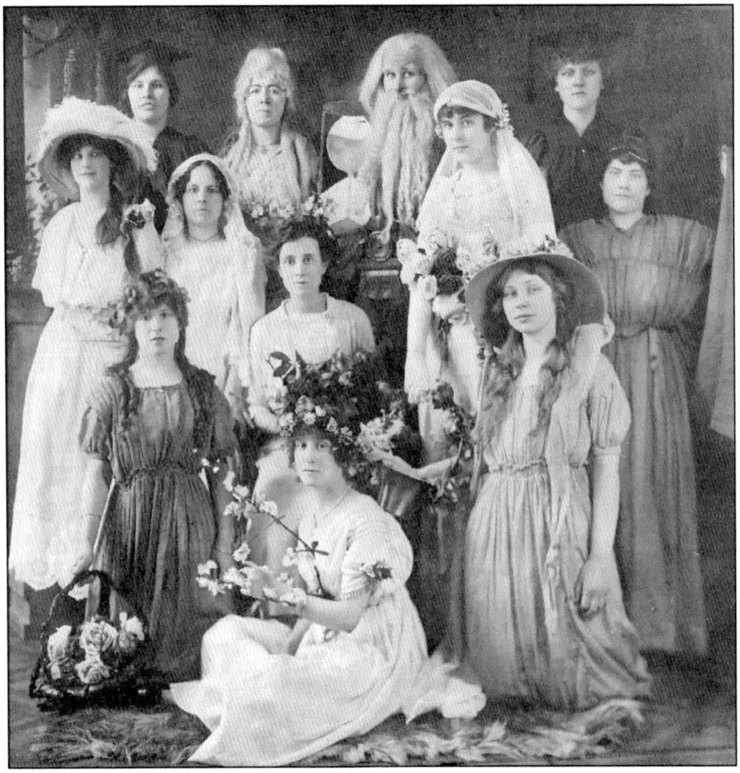

Among those pictured as part of the Rock Hall High School class play in 1912 is Mary Hognas Beekman, second row, second from the right. Mary was born in 1899. This play was part of her graduation from eighth grade. Mary was selected from the state of Maryland to serve in the army's ordinance corps, one of 50 girls from each state selected to the program. (Courtesy of H. Edward Beekman Jr.)

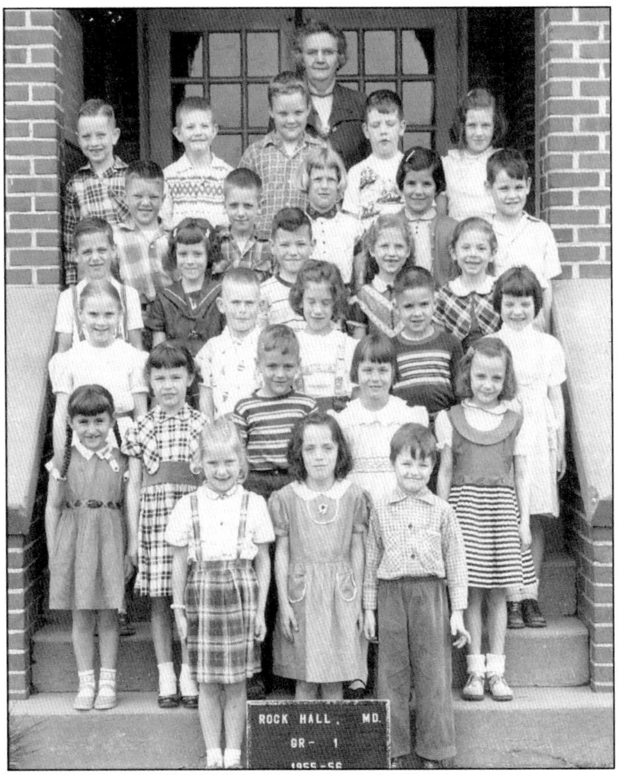

First grade Rock Hall Elementary School students in 1955–1956 included, from left to right, (first row) Diane Nordhoff Lloyde, Edna Coleman, and Morris Alvin "Buddy" Trego; (second row) Darlene Simns Freeman, Janie Hudson Thompson, Bruce Kendall, Caroline Parson Crouch, and unidenitified; (third row) Diane Moffett, Chris Nordhoff, Jerry Chandler, Tommy Lloyde, and Libby Creighton Kennard; (fourth row) David Mench, Betty Ann Jacquette Strong, Larry Legg, Donna Brady, and Patsy Edler Townsend; (fifth row) Marty Carter, Dickie Jacquette, Ruth Olsen, Bonnie Baker, and James Parson; (sixth row) Mark Cannan, Alfred Bredson, Steward Mayne, Randy Christian, Linda Chaires, and teacher Louise Kendall. (Courtesy of Jane and Carroll Thompson.)

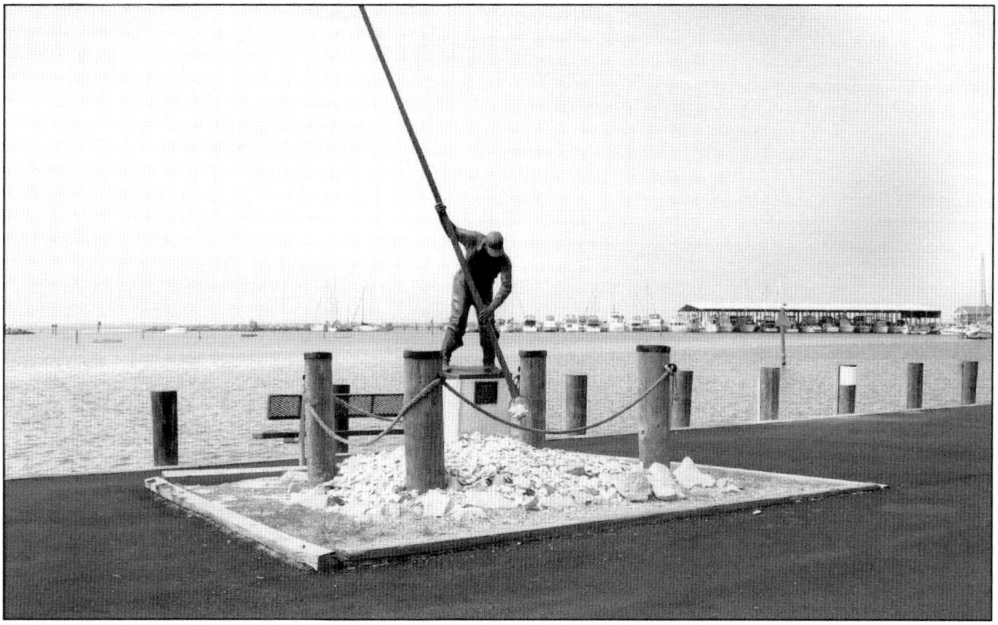

The statue and memorial titled *Oysterman* is displayed at the bulkhead on Rock Hall Harbor. It was modeled after waterman and boatbuilder Stanley B. Vansant. This life-size sculpture by Kenneth Herliny was dedicated in 1995 to the watermen and other working people of the Chesapeake Bay. (Courtesy of Patricia Joan O. Horsey.)

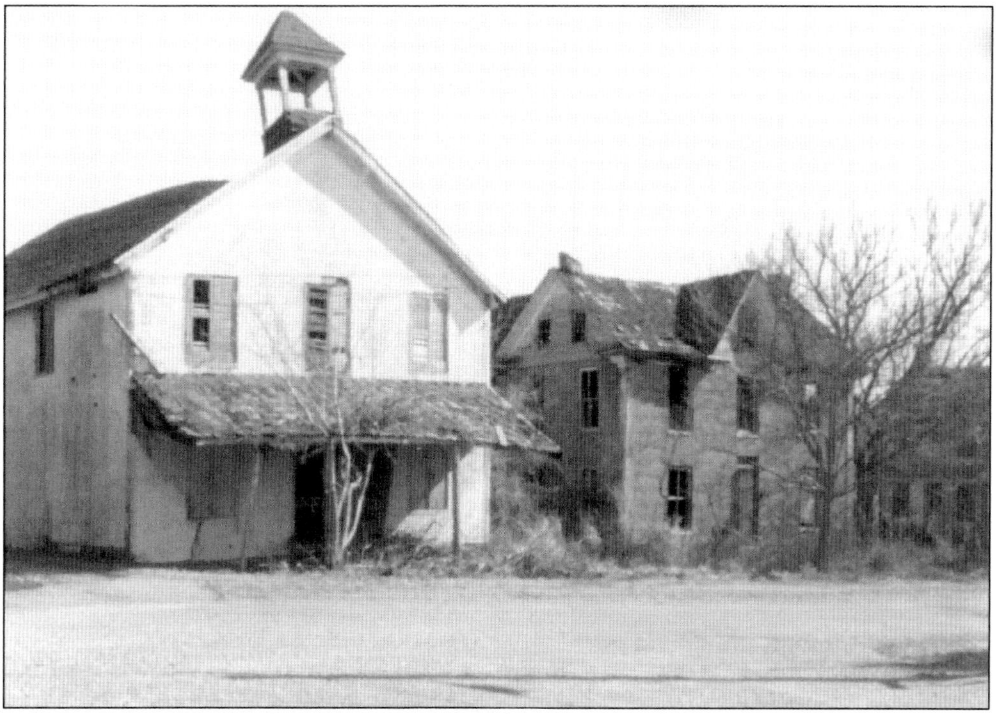

This is an image of Crouch's Store in Piney Neck. It was owned by Charles Wesley Crouch and later by Charles T. Crouch, grandfather and father respectively of Honey Wood. It was a general store and popular meeting place. (Courtesy of Madelyn Cornelius.)

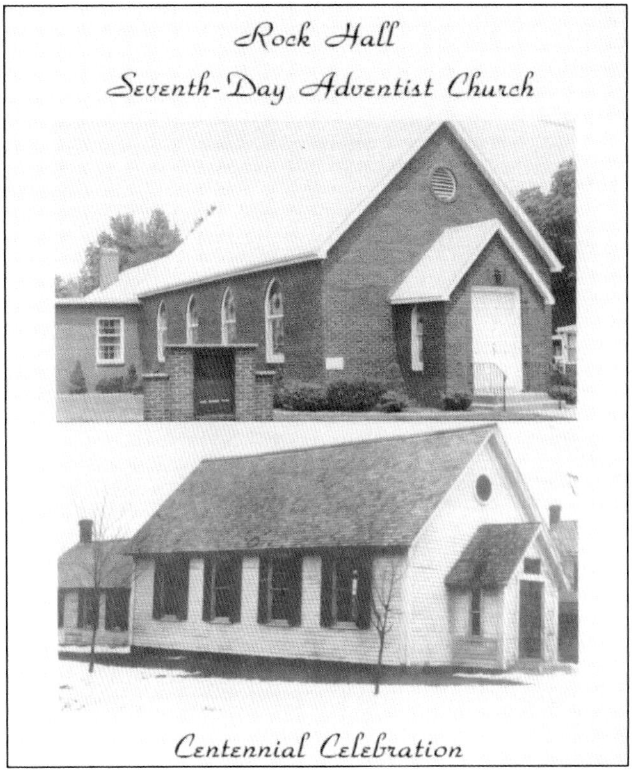

The Rock Hall Seventh-Day Adventist Church began in 1891 at Downey's Hall on Main Street. John Judefind donated the lot on Sharp Street and Judefind Avenue, where the church remains today. This church is the oldest in the Chesapeake Conference and celebrated its 100th year in 1992. (Courtesy of Rose Elma Cornelius and Madelyn Cornelius.)

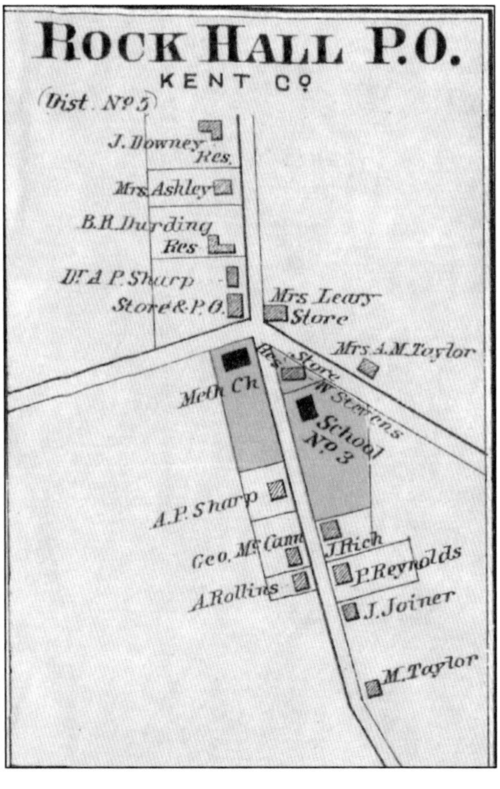

This 1876 map was taken from the atlas of Kent and Queen Anne's Counties, Maryland, published by Lake, Griffing, and Stevenson in 1877. District No. 5 in Kent County was listed as Edesville. The map of the entire district spans two full pages of this atlas. This map served as an insert that highlighted Main and Sharp Street, residences, and businesses. (Courtesy of Steve Figlin.)

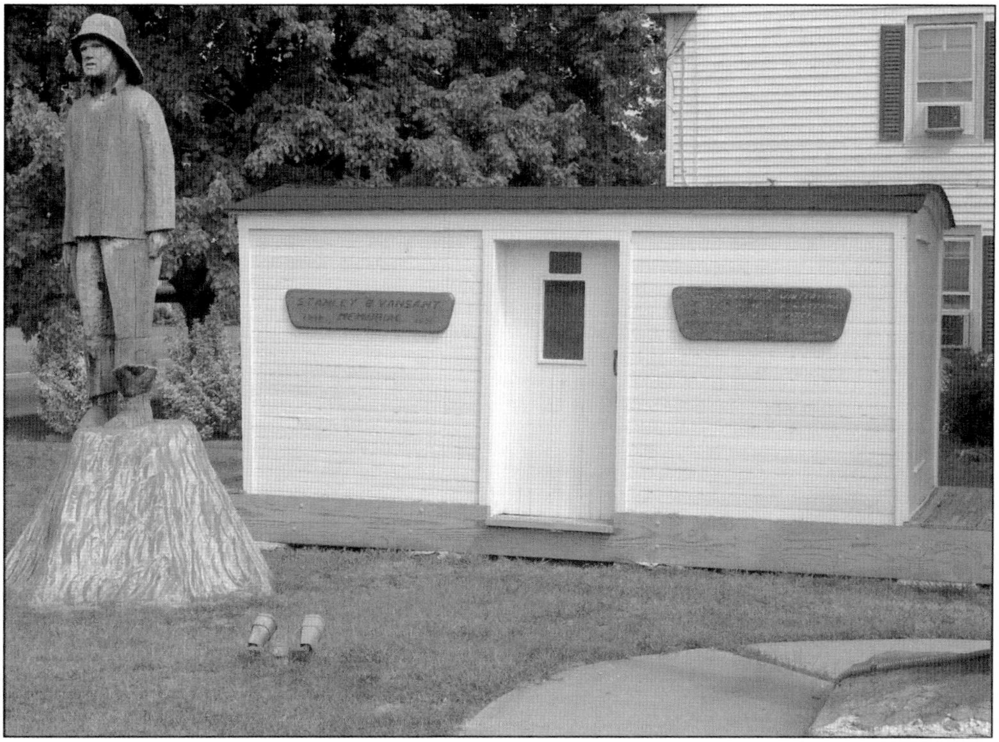

The Stanley B. Vansant Memorial is located on the corner of Route 20 and Main Street. This memorial includes a wooden statue of Captain Vansant and a fishing shanty, a wintertime or portable home for watermen that can be towed to suitable sites. This fishing shanty was refurbished by the Friends of Captain Vansant and the Rock Hall Lions Club. (Courtesy of Ed Kurowski.)

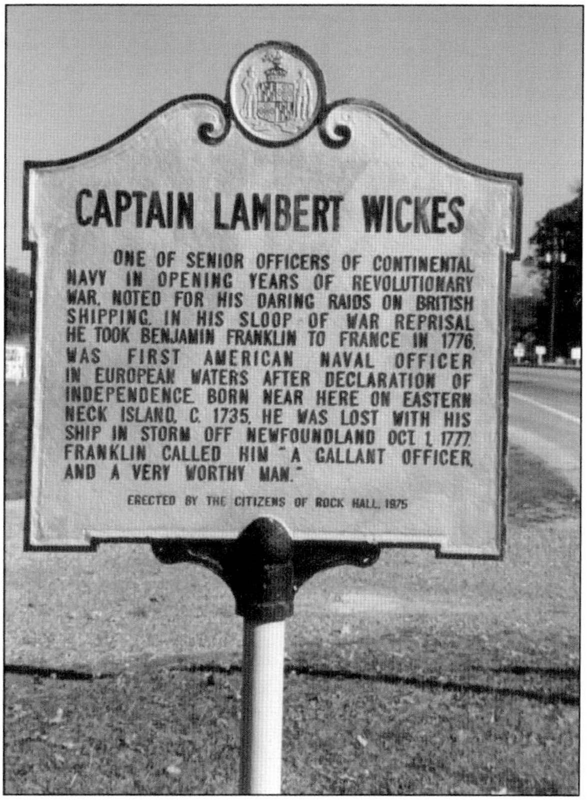

Capt. Lambert Wickes was born on Eastern Neck Island around 1735. His family home, Wickcliffe, was located on the southern part of Eastern Neck Island on the Chester River. He was noted for his daring raids on British shipping and was the first American naval officer in European waters after the Declaration of Independence. This marker was erected by the citizens of Rock Hall in 1975. (Courtesy of Ed Kurowski.)

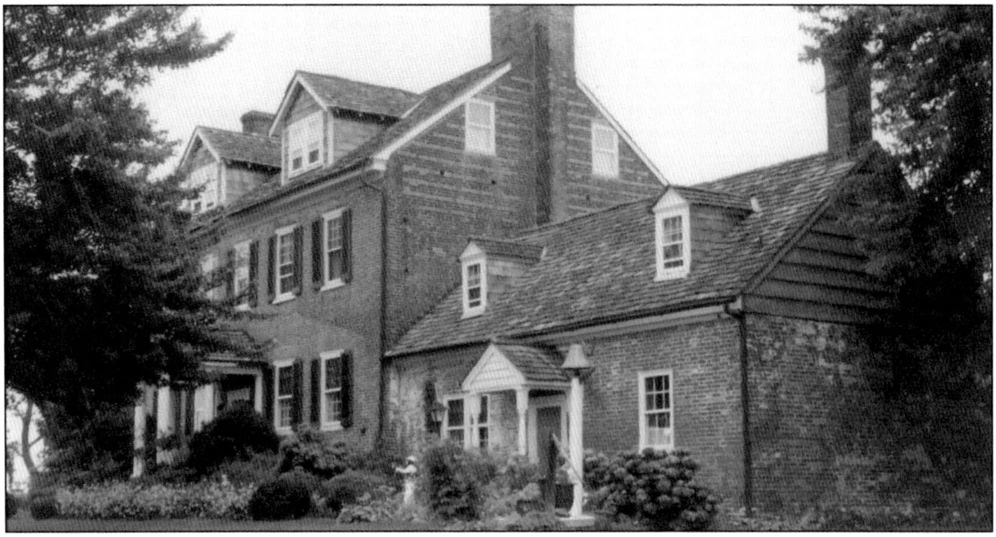

Trumpington is located on Eastern Neck just outside of Rock Hall. The farm was patented in 1659 and has remained in the same family for over 300 years. It is a Bicentennial Farm (1776–1976) and is on the National Register of Historic Places. The Willson-Strong family traces back to the original owner, Thomas Smythe. Smyth owned both Trumpington and Widehall in Chestertown, Maryland. The family has many original family records and hosted Jenifer Grinded Dolde as she wrote the book *Trumpington: A Legacy of Land on the Chesapeake Bay.* (Courtesy of Mildred Strong.)

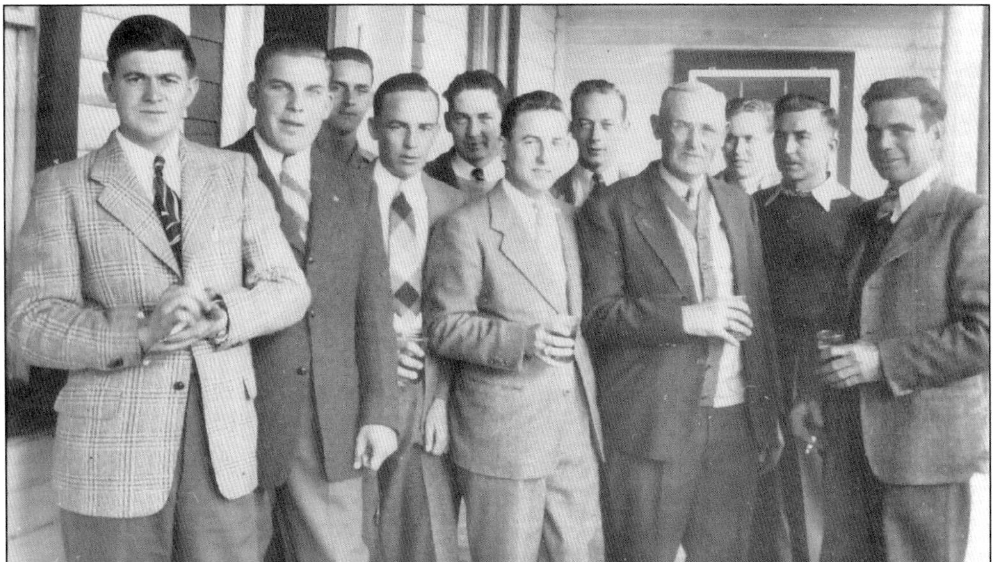

Pictured from left to right, (first row) Vaughan Hogans, Thomas "Dutch" Parsons, Bayard Parsons, George Parsons, Arthur Prettyman, Medcalf Jaquette, and Herman Hill; (second row) Edward Nordhoff, Weldon Kelley, Robert Scoons, and Otto Nordhoff met on the deck of the Rock Hall Yacht Club in 1946. This occasion was a meeting to discuss the refinancing of the club by issuing new stock. Rock Hall Yacht Club was founded in 1937 with Hillry Akers acting as chairman, George Ellsworth Leary as president, Frank Puppe as vice president, and Dr. William S. Brinsfield as secretary-treasurer. In 2007, Rock Hall Yacht Club commemorates 70 years during Rock Hall's 300th-anniversary celebration. (Courtesy Jeff and Margaret Hill.)

Two

THE WATER AND WATERMAN

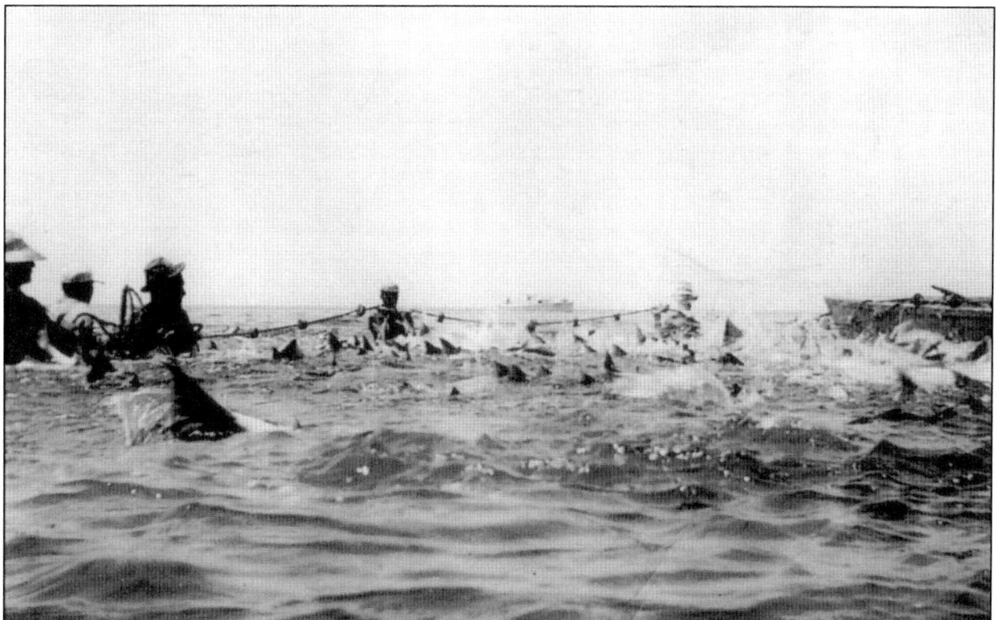

This group of watermen, including John Edward "Bootie" Elburn, is seine hauling in the Chesapeake Bay off Tolchester Beach in the 1940s. A seine is a large fishing net that hangs vertically in the water by attaching weights along the bottom edge and floats along the top. (Courtesy of Clay Larrimore.)

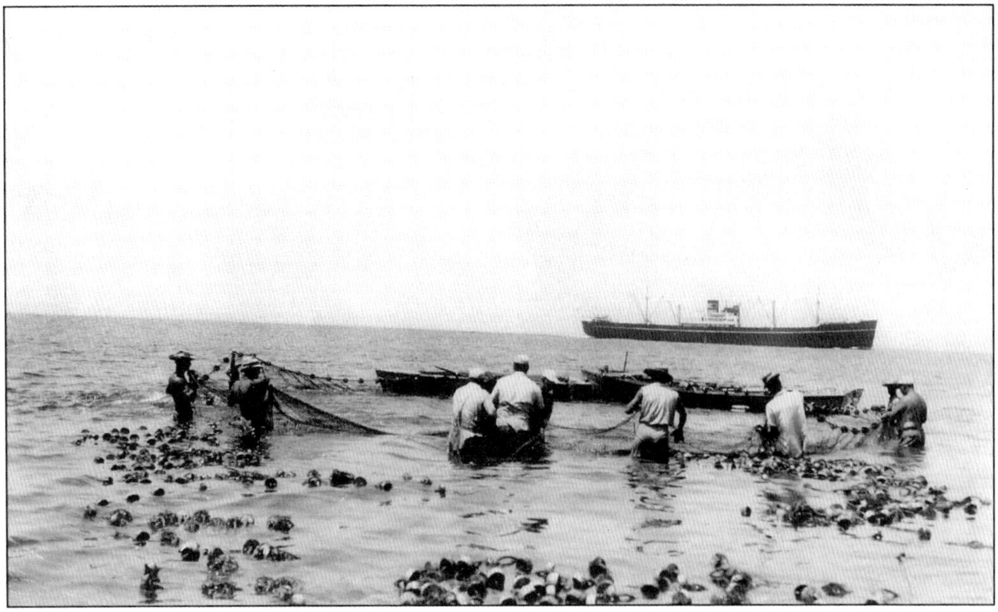

These watermen are seine hauling for rockfish off Tolchester Beach in the Chesapeake Bay in the 1940s. A typical day's catch was one to two tons of rockfish. (Courtesy of Clay Larrimore.)

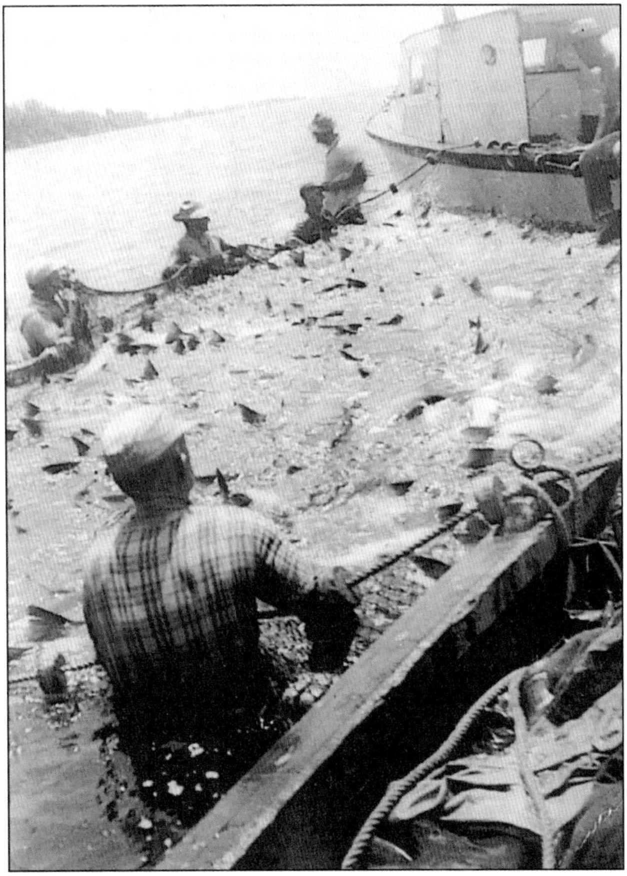

Bootie Elburn and his crew, including Bob Wagner and Robert Larrimore, are seine hauling for rockfish in the 1940s in the Chesapeake Bay between Tolchester and Swan Point near Rock Hall. (Courtesy of Clay Larrimore.)

This photograph was taken at Long Cove, Piney Neck, near Rock Hall in 1941. Looking over the seine haul catch of rockfish from the Chester River are, from left to right, Jim Edwards (with hat and bucket at about 12 years old), Clarence "Oak" Edwards (walking away), Robert "Kike" Edwards (straw hat), Bob Yerkie (with sailor cap), Don Yerkes, and Howard Beck (facing camera). (Courtesy of Clay Larrimore.)

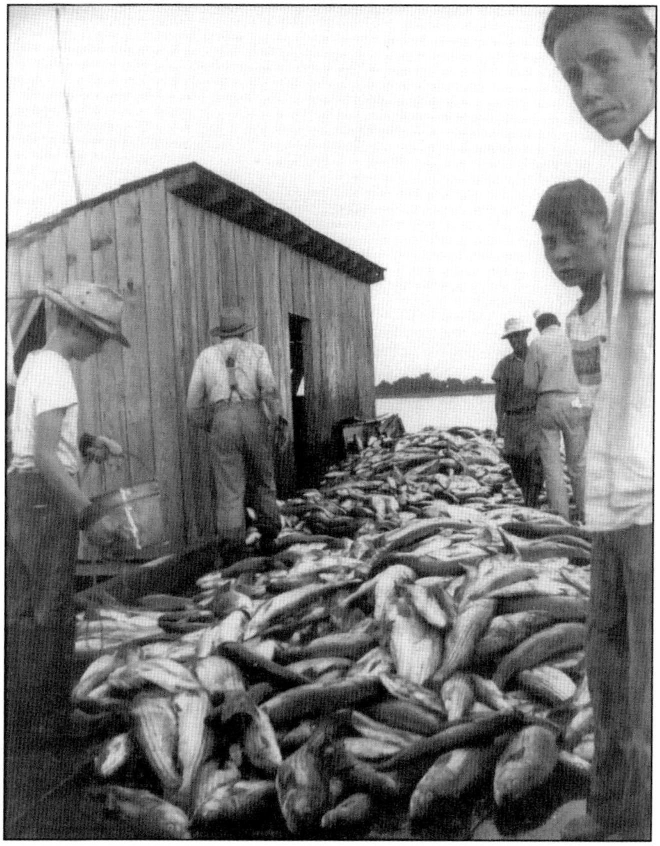

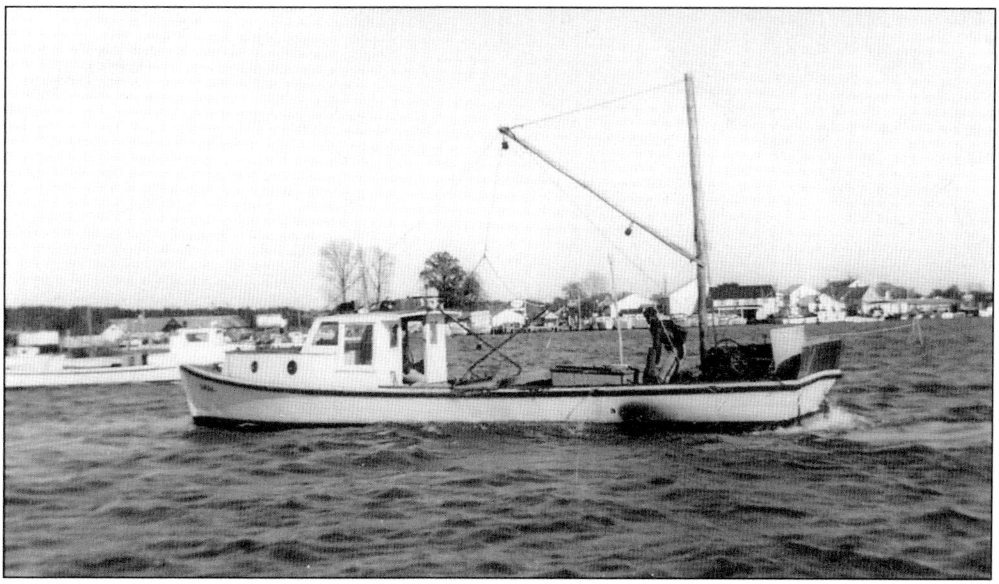

This photograph of an oyster boat, taken at Rock Hall Harbor, shows a patented tong rig developed by Pres Joiner of Rock Hall. The importance of this was great, as it automated the catch process and enabled it to be a much easier, one-man process. It is said that Captain Joiner enjoyed the time and freedom of working alone on the water. (Courtesy of Judy Hickman.)

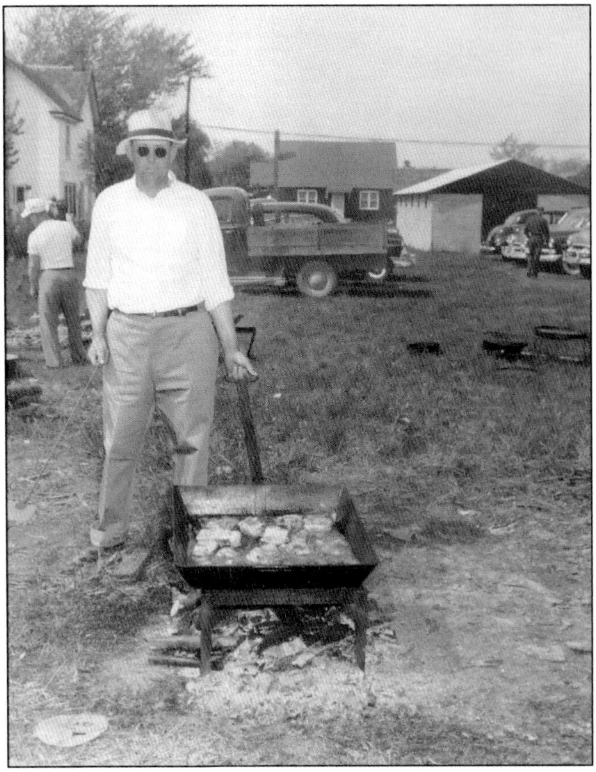

Maurice "Splint" Downey is shown frying fish. Frying whole or fish fillets is part of a traditional Rock Hall fish fry. Heavy homemade cast-iron skillets are used for the frying. (Courtesy of H. Edward Beekman Jr.)

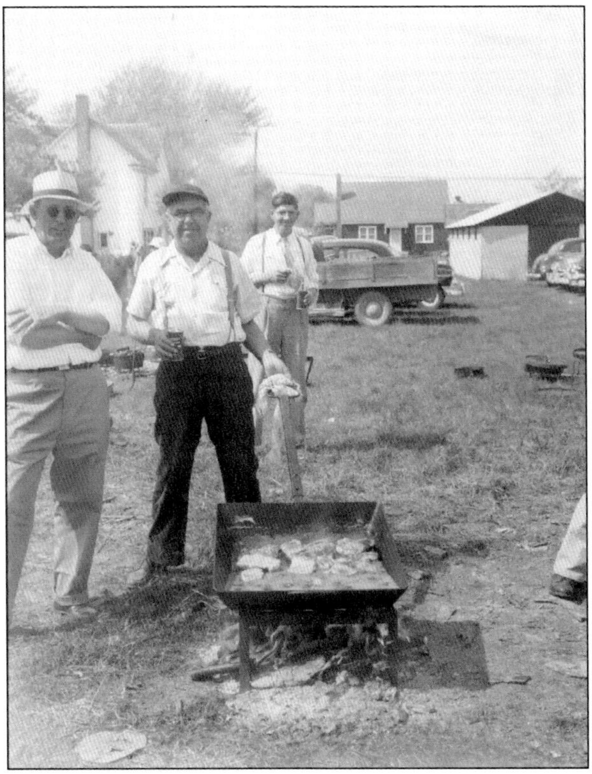

Deep frying the fish was part of the tradition at the popular fish fries held in Rock Hall. Fish fries remain a popular Rock Hall enjoyment. Friends, family, organizations, and churches continue this custom to this day. Pictured from left to right are Splint Downey, Charlie Jacobs, and Glenn Edwards. (Courtesy of H. Edward Beekman Jr.)

One of the traditional items served at a fish fry is shortbread, often dipped in molasses. Shortbread is made from a flour-based dough. It is formed into a round shape and baked in pans called dutch ovens. Baking bread here are, from left to right, Hank Goodman, Oliver Townsend, and Calvin Jacobs. (Courtesy of H. Edward Beekman Jr.)

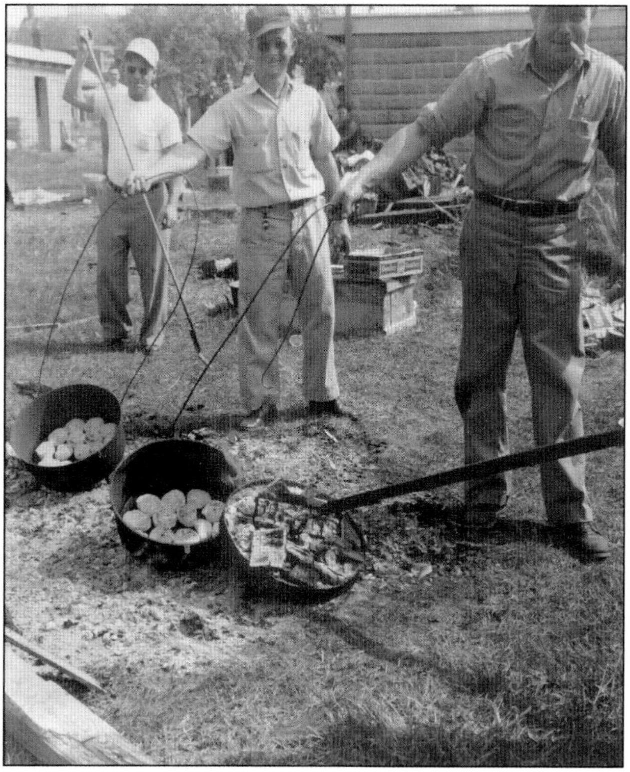

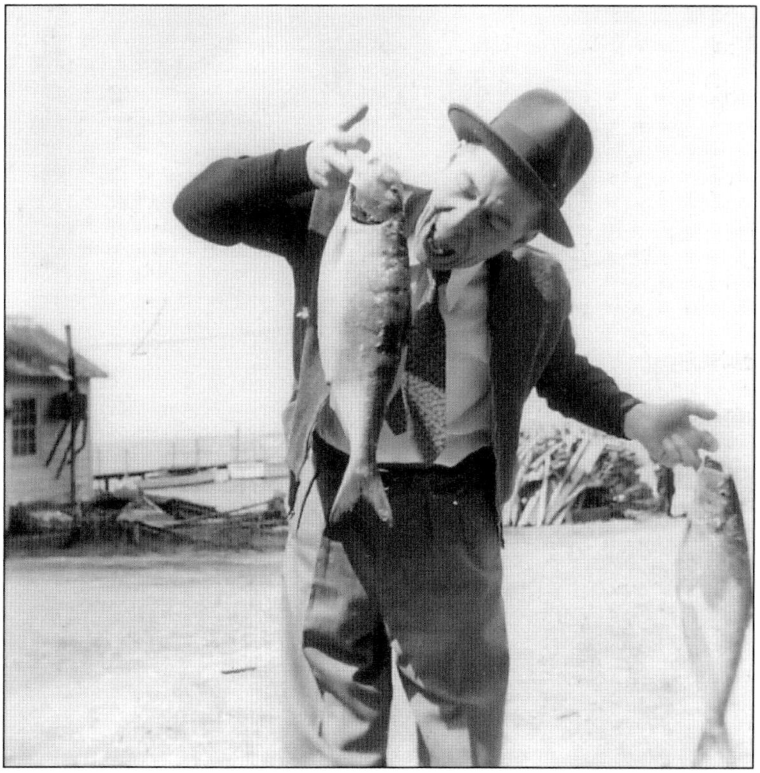

These fish are typical of the ones caught off Rock Hall for many years; Albert Hogans is ready to take a bite! (Courtesy of H. Edward Beekman Jr.)

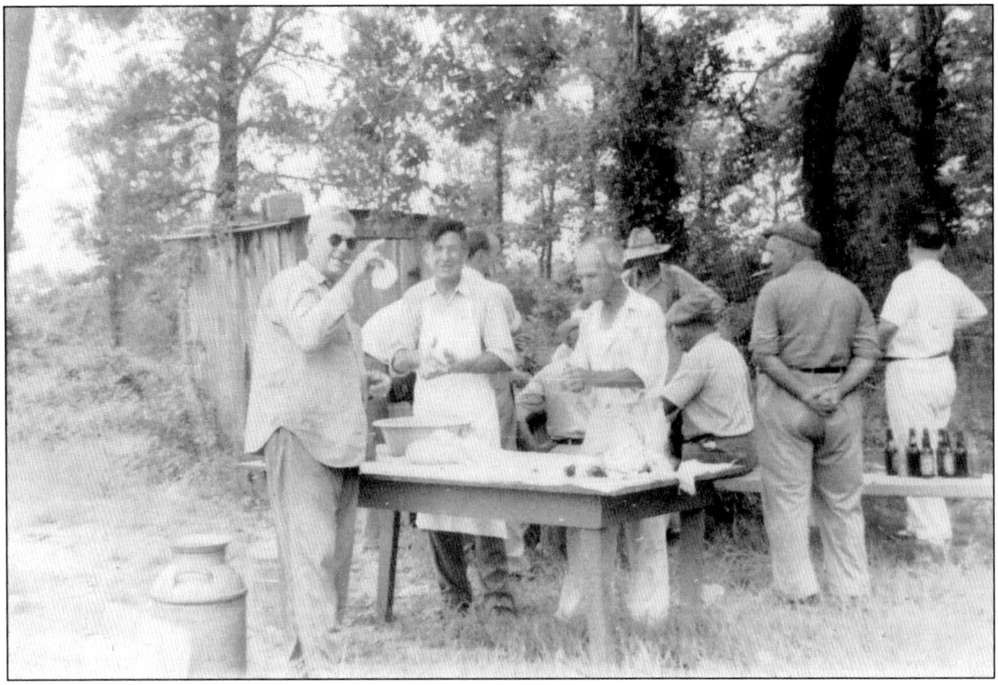

Among those preparing dough at a Rock Hall fish fry is Raymond Hersch (second from left). Raymond was John Hersch's father. John owned and operated the popular Hersch's Bar. (Courtesy of H. Edward Beekman Jr.)

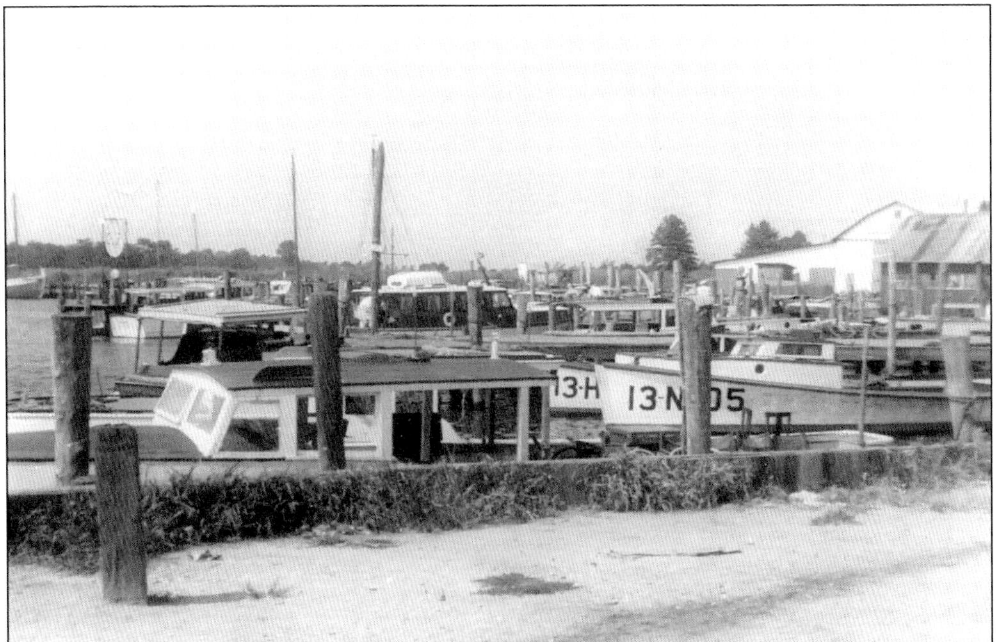

This photograph taken during World War II shows Rock Hall's waterfront, the watermen's workboats identified with large numbers. (Courtesy of H. Edward Beekman Jr.)

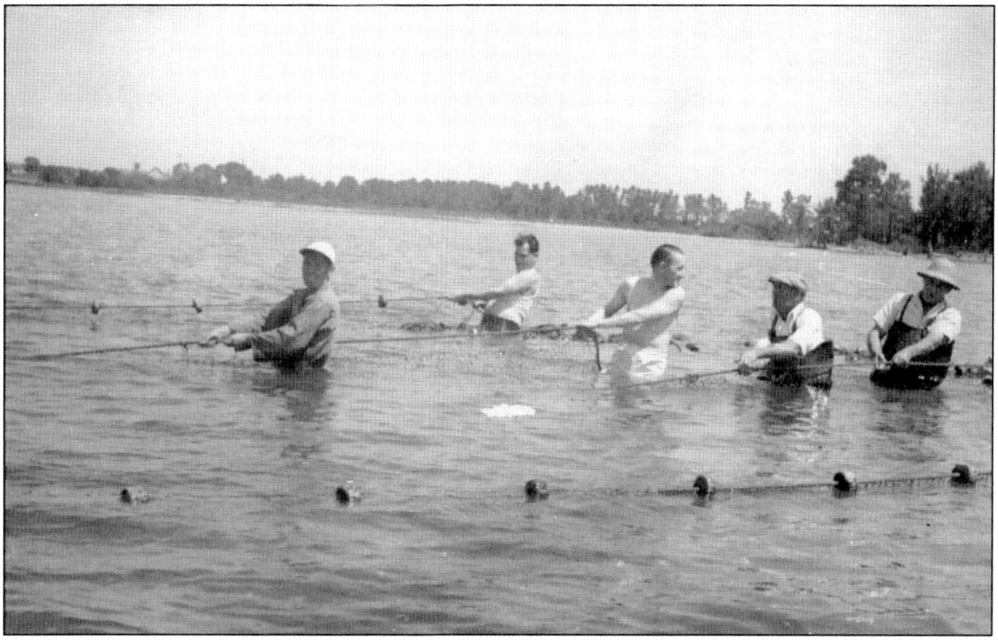

Among those pulling the seine at Rock Hall are Fred Crouch at left, Frank "Doc" Smith in center, looking backwards, and Earl Boulter behind Crouch. (Courtesy of H. Edward Beekman Jr.)

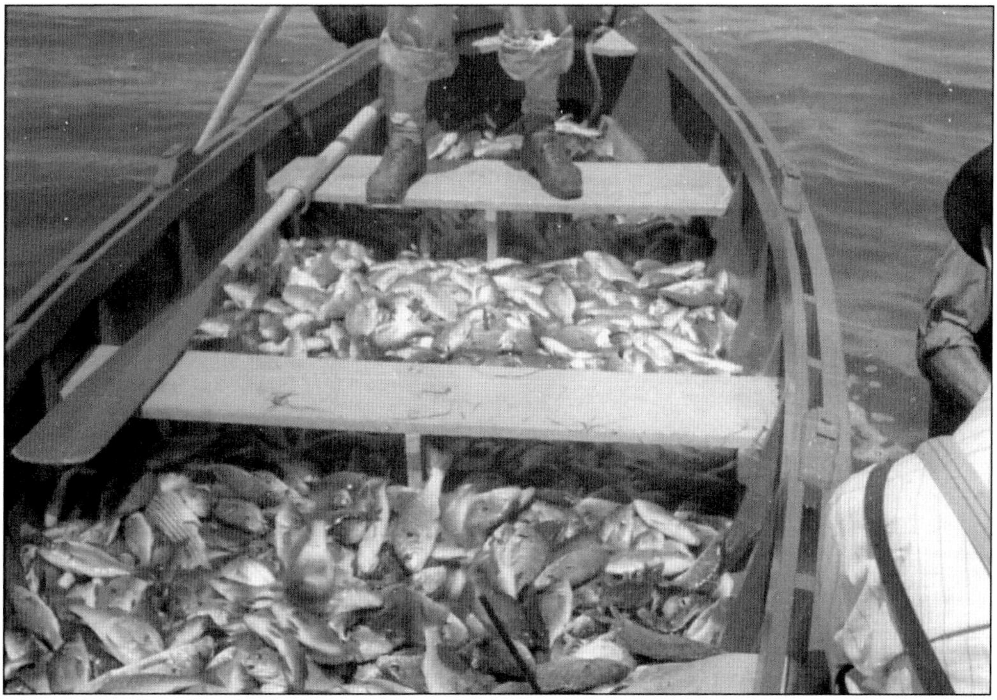

This is literally a boatload of perch and rockfish caught seining off Rock Hall. (Courtesy of H. Edward Beekman Jr.)

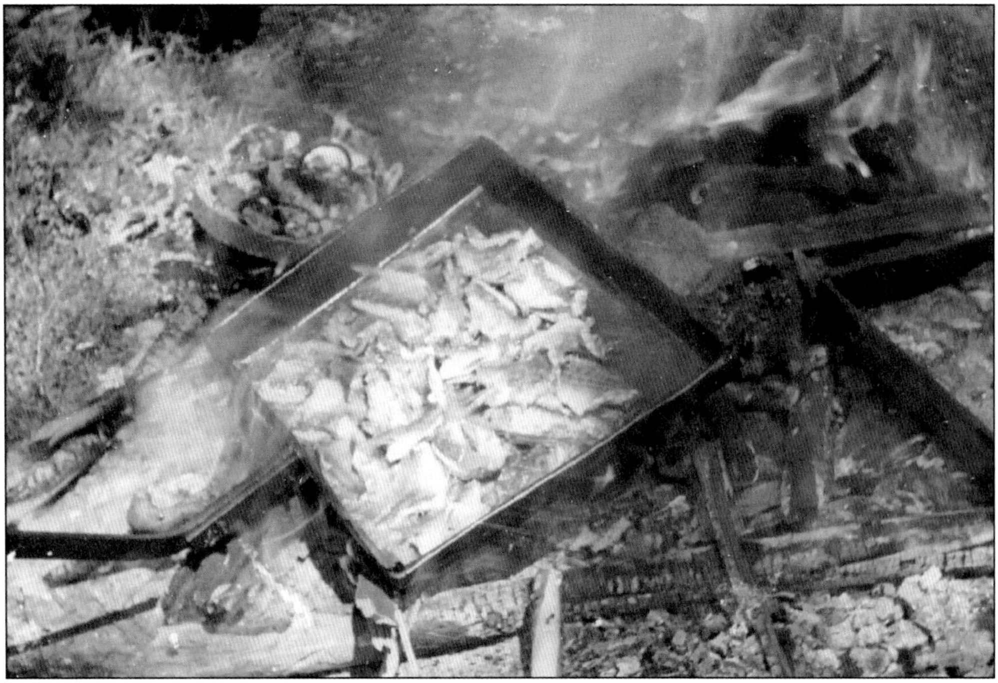

This is an up-close photograph of a pan of fish fried and ready to be served at one of the popular fish fries in Rock Hall. Here white perch is the catch of the day. (Courtesy of H. Edward Beekman Jr.)

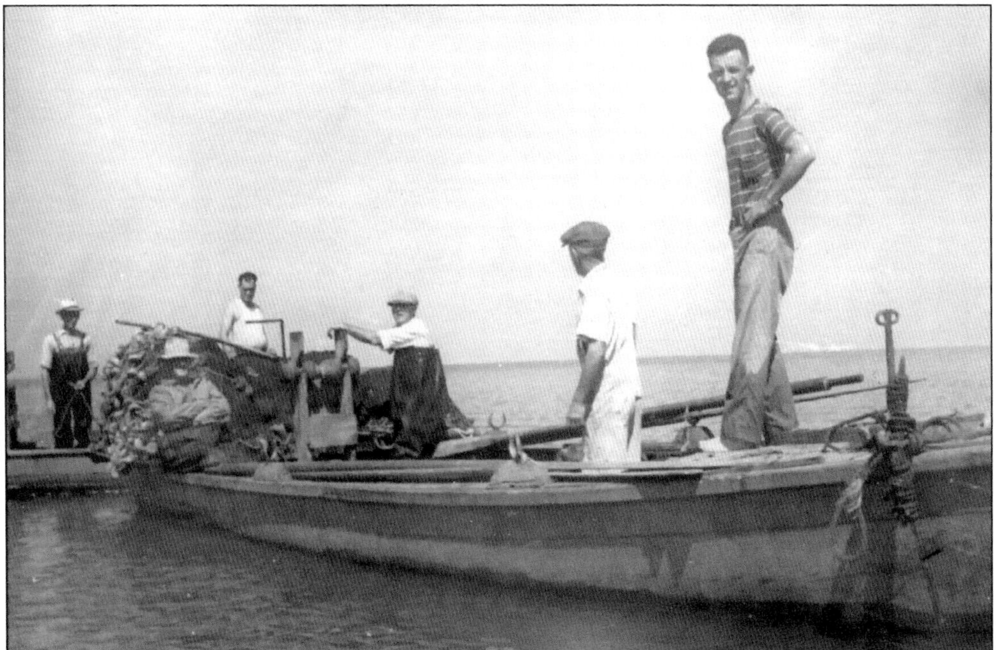

Rock Hall watermen return from a day of fishing. From bow to stern are George Urie, Earl Boulter, and Tommy Legg. The picture was taken off the beach at Huntingfield Farm. (Courtesy of H. Edward Beekman Jr.)

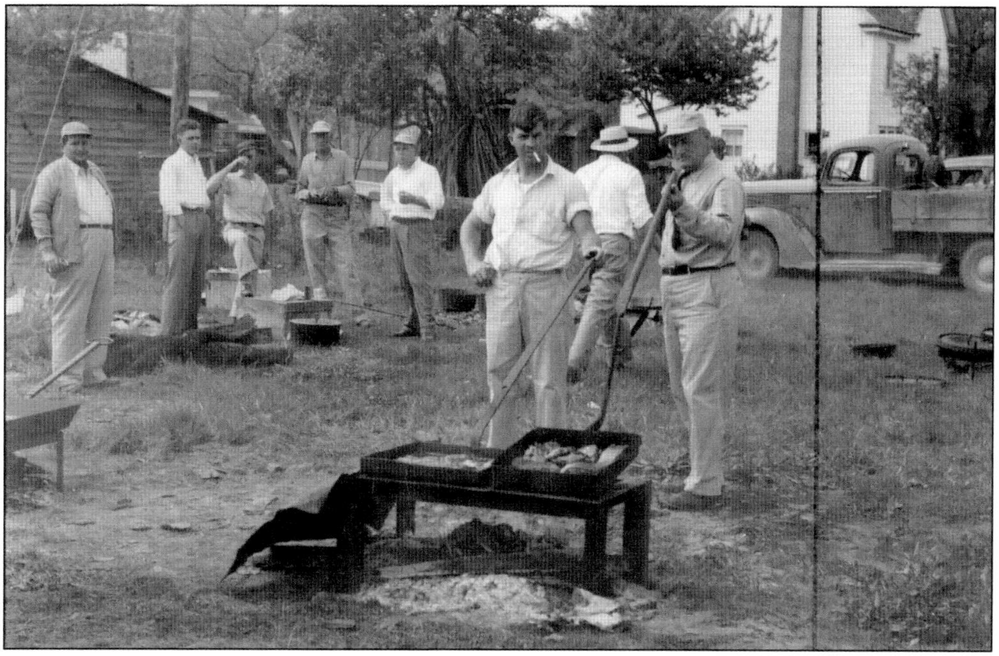

Watermen of Rock Hall watch as fish is fried for a fish fry. It is common for the men to catch, prepare, cook, and serve the fish and bread at fries. Those pictured are Charlie Clark (at left, in sweater and cap), Jiles Warner, Oliver Townsend, Roby Kelley, Carter Bryden, Jimmy Hurtt, and Allen Urie. (Courtesy of H. Edward Beekman Jr.)

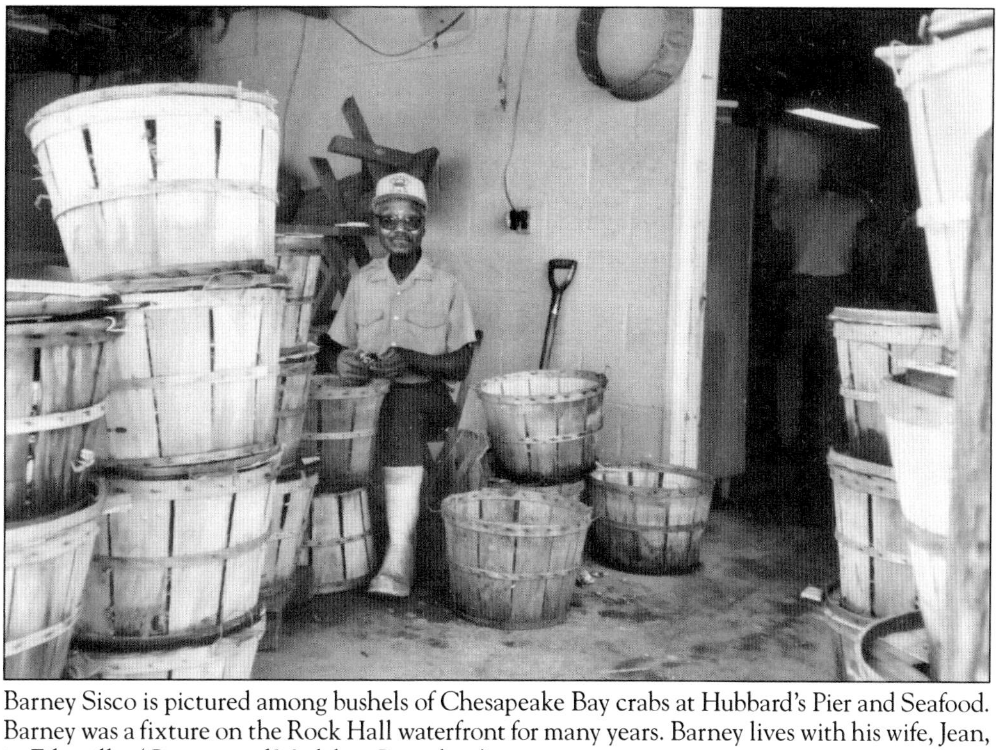

Barney Sisco is pictured among bushels of Chesapeake Bay crabs at Hubbard's Pier and Seafood. Barney was a fixture on the Rock Hall waterfront for many years. Barney lives with his wife, Jean, in Edesville. (Courtesy of Madelyn Cornelius.)

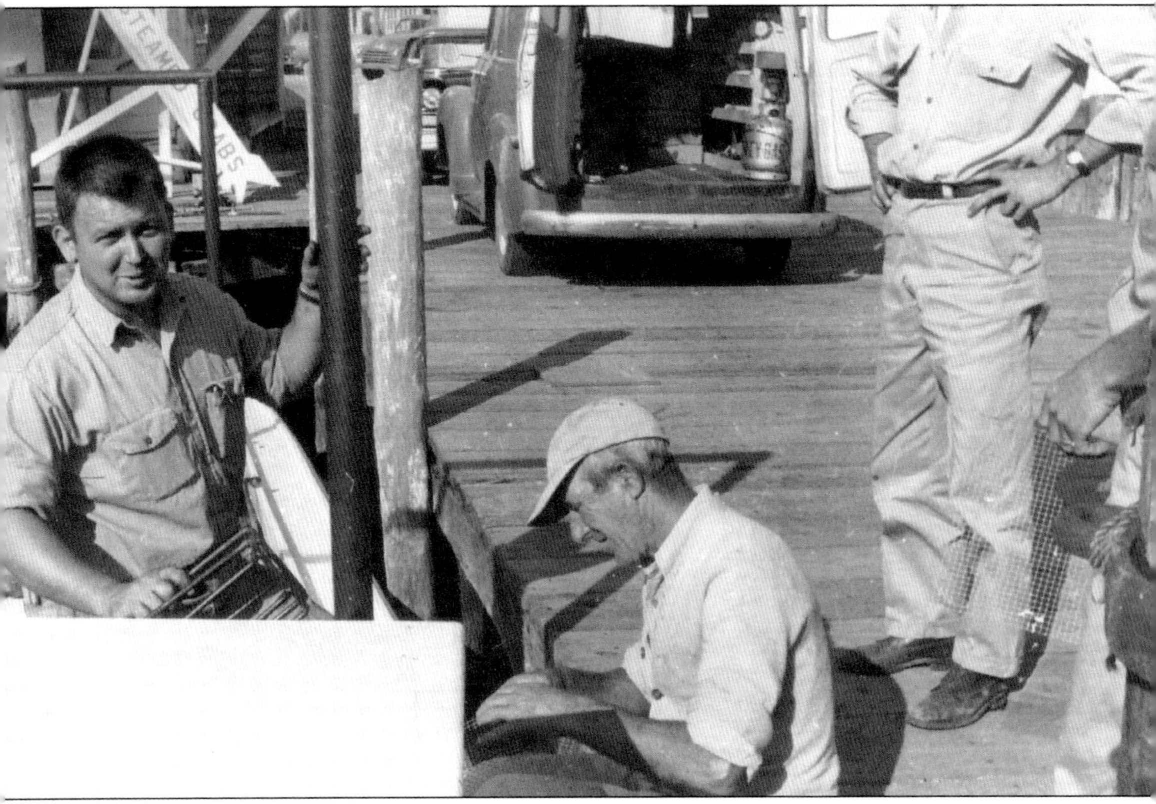

Jimmy Crouch works with Capt. Max Jacobs on his boat *Pres*. Jimmy worked as a general and marine electrical and plumbing contractor with his father, Cecil Crouch. Captain Jacobs was a lifelong waterman. His grandson is Mayor Jay Jacobs. (Courtesy of Betty Jacobs.)

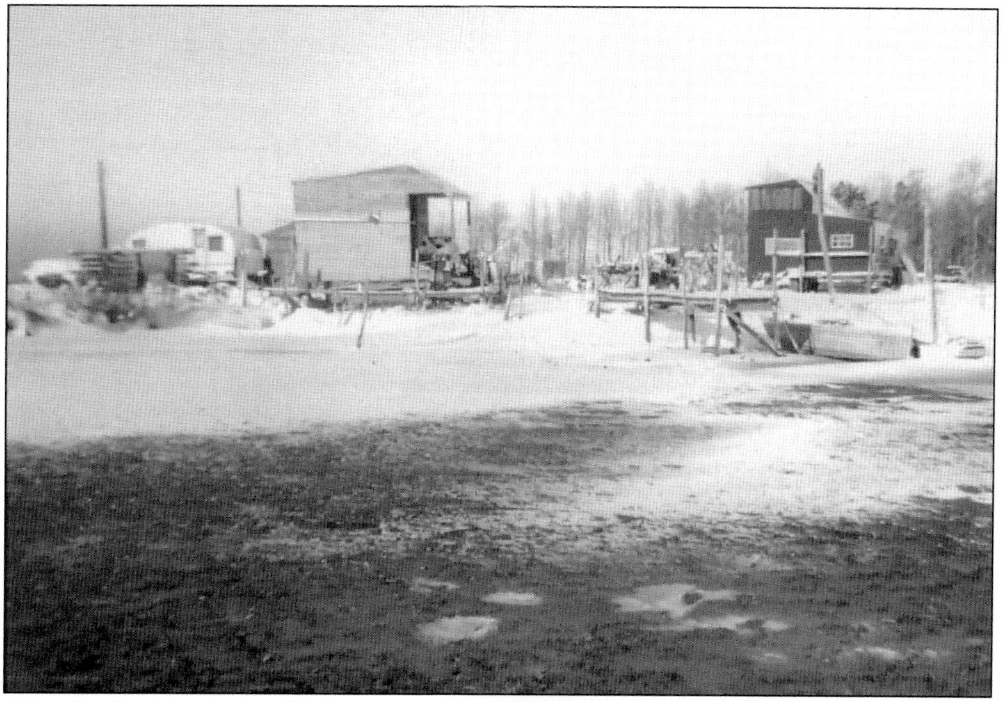

Cain's Seafood, located on Walnut Street at Rock Hall Harbor, is pictured during a snowstorm in 1958. Bill Cain founded the company in 1957 after fishing the preceding year in Rock Hall with Capt. Charles Blackiston. The business operated year-round wholesaling and retailing local seafood and offered slips for off-load and rent. The Cain family operated the business until 1995. The facility is now privately owned. (Courtesy of Madelyn Cornelius.)

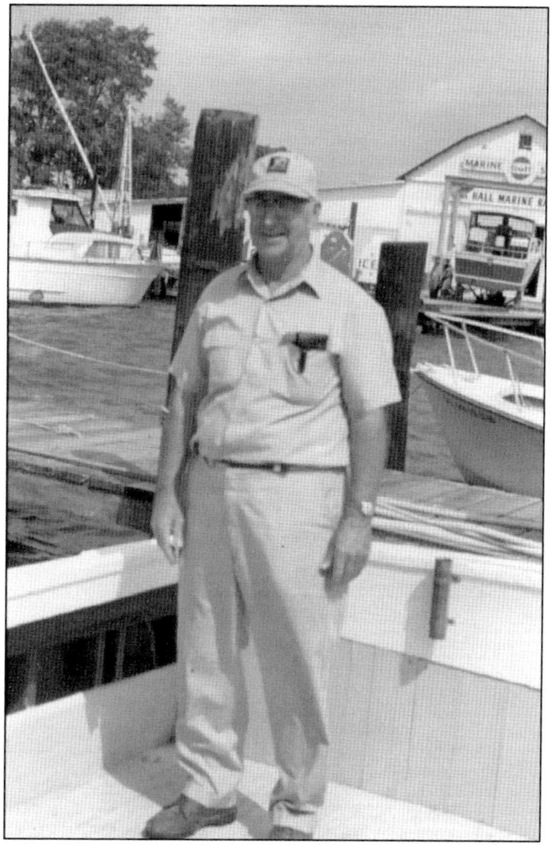

Capt. Roby Cornelius is pictured aboard his boat, the *Rose Elma*, in 1974. This picture was taken at his slip at Rock Hall Marine Railway. Captain Roby began his career on the water when he was 11 years old. He was a commercial and charter captain who was also famous for making beaten biscuits with his wife, Rose Elma. (Courtesy of Madelyn Cornelius.)

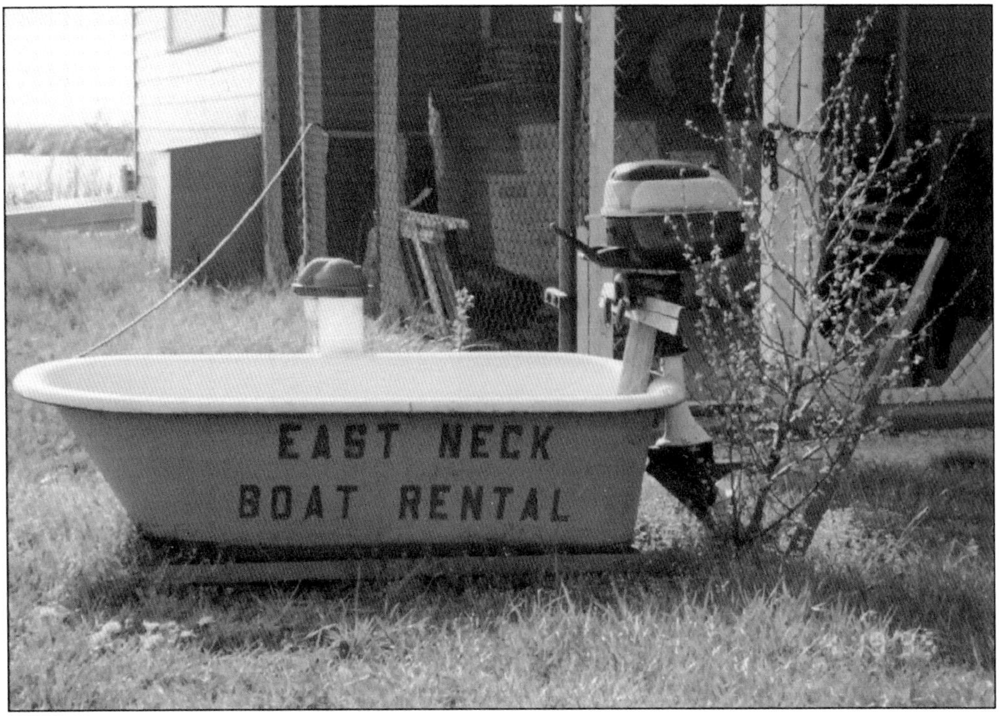

This unique sign advertising East Neck Boat Rental greets those arriving at the Eastern Neck Island Bridge south of Rock Hall. The public can rent boats and "soft crab" (catch soft crabs) along the Eastern Neck Island Narrows flats, a popular soft-crab spot. (Courtesy of Madelyn Cornelius.)

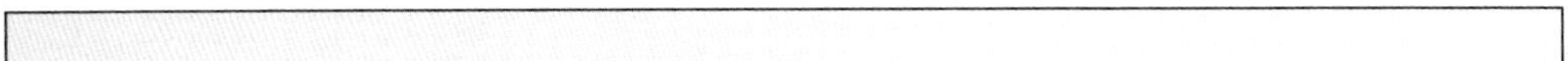

The Eastern Neck Island Bridge sits between the Chester River and the Chesapeake Bay and takes visitors to the Eastern Neck National Wildlife Refuge, just a few miles from Rock Hall. This 2,285-acre island refuge is a major feeding and resting place for migratory and wintering waterfowl and is home to the endangered Delmarva fox squirrel and the threatened bald eagle. (Courtesy of Madelyn Cornelius.)

The *Hey Rube* is pictured in Rock Hall Harbor at the Sharp Street Wharf near an icebreaker boat that had been sent to clear the harbor of ice so the watermen could get out in the Chesapeake Bay. (Courtesy of Jack Jester.)

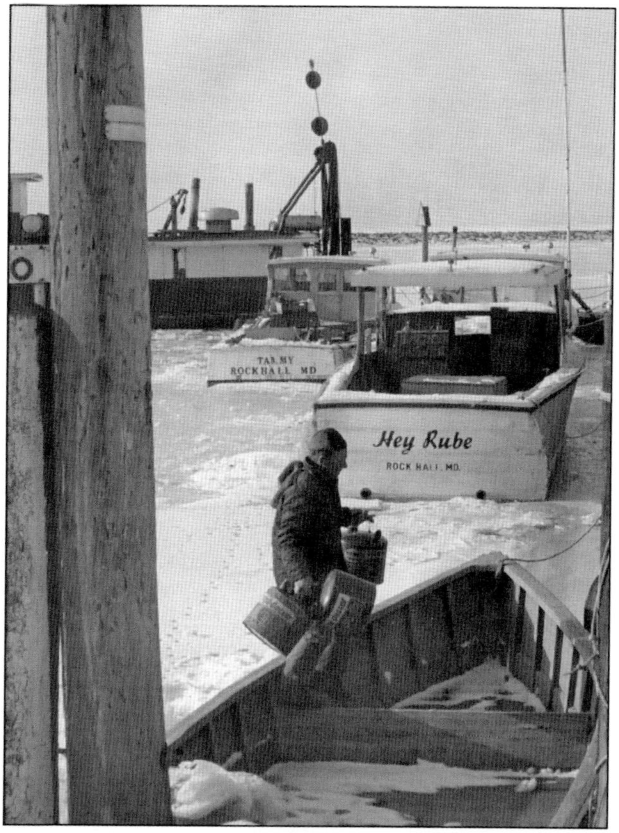

Roby Cornelius Jr. and his wife, Madelyn, who worked as a team year-round in the seafood business, also operated a goose-picking company at their home on North Main Street in Rock Hall for many years. Madelyn, who has enjoyed photography all her life, is a devoted member of the Rock Hall Seventh-Day Adventist Church and continues making and offering the famous coconut cakes baked by her mother-in-law, "Miss" Rose Elma. The recipe is a family secret. Family and Rock Hall traditions and heritage are most important to Madelyn. (Courtesy of Madelyn Cornelius.)

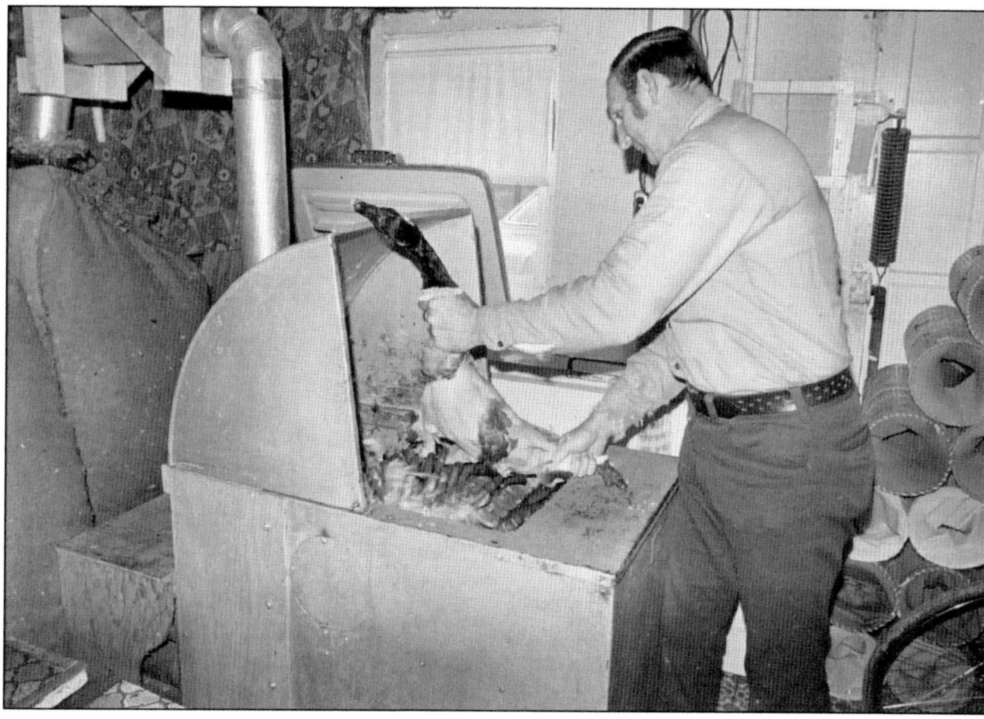

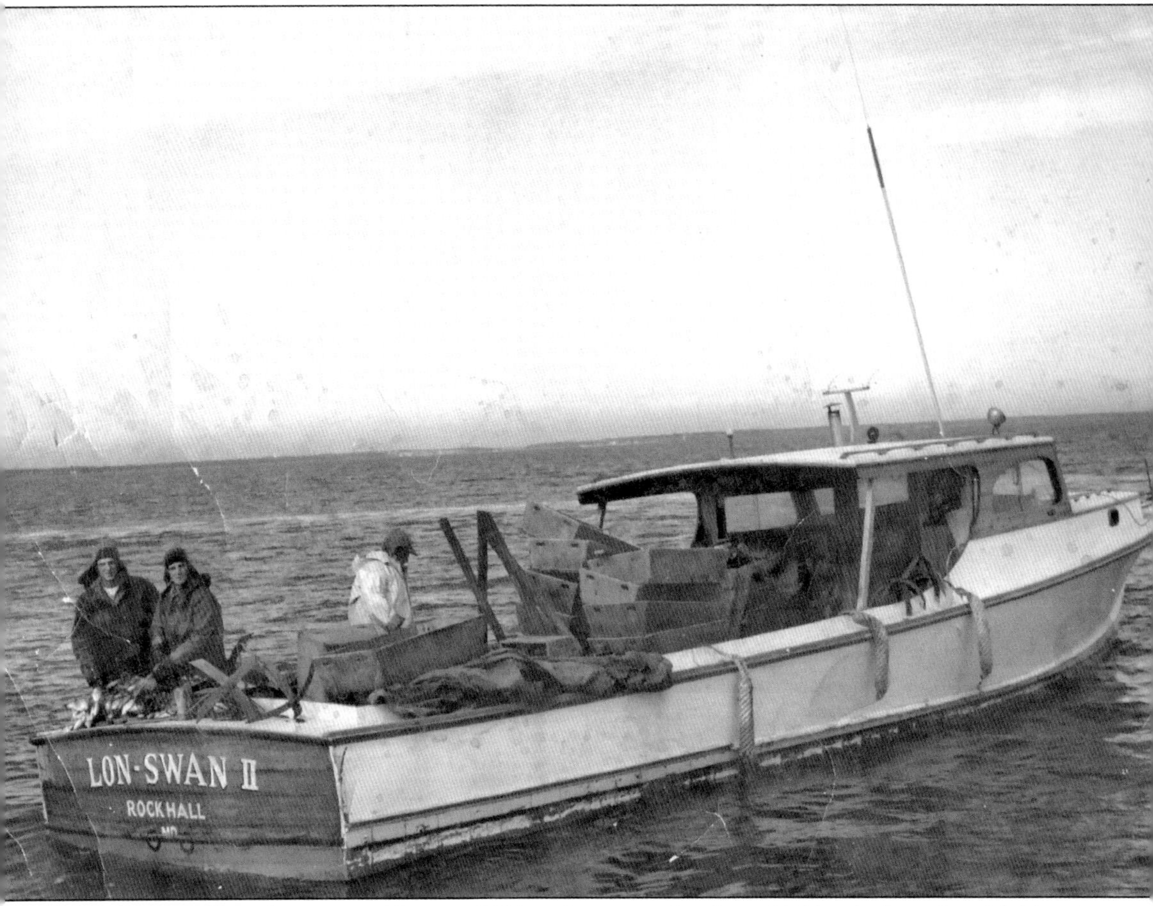

The *Lon Swan II* is pictured here in 1964 with its captain, Cope Hubbard, aboard and fishing in the Chesapeake Bay. Captain Hubbard, a longtime Rock Hall waterman, was the grand marshal in the 2007 Rock Hall Fourth of July Parade, which also celebrated the town's 300th anniversary. Cope had two brothers, Wilkins and Alonzo "Lon." The three brothers owned the *Lon Swan I* in partnership, and it was built by Lon in his backyard. The *Lon Swan II* was built in Wingate, Maryland, by Harvey Hurley for Cope. Lon also built two other boats, the *Gen Mac* and the *Oneida I*, for his brother-in-law, Capt. Naudain Francis. The Hubbard brothers were also in business together as Hubbard's Pier and Seafood. (Courtesy of Jack Jester.)

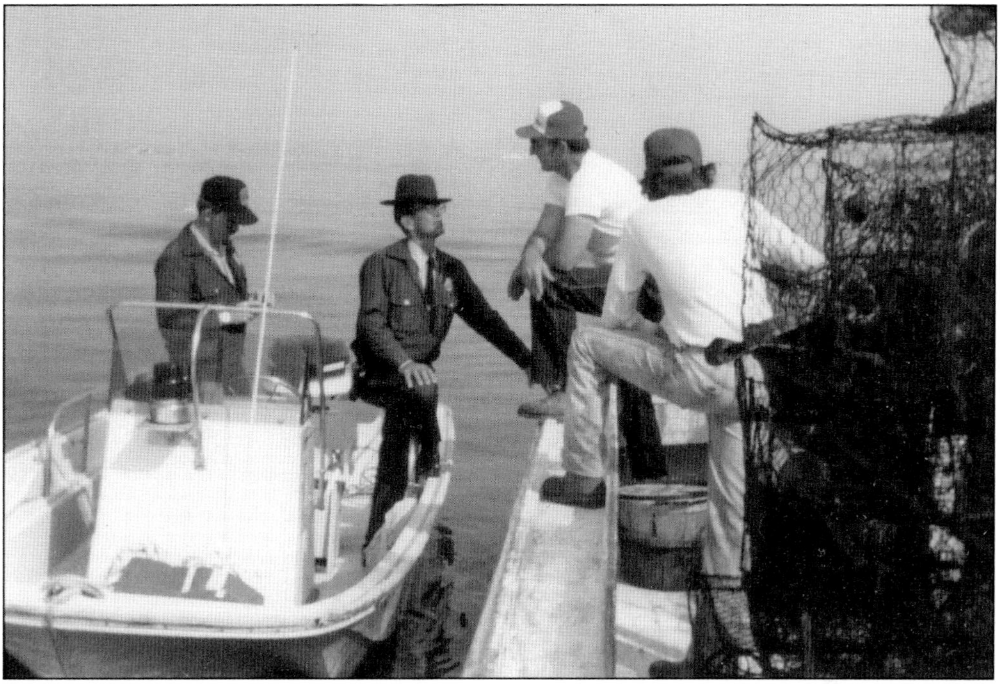

From left to right, Maryland marine police officers Ted Capel and Meryl Stevens check out watermen Billy Cain and Roby Cornelius Jr. aboard Roby's boat, the *Robyn De*, crabbing in the Chesapeake Bay just off Rock Hall. (Courtesy of Madelyn Cornelius.)

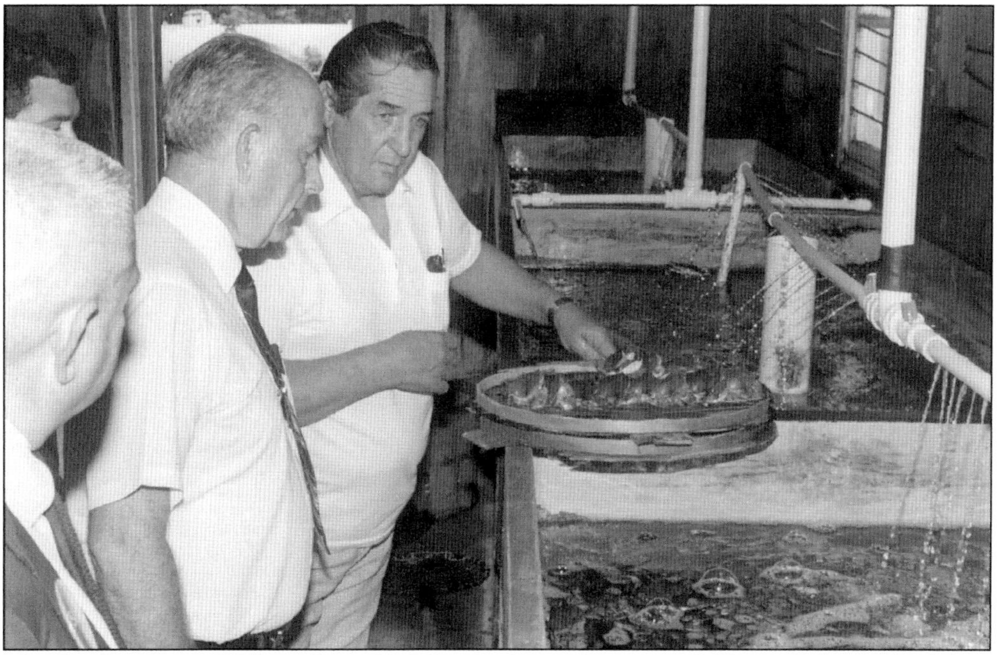

Maryland governor William Donald Schaefer (center) visits with Ernie Coleman (right) to learn more about soft-crab sloughing operations in the 1980s. Also pictured is longtime former Chestertown mayor and Kent County Economic Board chairman Elmer E. Horsey (left). (Courtesy of Madelyn Cornelius.)

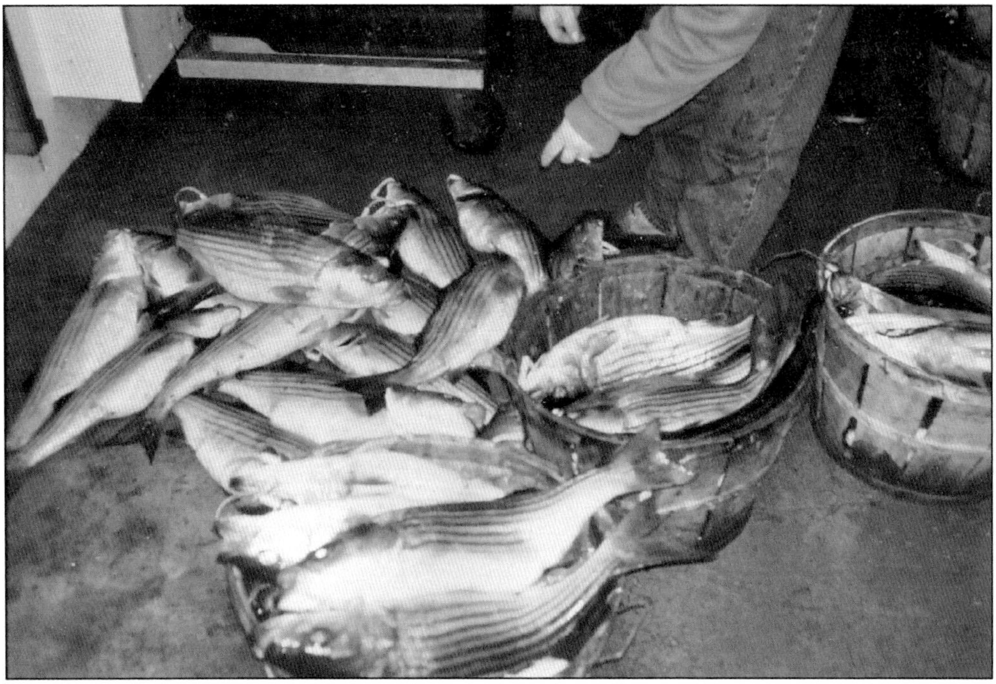

A successful day of fishing for rockfish in the Chesapeake Bay produced several baskets ready to ship to buyers at Hubbard's Pier and Seafood. (Courtesy of Madelyn Cornelius.)

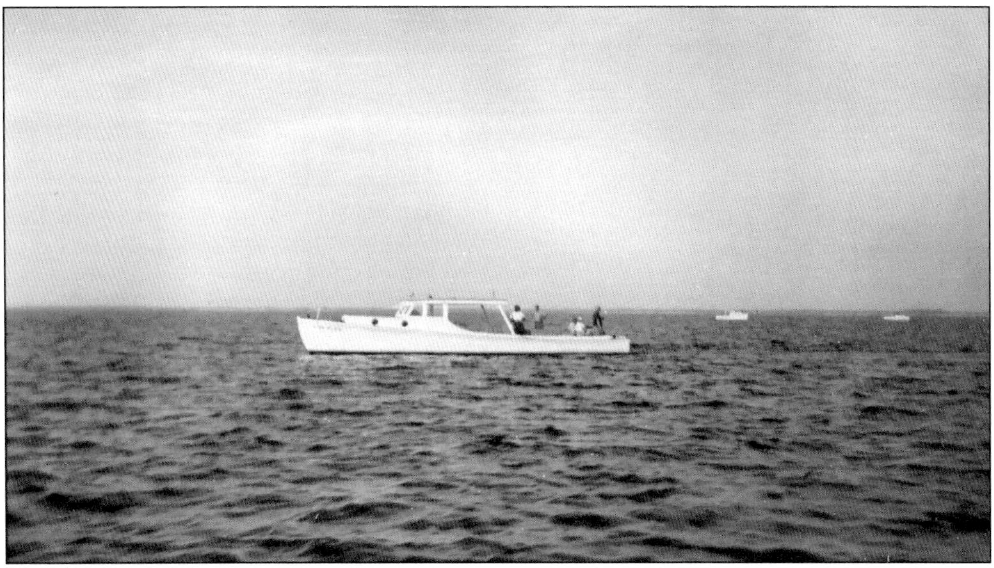

The *Rose Elma*, owned by Capt. Roby Cornelius, is pictured in the Chesapeake Bay just off Rock Hall. The *Rose Elma*, named after Roby's wife, was built in Chestertown. His other boat, the *Myrna*, named after his daughter, was built at Hooper's Island, Maryland. (Courtesy of Madelyn Cornelius.)

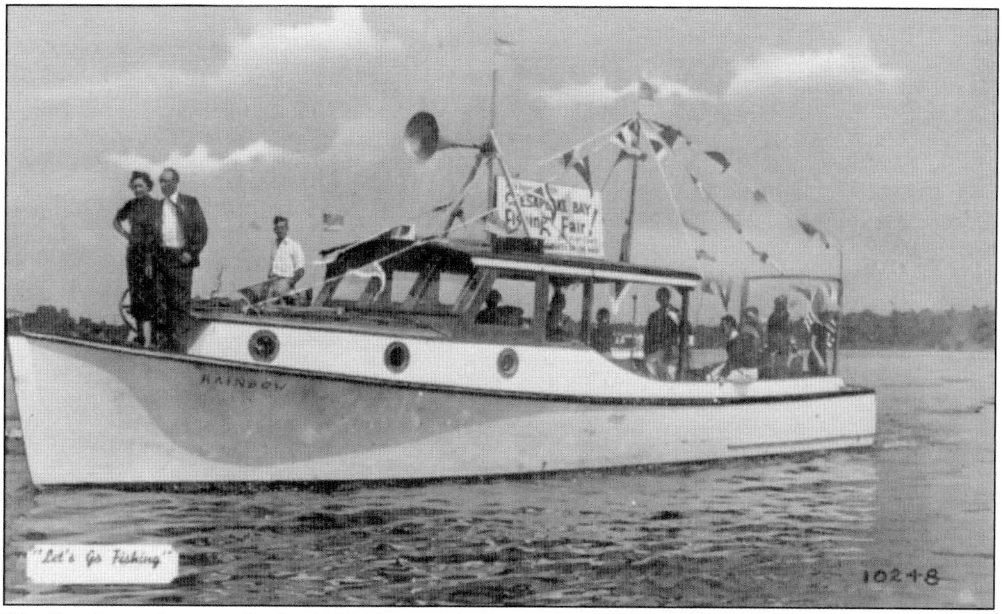

The *Rainbow* advertises for the 1938 Chesapeake Bay Fishing Fair. Capt. Grover Carter built the boats *Rainbow* and *Silver Moon* in partnership with Capt. Josh Thomas. In 1940, the federal government bought the *Rainbow* for use during the war. Capt. Carter bought the boat back in 1946. The boat was later owned by Capt. Farnsworth "Fonnie" Sewell. (Courtesy of Dorothy McKinney.)

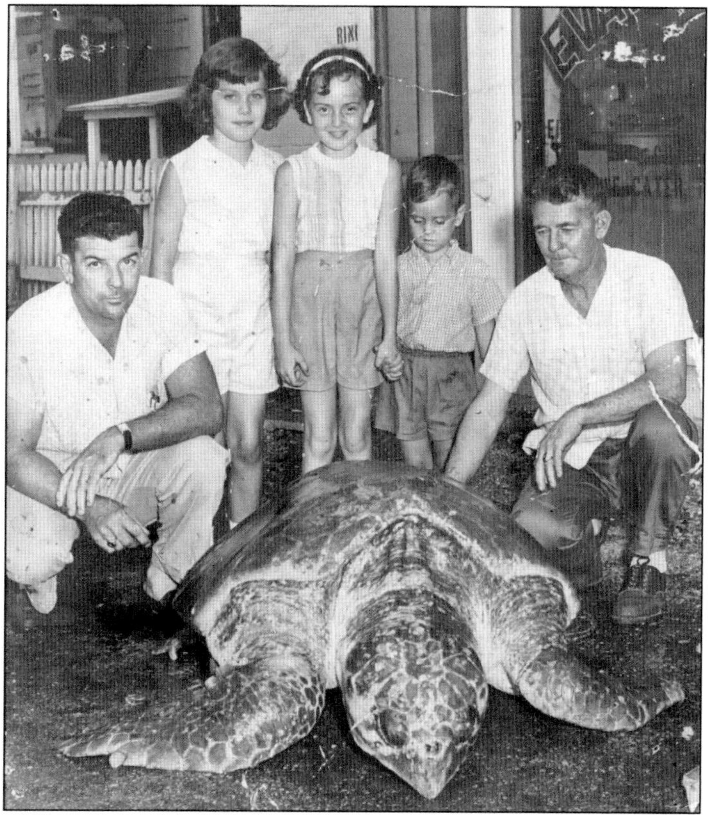

This photograph was taken at Evans Seafood, now Waterman's Crab House in Rock Hall. Looking at the giant turtle presumably taken from the nearby waters of the Chesapeake Bay are, from left to right, Roy Evans, owner of Evans Seafood; Carol Cox; Cheryl Anderson Jacobs; Johnny Anderson; and Roy's father, Willard Evans. (Courtesy of Madelyn Cornelius.)

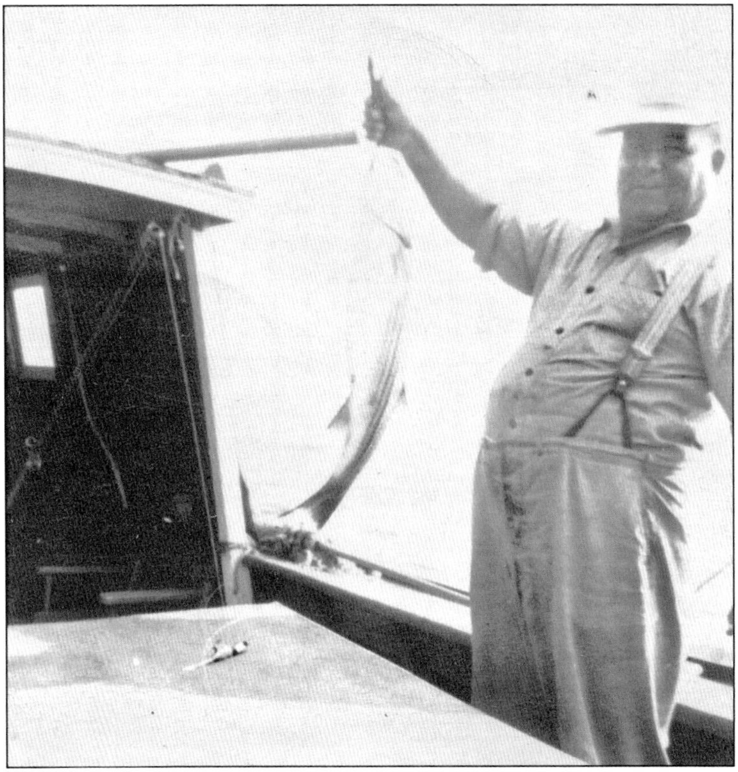

Capt. Frank Jacob shows off his catch on his boat, *Let's Go*. The boat was named by his friend Nobby Glenn. Nobby told Captain Frank "you should name your boat *Let's Go*, because every time you come get me you say, 'Let's Go!' " (Courtesy of Bobby Jacob.)

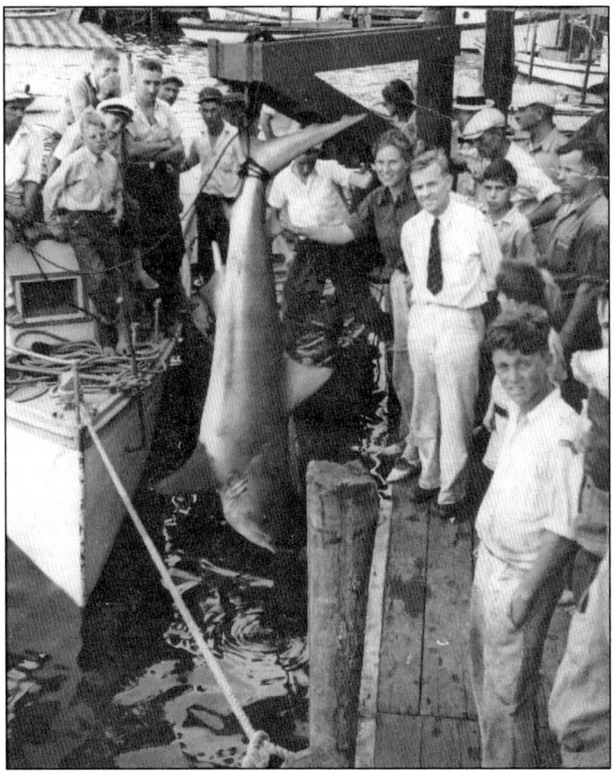

This shark, caught off Rock Hall and brought in by Capt. Frank Jacob on his boat *Let's Go*, was displayed at Rock Hall harbor. Among those pictured are Burgess Tucker and Captain Frank. (Courtesy of Jack Jester and Bobby Jacob.)

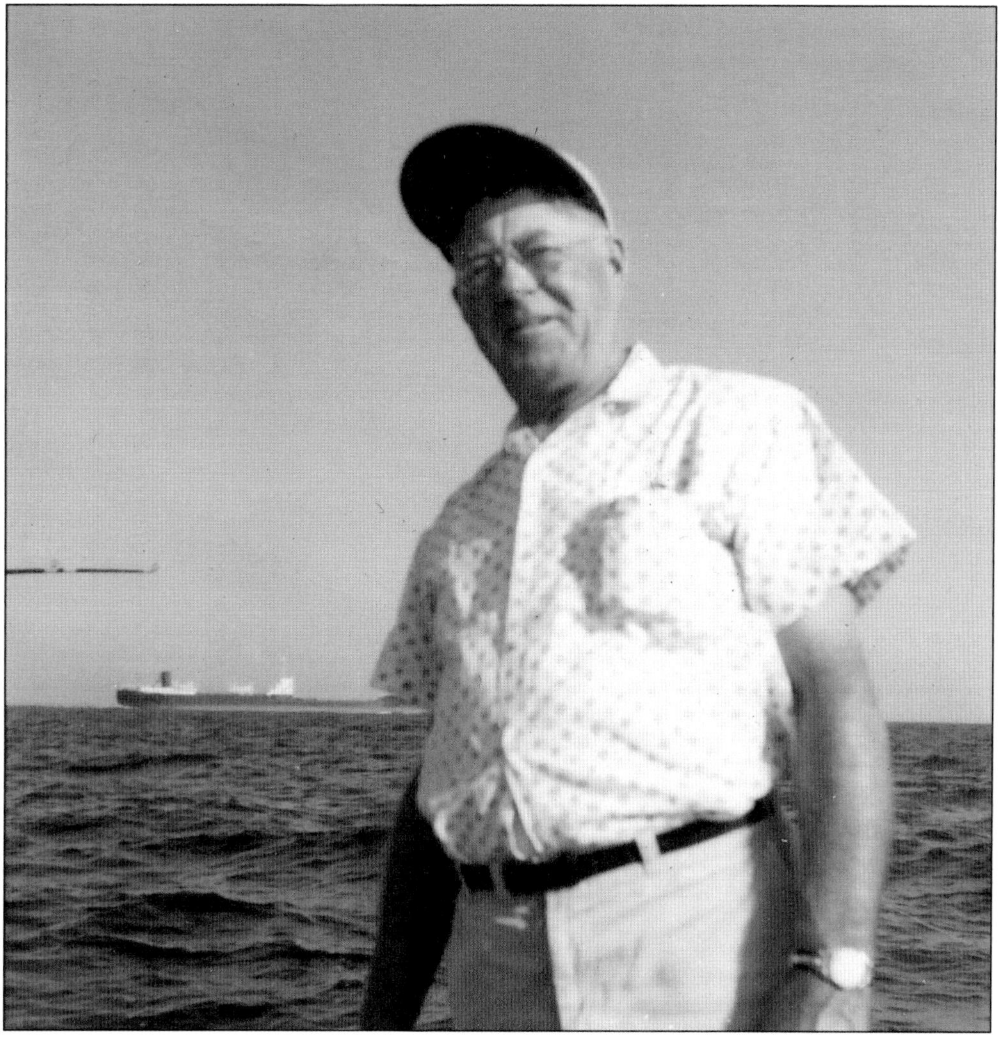

Capt. Buck Brady was the captain of the boat *Frances*, now on display at the Waterman's Museum in Rock Hall. The *Frances* is now known as *Old Buck*. Captain Buck was brother to other successful watermen Capt. Medford "Muffy" and Capt. Charley Brady. (Courtesy of Honey Wood.)

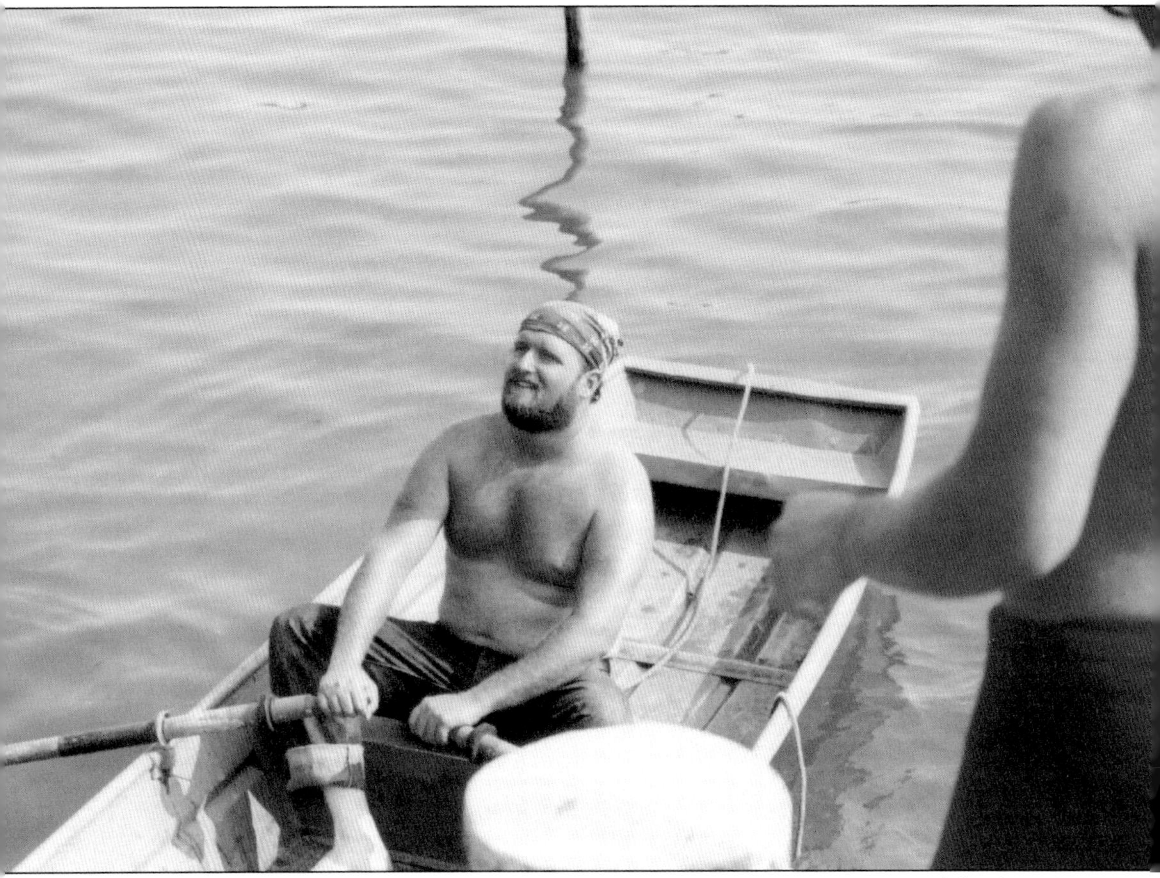

Capt. Jerry Creighton is pictured as he competes in a rowing contest at one of the first Kent County Waterman's Days in Rock Hall. Waterman's Day is a Fourth of July happening and one of the largest events in Kent County that continues today. Captain Creighton is the official photographer for the Kent County Waterman's Association, and he owns J and J Seafood in Galena, Maryland. (Courtesy of Jerry Creighton.)

Three

BUSINESS

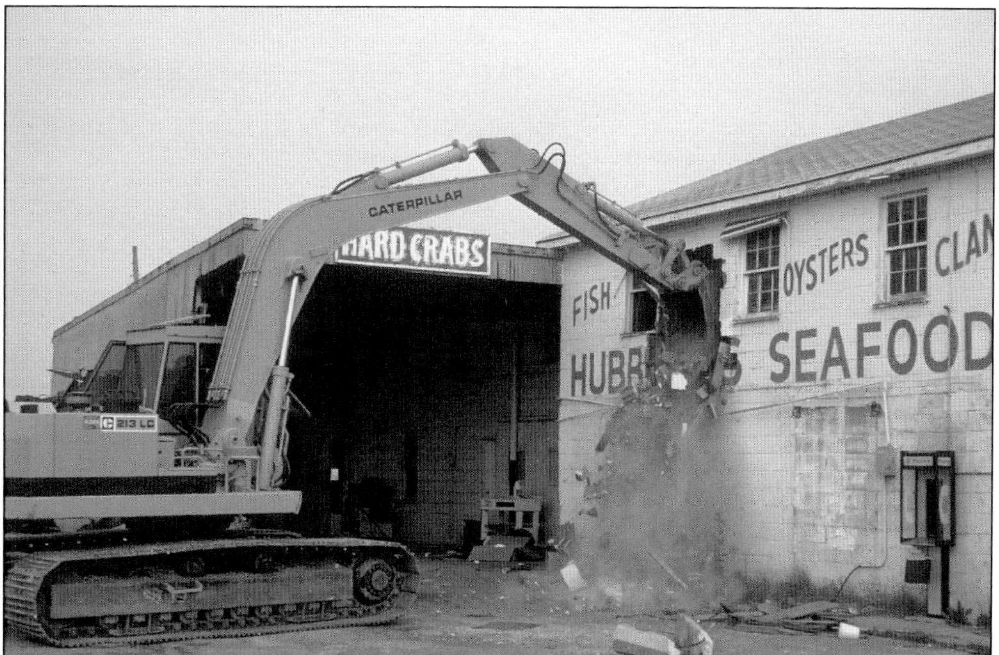

A longtime Rock Hall seafood business, Hubbard's Pier and Seafood closed and was torn down in the early 1980s. Locals remember this day as the end of a wonderful era. Many gathered to say goodbye and take photographs. (Photograph courtesy of Heather R. Davidson.)

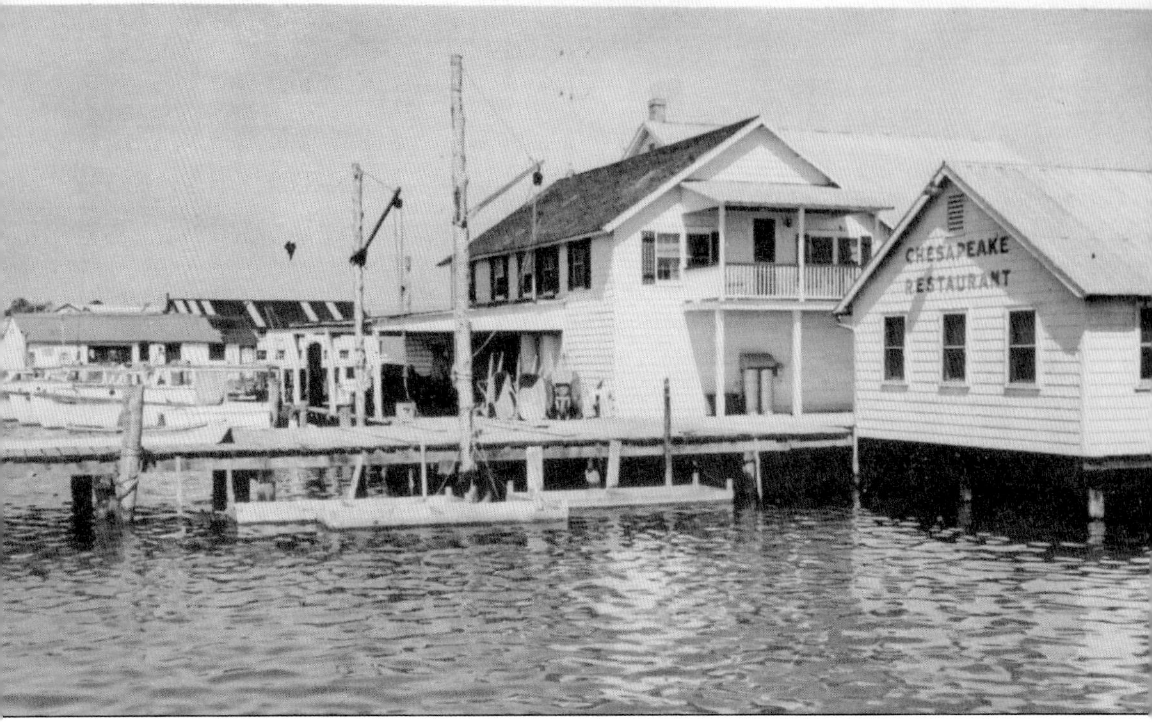

At least 30 boats could be chartered from the Chesapeake Restaurant. Their advertisements boasted "fishing tackle, boat accommodations, bait and all kinds of guide information." The Chesapeake Restaurant, along with Bud's Seafood, no longer exists. Rock Hall Landing Marina is now located in this area. (Courtesy of Jack Jester, Ida Mae Dulin, and Dorothy McKinney.)

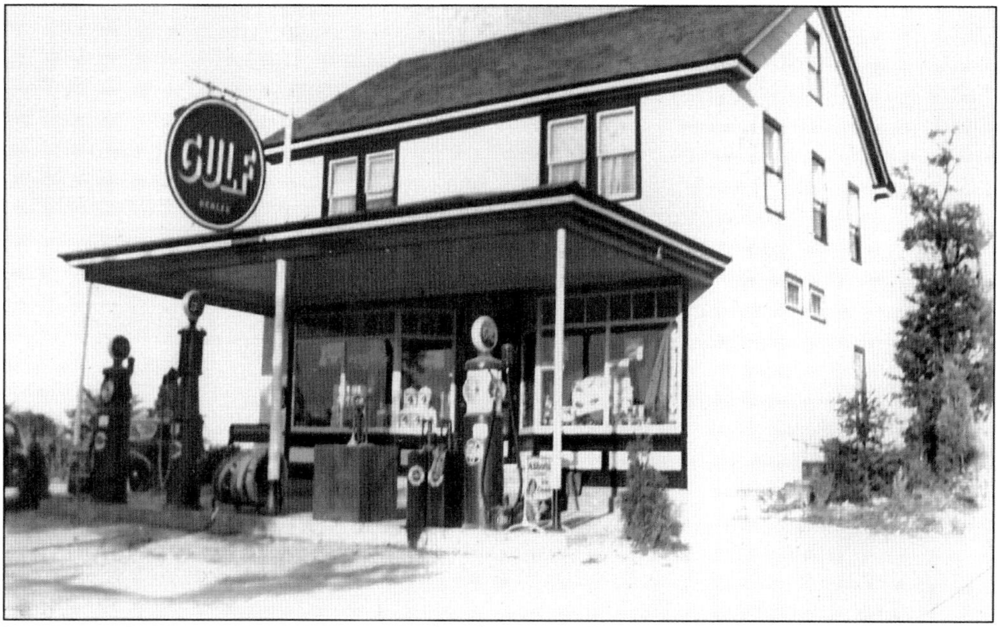

Jacquette's Store, on Route 20 just outside of Rock Hall in an area referred to as Edesville, is pictured with its Gulf gas pumps. The store, originally owned by J. C. Stewart, was later purchased by LeRoy Jacquette. Medcalf, Jacquette's son, became the proprietor after "Mr. Roy's" retirement. (Courtesy of Julie J. Stephens.)

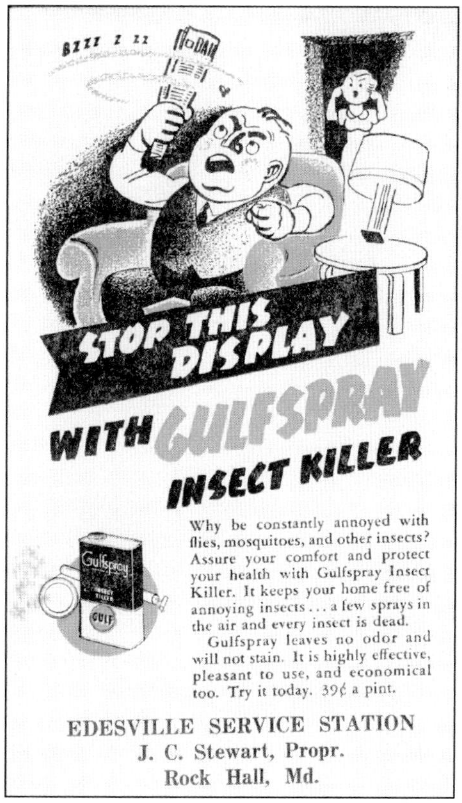

Also known as Jacquette's Store, the Edesville Service Station—J. C. Stewart, proprietor—advertised Gulfspray for sale. It is now owned by the Barry family. (Courtesy of Ida Mae Dulin.)

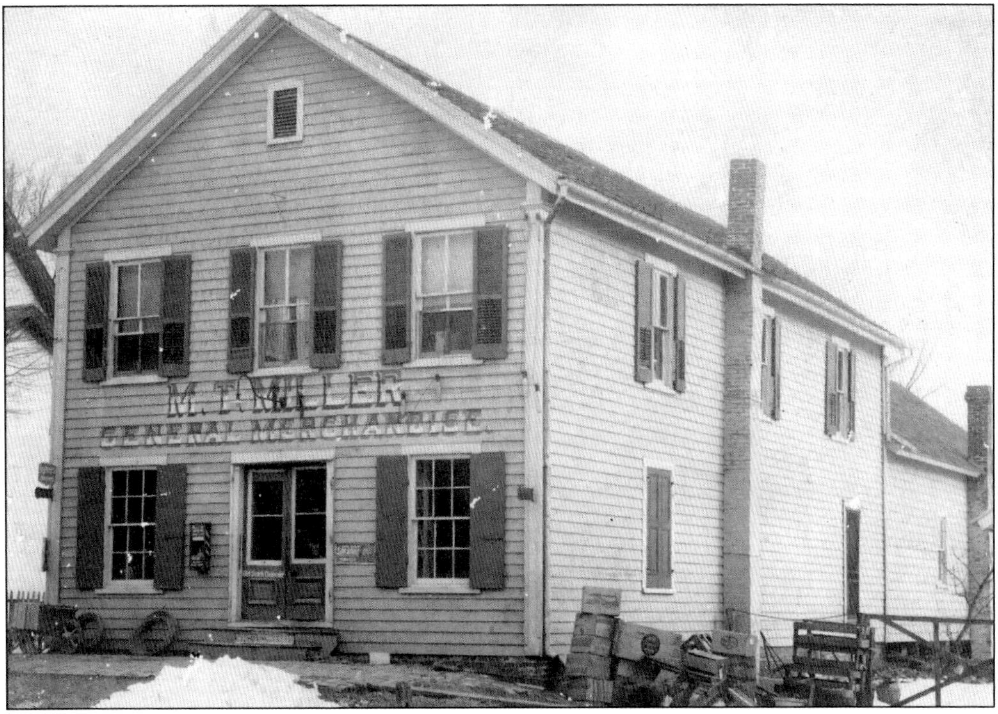

Miller's Store was located on Sharp Street where the Rock Hall Lions Club building stands today. It was owned and operated by Marion T. "Manny" Miller, who was married to Julia Burgess Miller. (Courtesy of Ida Mae Dulin and Dorothy McKinney.)

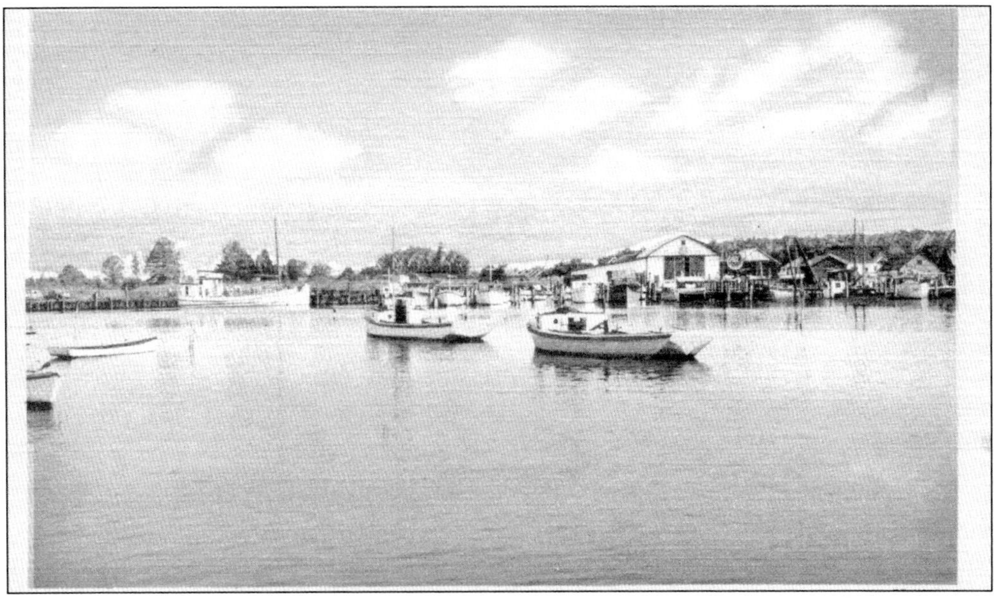

The Rock Hall Marine Railway was founded in 1928 on Hawthorne Road by G. Ellsworth Leary, George N. Coleman, and J. A. Stevens. In 1929 and 1937, J. A. Stevens and George N. Coleman, respectively, sold out to G. Ellsworth Leary, who, upon his death in 1955, left the business to his son, George E. Leary. Rock Hall Marine Railway is still owned and operated by the Leary family—Elmer and Ann and their children, Ricky and Debbie. (Courtesy of Jack Jester.)

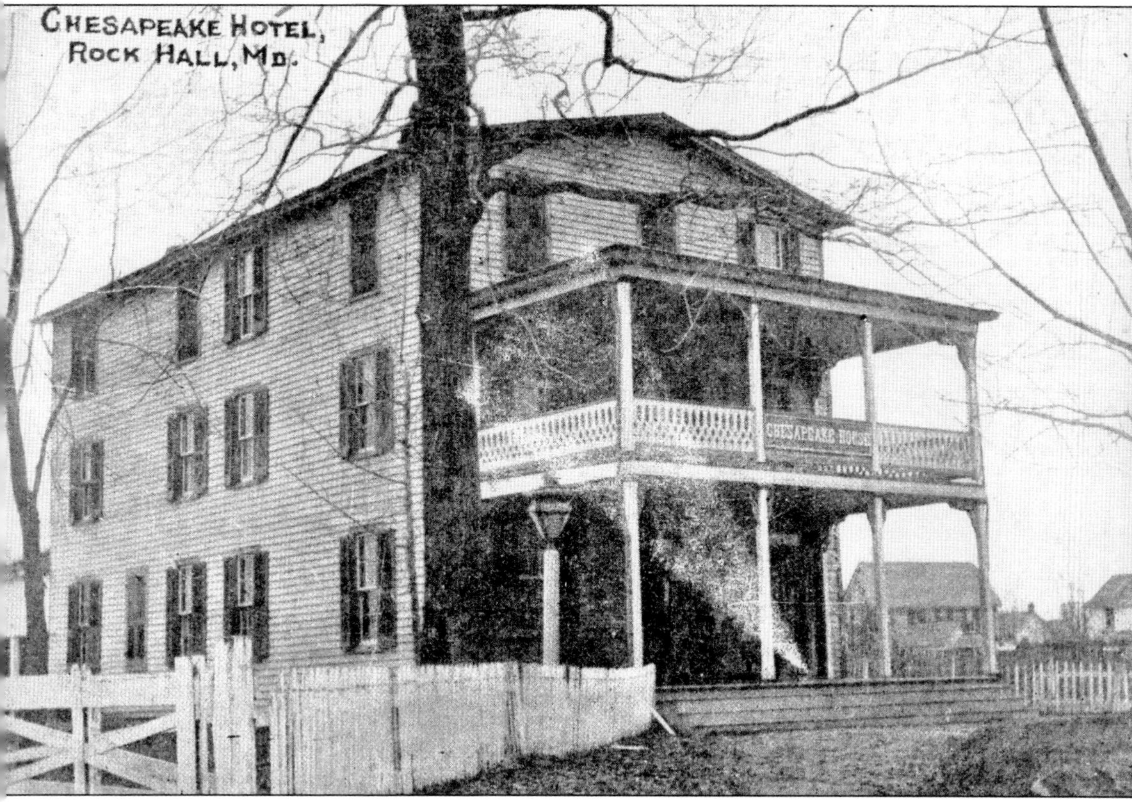

The Chesapeake Hotel, both a hotel and boardinghouse, was located on North Main Street in Rock Hall. When he first began his career as a waterman, Emory "Pie" Edwards remembers during an oyster blight in the Chester River that Piney Neck watermen would come to the Rock Hall bayside off Swan Point to oyster. Instead of going back to Piney Neck each night, they would rent rooms at the Chesapeake. (Courtesy of Ida Mae Dulin and Dorothy McKinney.)

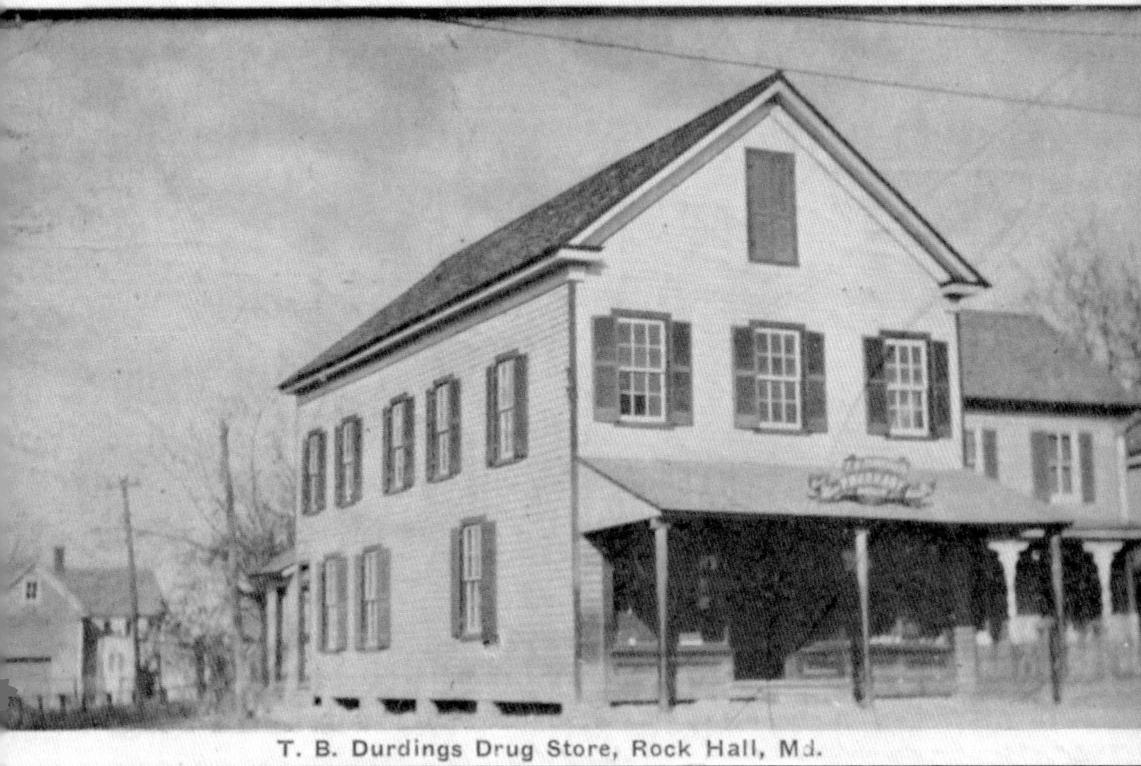

T. B. Durding's Drug Store was the first pharmacy in Rock Hall. It was also the first to have a pay phone and at one time housed the post office. Originally built by Alpheus Phineus Sharp, founder of Sharp and Dohme Pharmaceutical Company, the building was purchased by the Durdings in 1870 and stayed in the Durding family until late 1987, when Art and Mary Sue Willis purchased both Durding's (which they renovated) and Myer's Market. The pharmacist license of Annie T. Durding, dated July 1, 1902, remains on display at Durding's. (Courtesy of Ida Mae Dulin and Dorothy McKinney.)

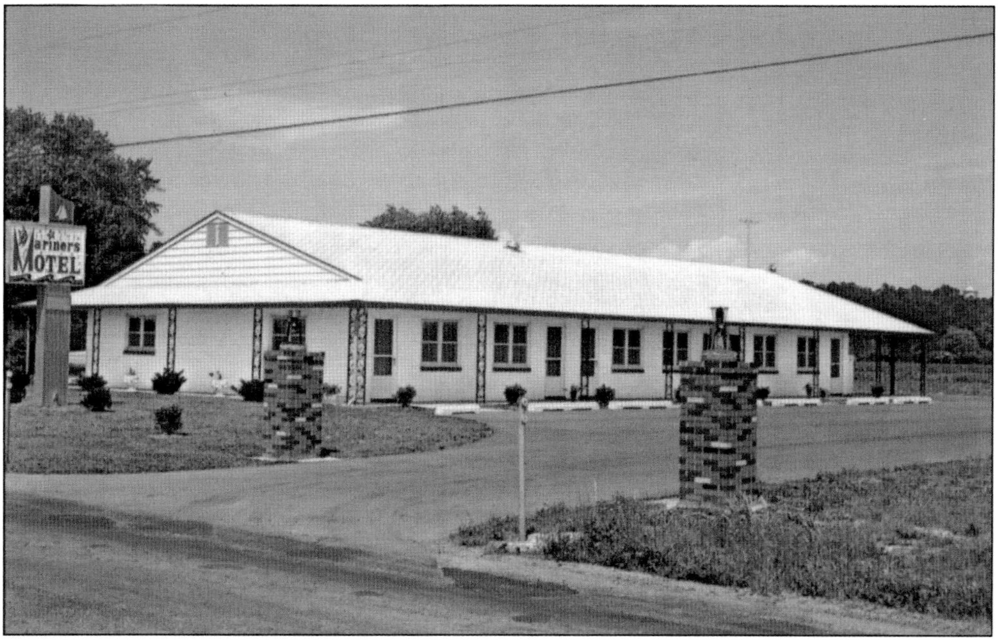

Built by Hilton Crouch in the 1960s, Mariner's Motel is still welcoming visitors to Rock Hall. (Courtesy of Madelyn Cornelius.)

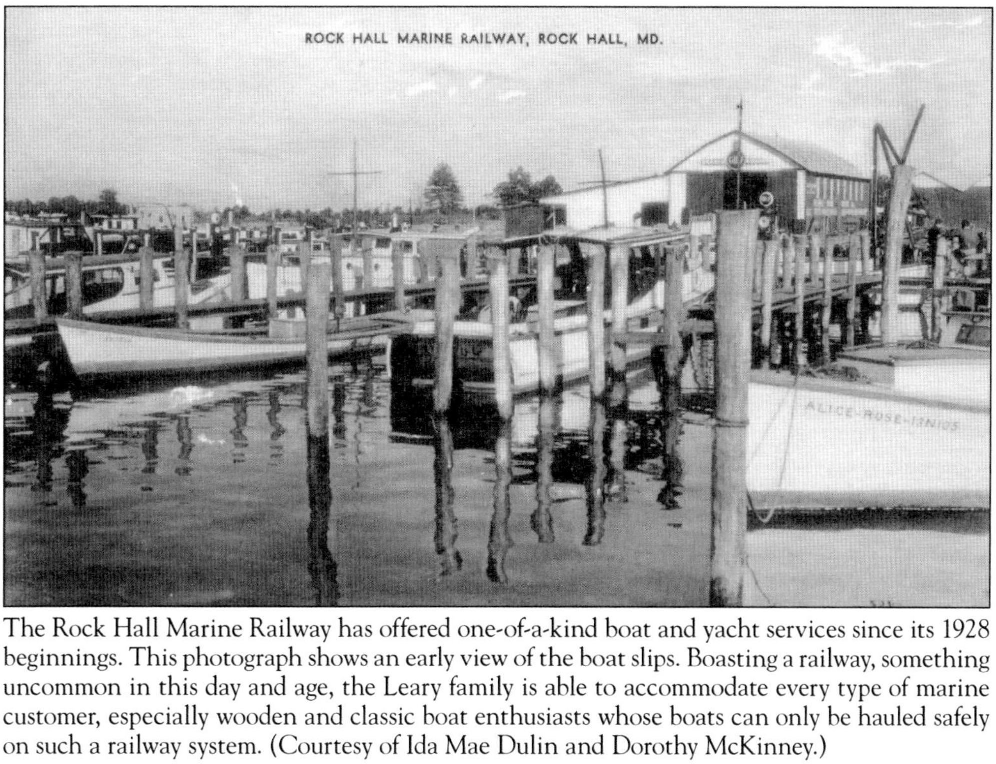

The Rock Hall Marine Railway has offered one-of-a-kind boat and yacht services since its 1928 beginnings. This photograph shows an early view of the boat slips. Boasting a railway, something uncommon in this day and age, the Leary family is able to accommodate every type of marine customer, especially wooden and classic boat enthusiasts whose boats can only be hauled safely on such a railway system. (Courtesy of Ida Mae Dulin and Dorothy McKinney.)

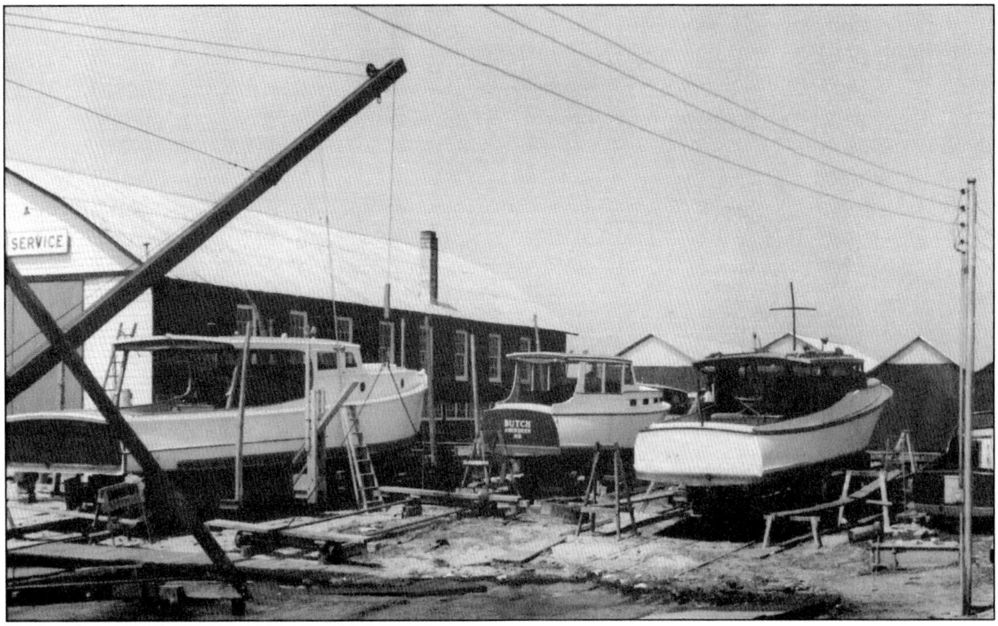

This photograph of the Rock Hall Marine Railway was taken in 1954. Drive by the Rock Hall Marine Railway any day of the week and there are likely buy boats, traditional cruisers, and modern-day boats all being serviced in this traditional Rock Hall way utilizing the railway system and skilled boat carpenters. This allows for large, heavy, wide, or wooden boats to be hauled safely and maintained and repaired to Bristol condition. (Courtesy Jack Jester.)

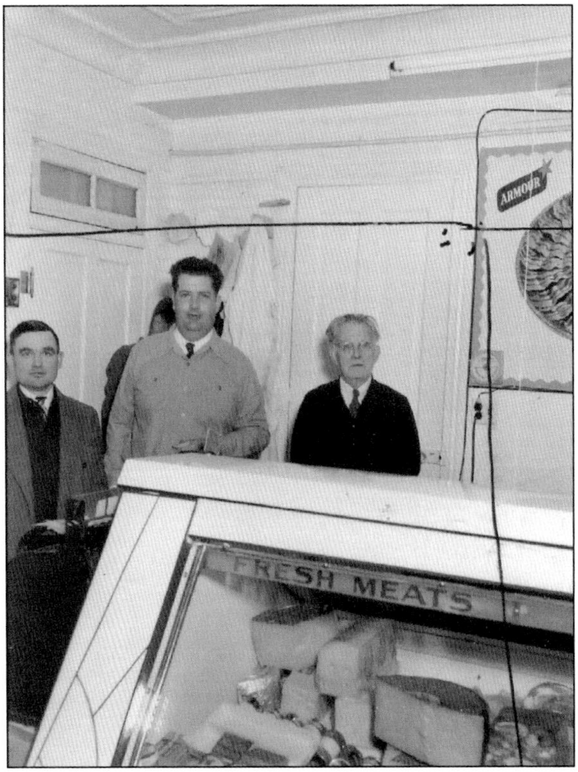

Casey Dowling (center) and Joseph Hogans (right) are seen at Dowling's Grocery Store on Main Street in Rock Hall in the late 1940s. Dowling's offered wonderful meats and made the famous hamburgers for Hersch's Bar. (Courtesy of H. Edward Beekman Jr.)

This photograph was taken in Hersch's Bar on Main Street, Rock Hall. From back to front are Pip Kendall, Maurice Pascall, and Frank Jester. Hersch's was a popular spot for hamburgers, beer, cocktails, pool, and pinball. John Hersch owned the bar. John was husband to "Miss Virginia" of Miss Virginia's Crabcake fame. (Courtesy of H. Edward Beekman Jr.)

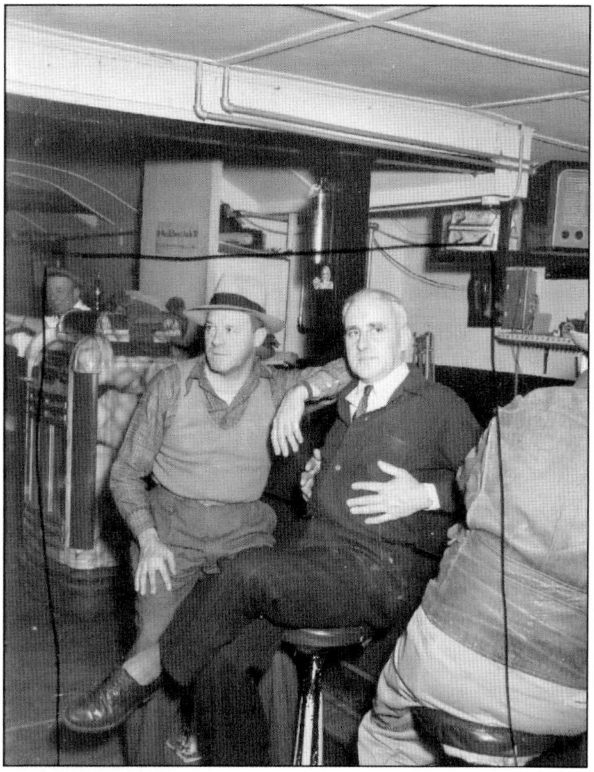

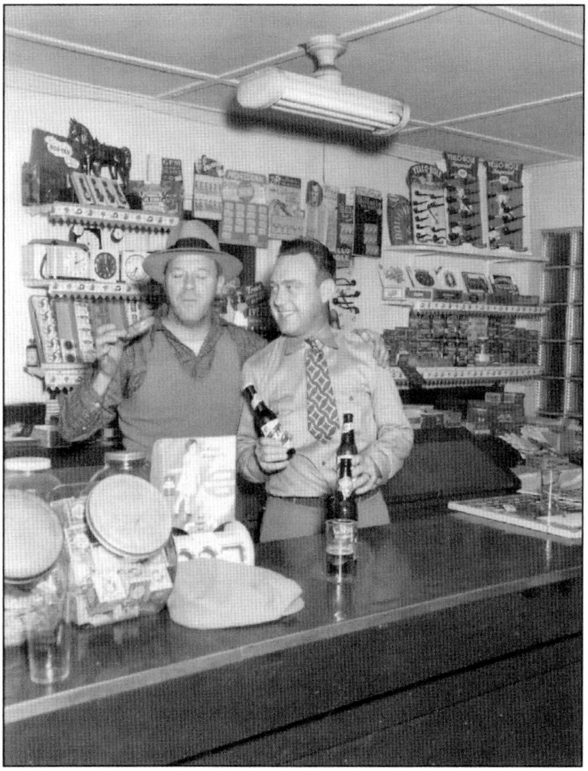

John Hersch, right, is behind the counter at Hersch's Bar on Main Street in Rock Hall with Maurice Pascall. The bar was located next to what is now Bay Leaf Gourmet. Bay Leaf is now owned and operated by Maurice Pascall and Chris Burgess. (Courtesy of H. Edward Beekman Jr.)

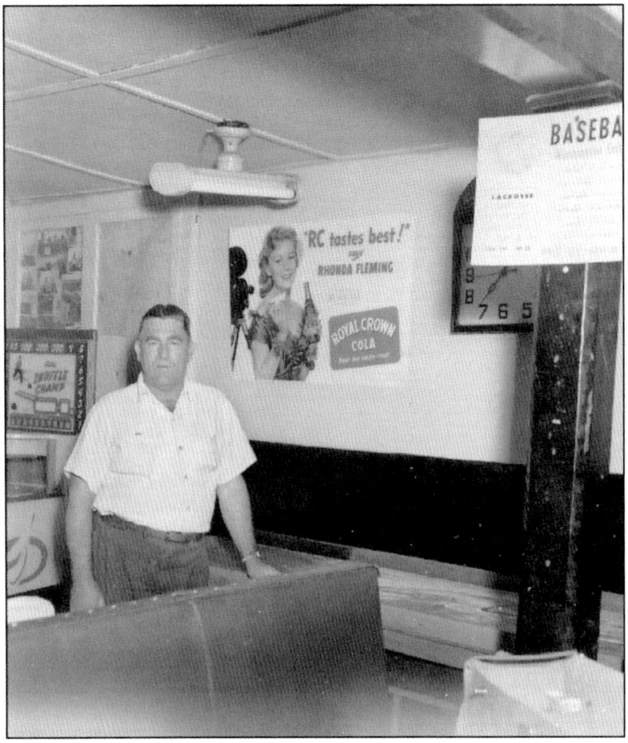

Hersch's Bar was a popular meeting place in Rock Hall. Royal Crown Cola was a popular drink at the time. Enjoying an afternoon is Willard "Peaches" Ashley. (Courtesy of H. Edward Beekman Jr.)

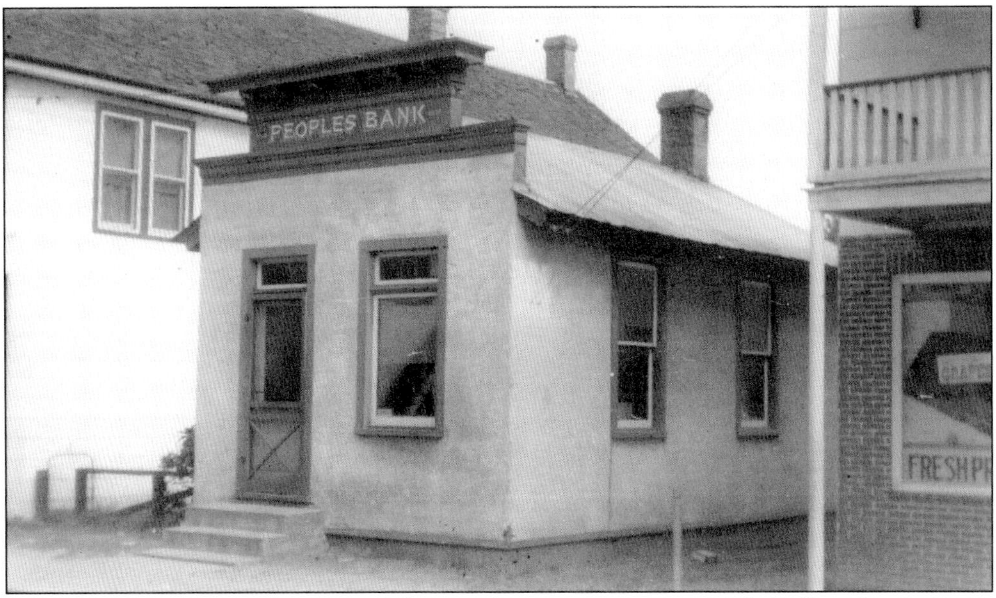

The Peoples Bank opened in part of the Joseph Downey Store in Rock Hall in April 1911. It moved to the location in this photograph in June 1921. Mary Davis Dodson was the first cashier. Upon retiring, her place was filled by Florence Hogans, who held the position until Herbert A. Urie was appointed as cashier. Urie served as cashier until his death in December 1946, and Robert D. Collyer was then appointed to the position. This building is currently the Bay Leaf Gourmet, a popular café owned by Maurice Pascall and Chris Burgess. (Courtesy of H. Edward Beekman Jr.)

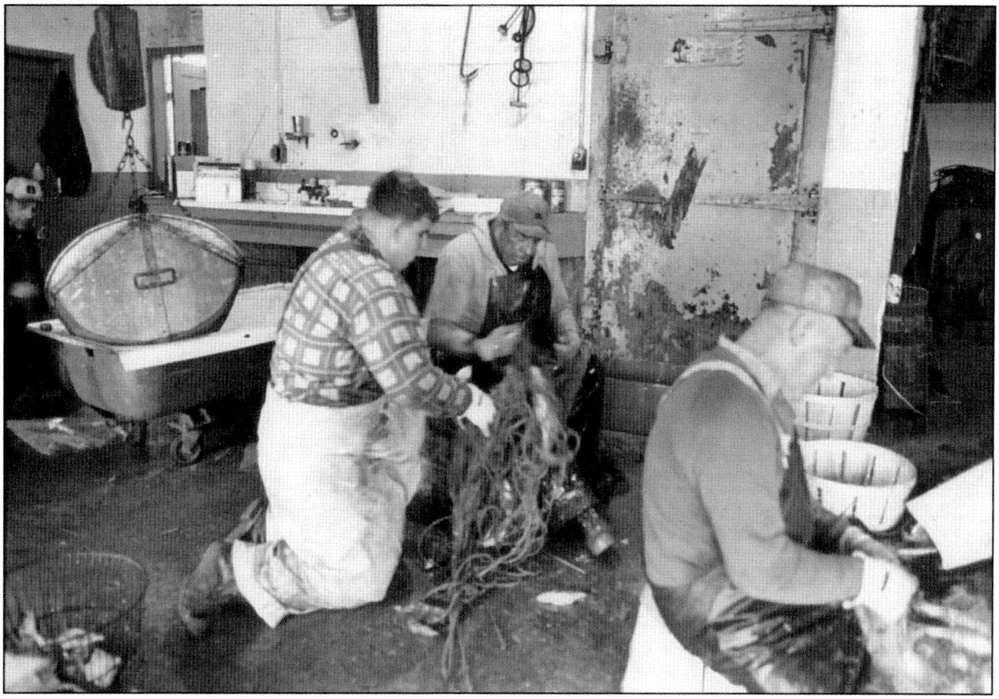

Watermen working at Crouch's Fish House included Tommy Baker and Teddy Creighton. Crouch's Fish House, located next to Hubbard's Pier and Seafood, sold wholesale and retail fish. It was owned by Irving and Hilton Crouch. (Courtesy of H. Edward Beekman Jr.)

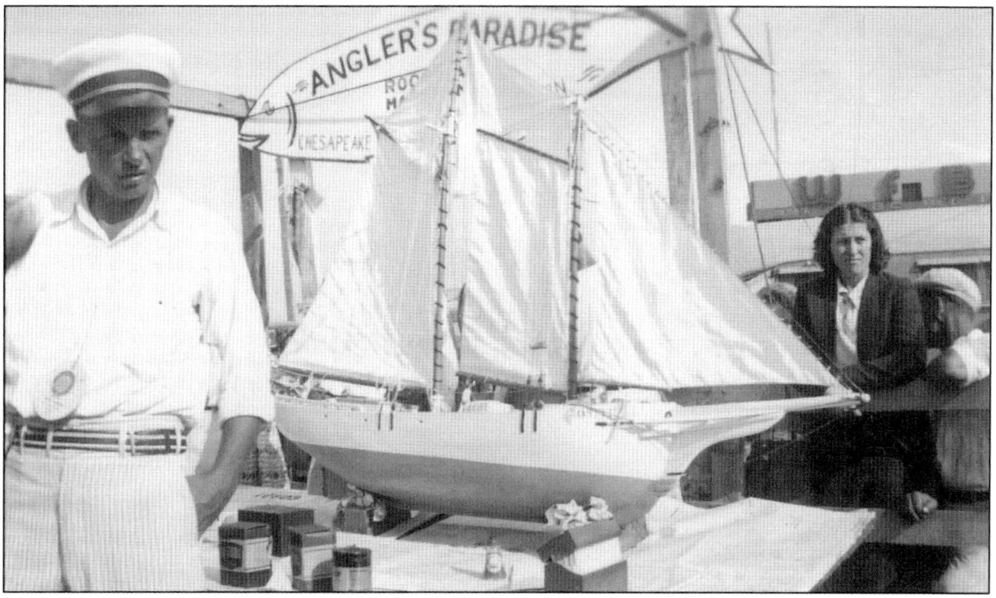

A model sailboat is displayed at the Chesapeake Fishing Fair in 1938, held in Rock Hall. The Chesapeake Bay Fishing Association selected the Swan Point area of Rock Hall for the festivities. The event included fishing, feasting, dancing, and exhibitions. (Courtesy of H. Edward Beekman Jr.)

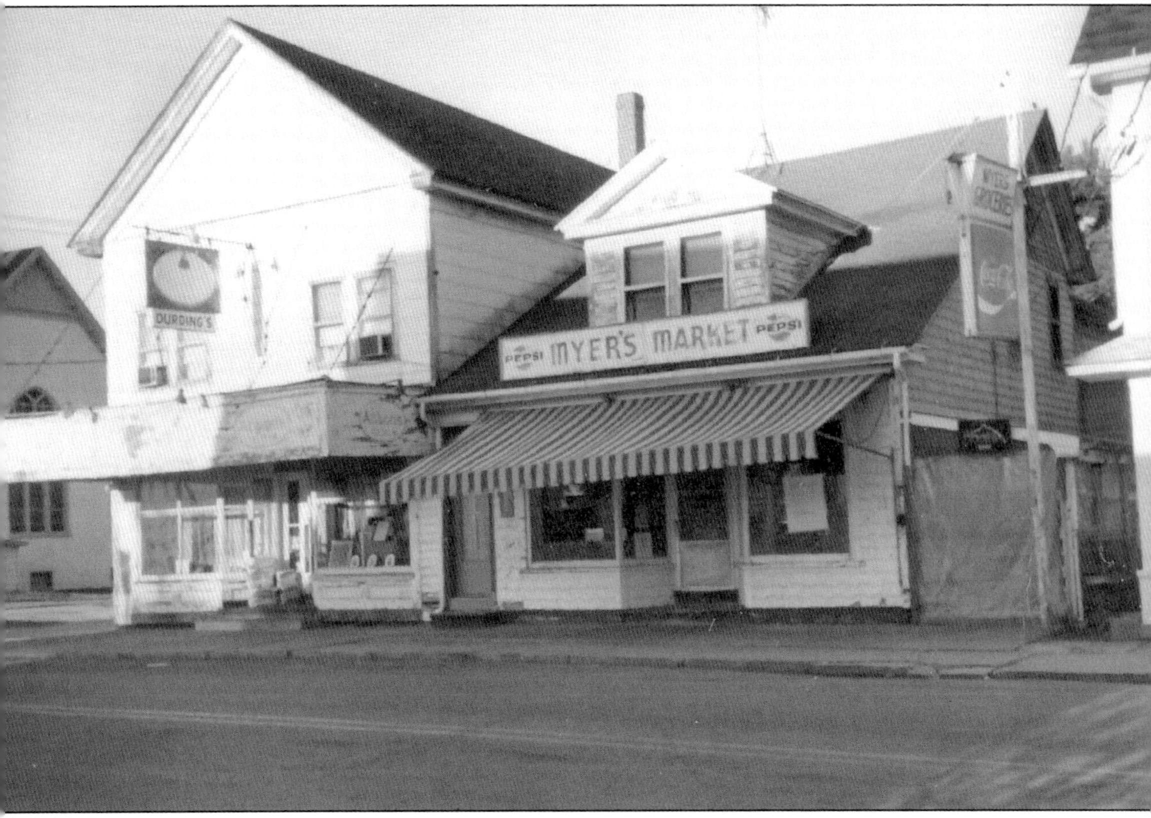

Pictured here in the early 1980s are two popular stores on Main Street—Durding's and Myer's Market. Durding's is still in operation and is known for its ice cream. Myer's Market no longer exists. After this picture was taken, Art and Mary Sue Willis purchased both buildings. The property has been lovingly restored and operates as Durding's Store. (Courtesy of Madelyn Cornelius.)

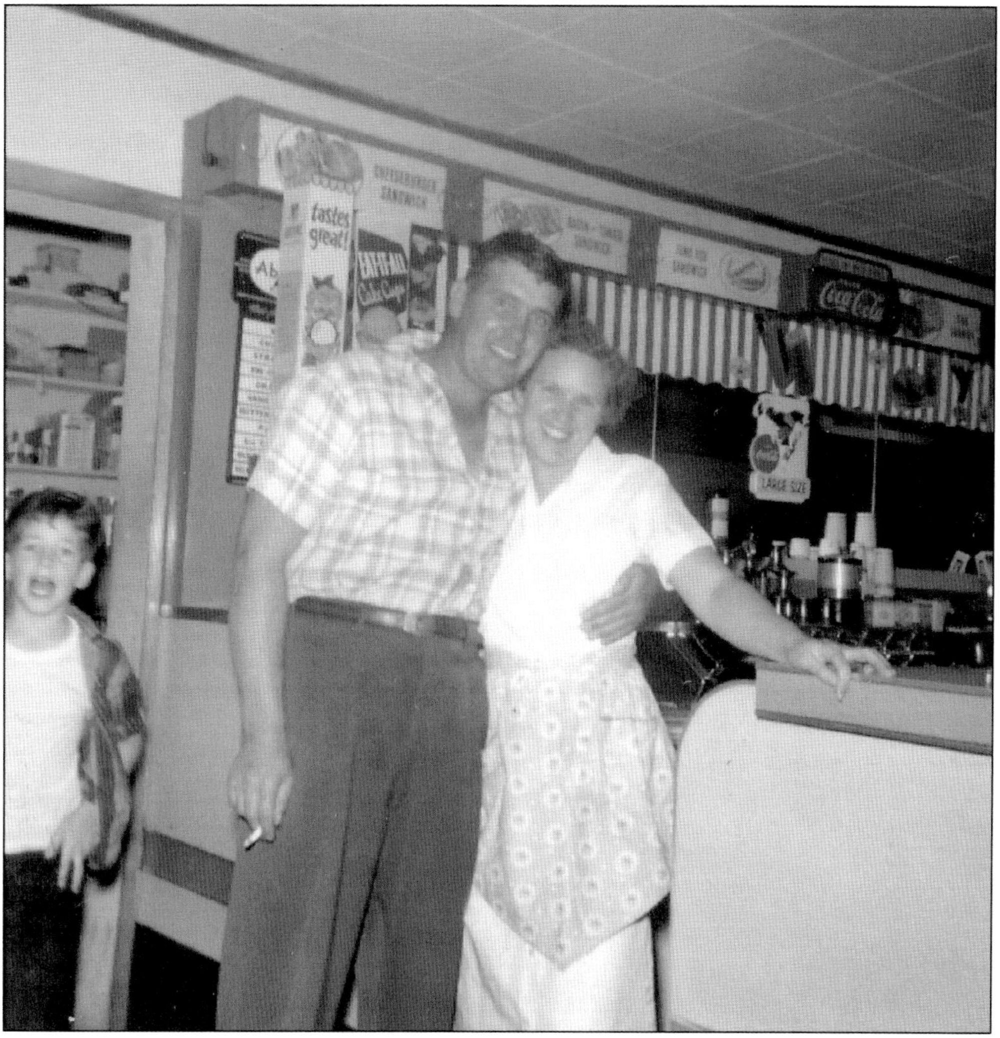

Gerry and Johnny Dierker are pictured at Hubbard's Pier and Seafood in 1959 standing next to a young Wilkins Hubbard. Rock Hall Landing Marina is now located where Hubbard's Pier and Seafood once stood. Dr. Wilkins Hubbard is the son of former Hubbard's Pier owners Edna Marie and Wilkins Hubbard Sr. After the passing of Wilkins Sr., Edna Marie operated the business. (Courtesy of Madelyn Cornelius.)

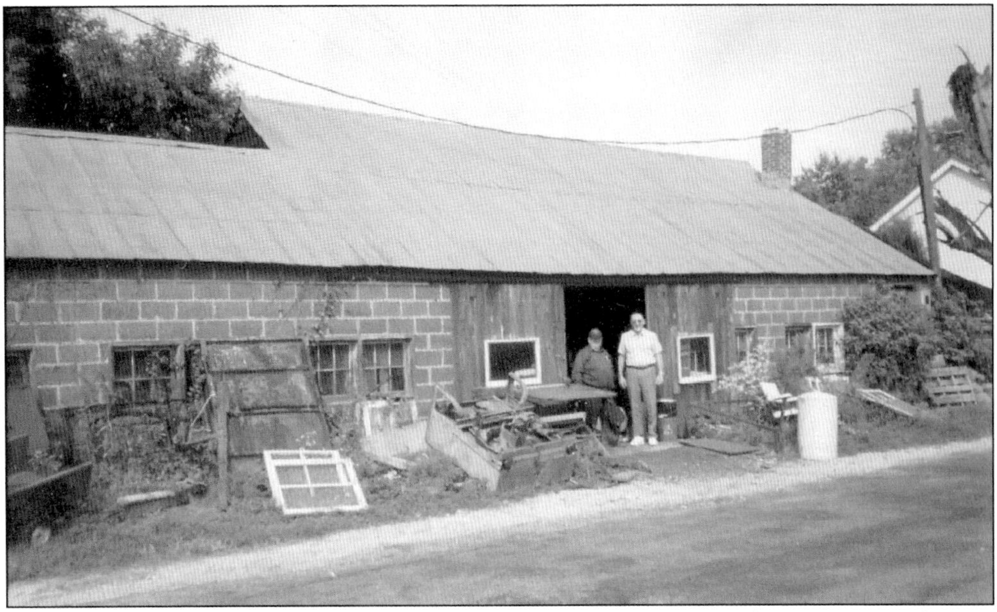

Martin Wagner is pictured in front of his Wagner Blacksmith and Machinery Repair Shop on Maryland Route 20 just outside of Rock Hall. He was a master machinist and blacksmith, working with a forge, torch, and anvil. He created many new products for farmers and watermen, such as anchors, rigs, and spades. (Courtesy of Madelyn Cornelius.)

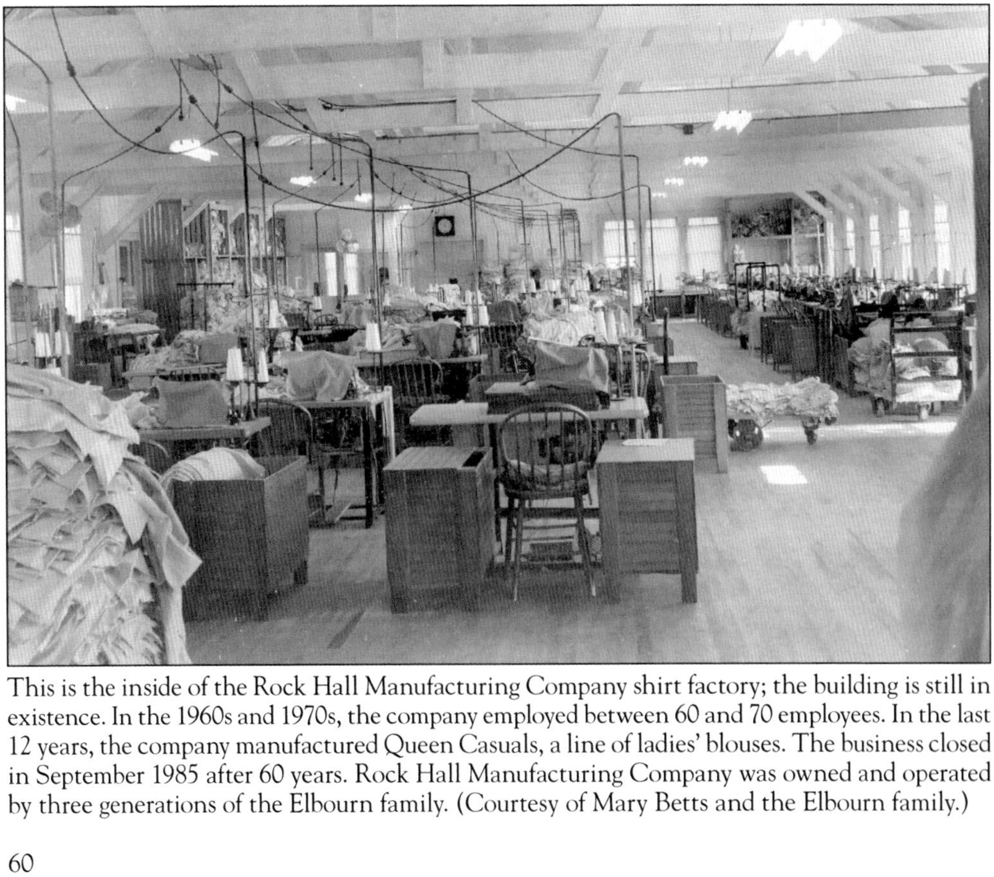

This is the inside of the Rock Hall Manufacturing Company shirt factory; the building is still in existence. In the 1960s and 1970s, the company employed between 60 and 70 employees. In the last 12 years, the company manufactured Queen Casuals, a line of ladies' blouses. The business closed in September 1985 after 60 years. Rock Hall Manufacturing Company was owned and operated by three generations of the Elbourn family. (Courtesy of Mary Betts and the Elbourn family.)

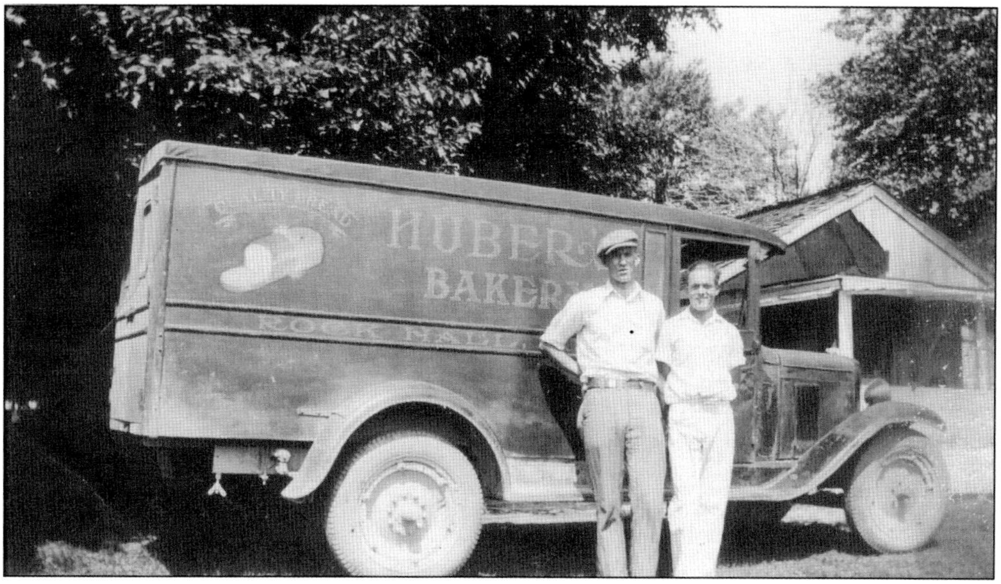

The Huber Bakery was located on Crosby Road outside of Sharptown, reportedly close to the site of the Sharptown School. Bread was delivered and placed in mailboxes for 5¢ per loaf. (Courtesy of Dorothy McKinney.)

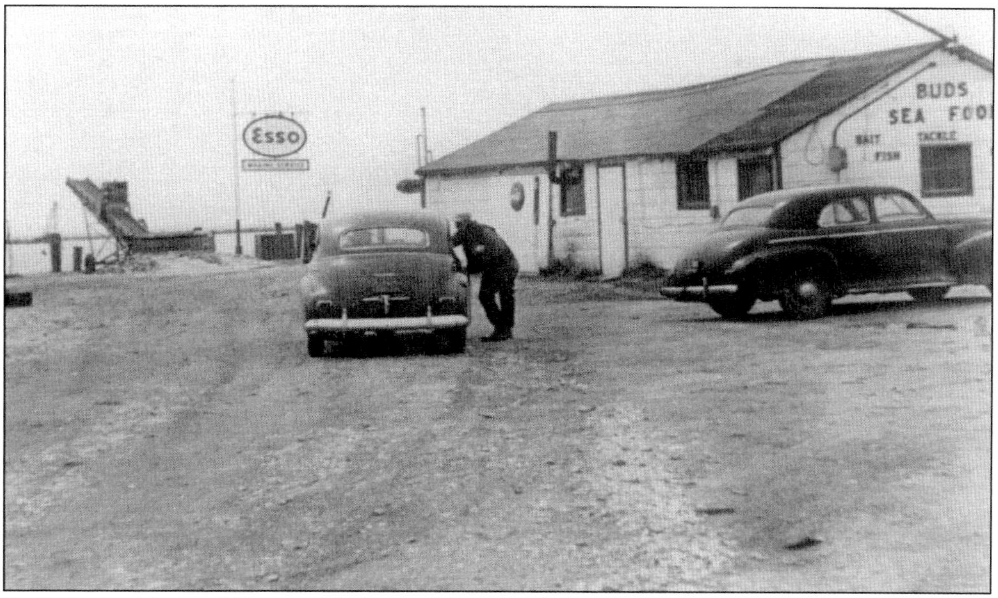

Bud's Seafood featured "bait, tackle, boats, fish and crabs." It was located at Rock Hall Harbor, which was developed into Rock Hall Landing. (Courtesy of Jack Jester and Madelyn Cornelius.)

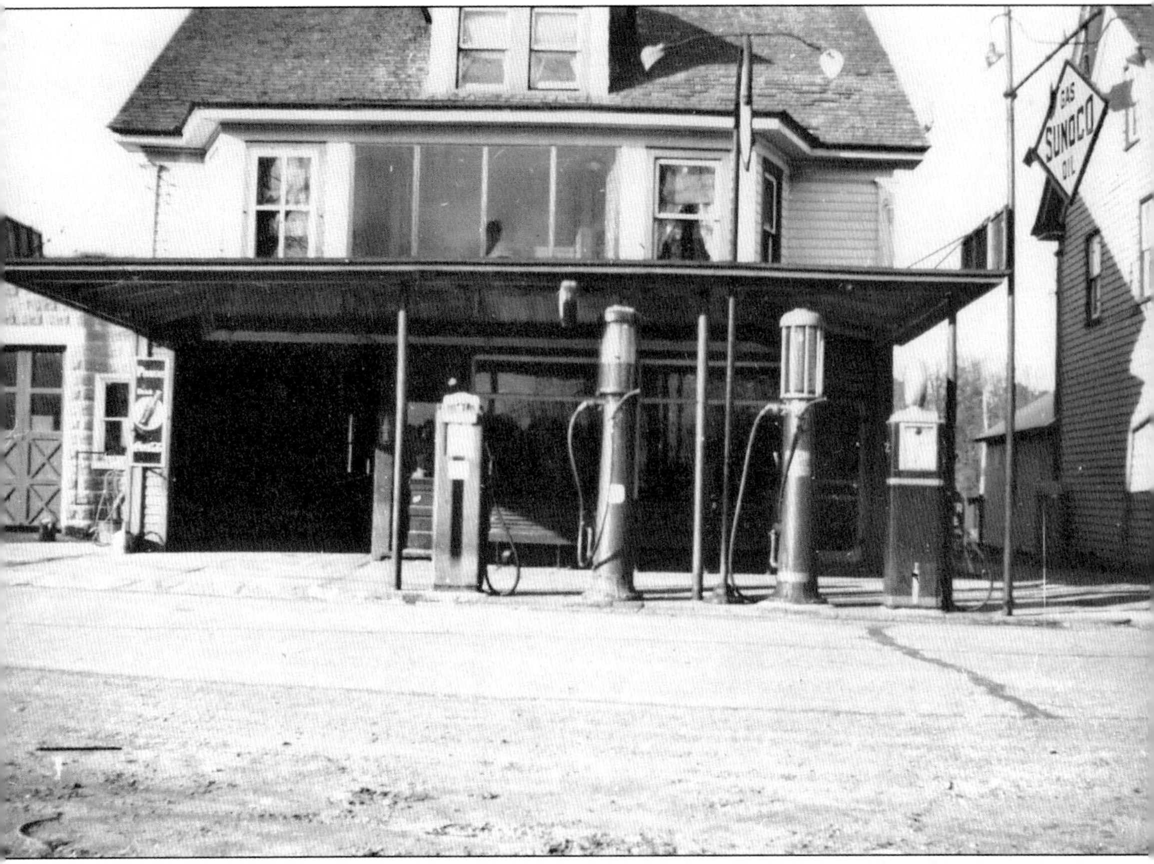

Tuckers Rock Hall Garage has remained in the same location since its founding in 1924. It was the oldest established service station in Rock Hall, founded by Thomas A. Tucker. After Thomas's death, the business was operated by his wife and sons Burgess and Elwood Lee Tucker. Burgess and Betty Tucker still own the facility, and it is operated today as Rock Hall Parts Plus. (Courtesy of Betty Tucker.)

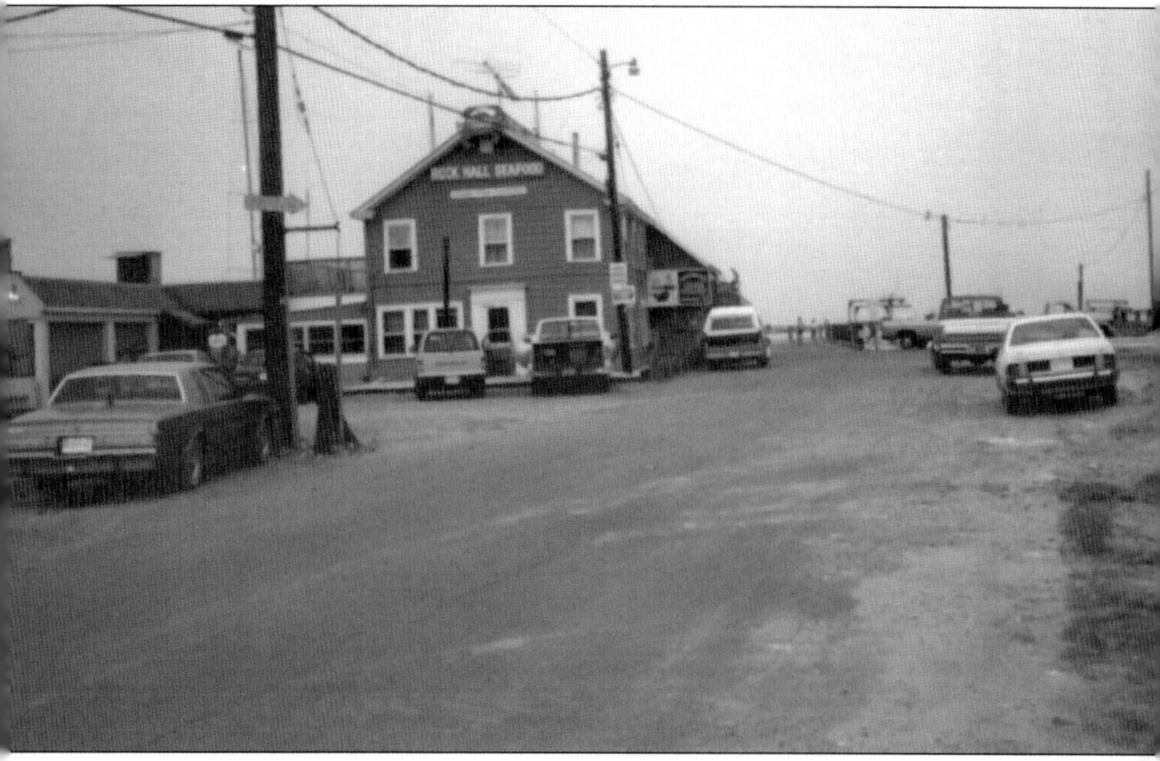

In the mid-1980s, Rock Hall Seafood was located at the Sharp Street Wharf, where Waterman's Crab House is now. This photograph was taken when the harbor and buildings to the right of the structure were cleared for what is now Rock Hall Landing. (Courtesy of Madelyn Cornelius.)

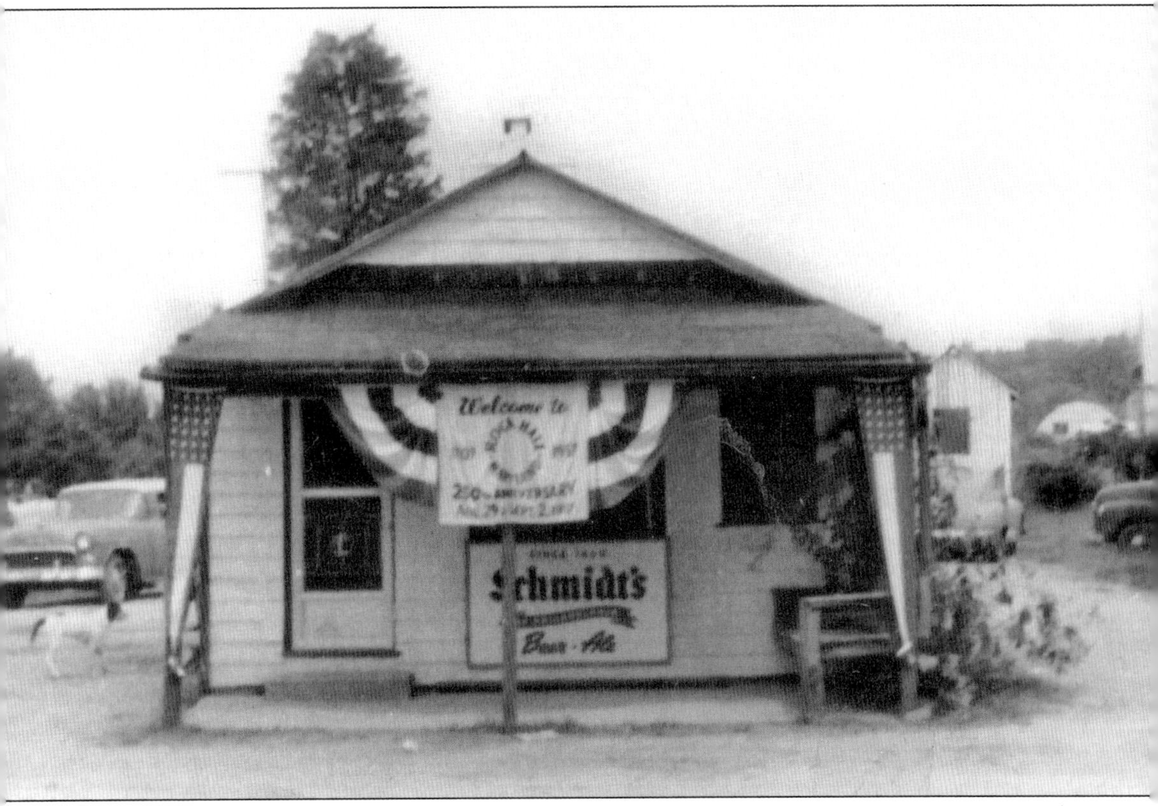

Celebrating 75 years in 2007, Coleman's Tavern, or "Maggie's," is owned and operated by Carolyn Jones, granddaughter of the original owner, and boasts the coldest beer and good old times in Rock Hall. Opening in 1932 as Coleman's Beer Garden, the family sold and delivered ice and coal as well as serving libations and homemade ice cream in the tavern. Coleman's was the original ice business in Rock Hall before both Joyner's and Rock Hall Ice opened. This image depicts the tavern during Rock Hall's 250th anniversary celebration. Coleman's Tavern was treated to a special 75th-birthday concert at the Mainstay during Rock Hall's 300th-anniversary celebration. The Mainstay is a popular center for performances, art shows, community activities, and cultural events. (Courtesy of Carolyn Jones.)

Four

PEOPLE

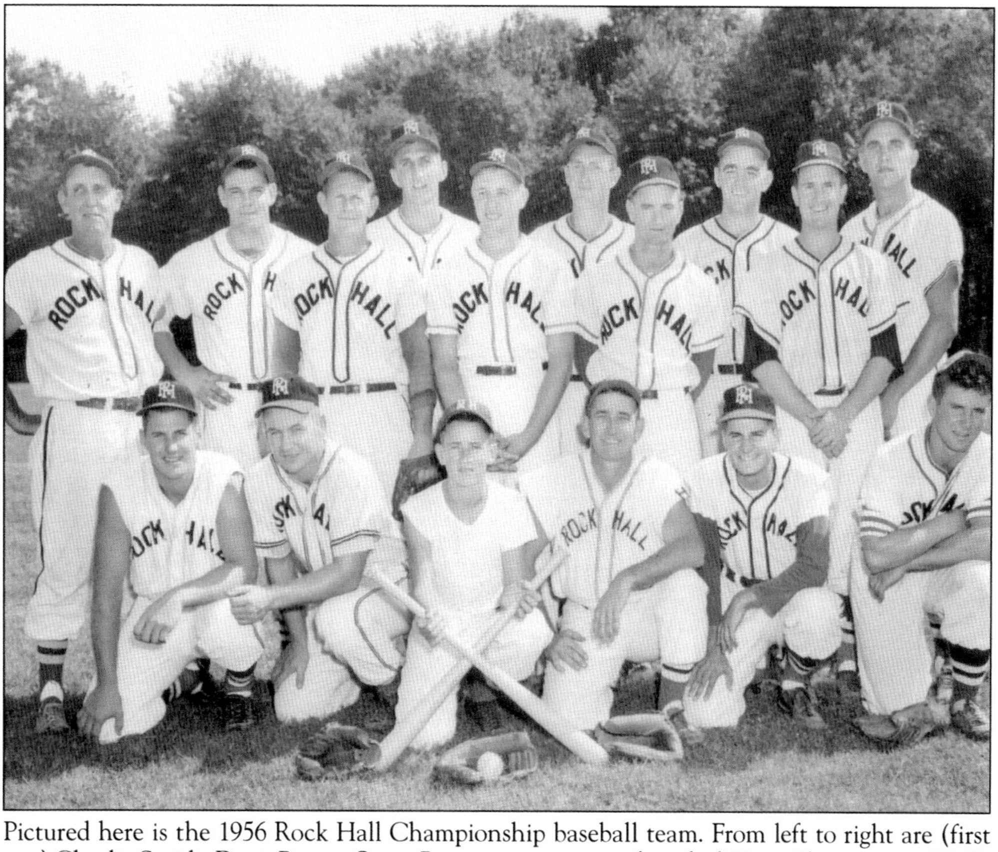

Pictured here is the 1956 Rock Hall Championship baseball team. From left to right are (first row) Charlie Smith; Davis Porter; Owen Porter, manager; unidentified; Dave Sharretts; and Billy Edwards; (second row) Bill Loller, Billy Usilton, William Joseph "Paddles" Orr, Roby Cornelius, Bob Puppe, George Glenn, Jim Edwards, Vaugh Steadman, Bucky Larrimore, and John Brice. (Courtesy of Clay Larrimore.)

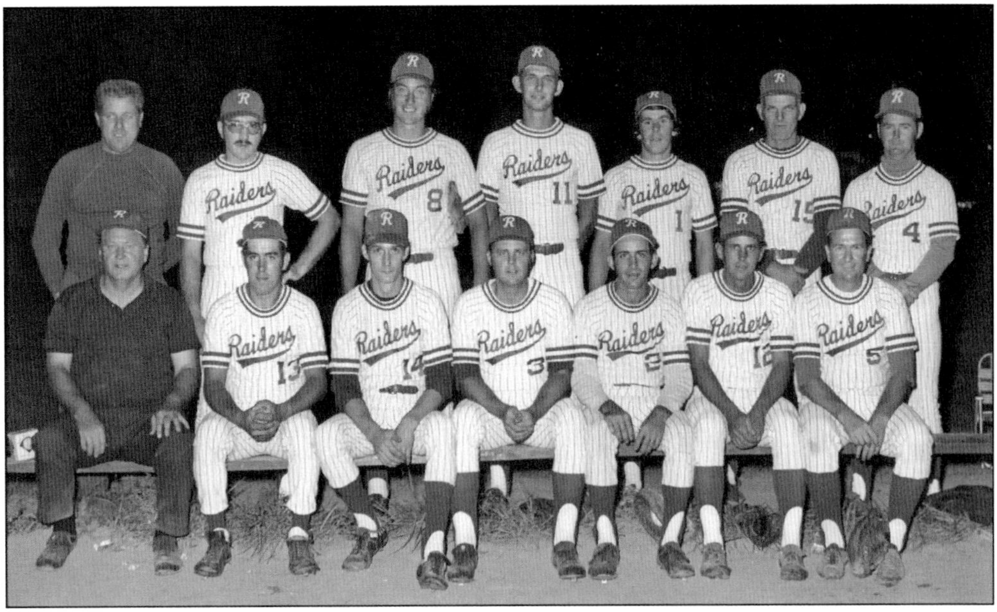

The Rock Hall Raiders are pictured in 1974, when they won the Kent County Championship. From left to right are (first row) Jesse Jones (coach and manager), Rabbit Mench (left field), Billy Reed (pitcher), George Jones (first base), Jimmy Leager (short field), Bobby Bramble (second base), and Bucky Larrimore (catcher/coach); (second row) Bob Puppe (pitcher/coach), Gordon Kimble (first base/coach), Clay Larrimore (catcher), Ed Pickering (center field), George Reihl (third base), Harry White (pitcher), and Charles Edwards (shortstop). (Courtesy of Clay Larrimore.)

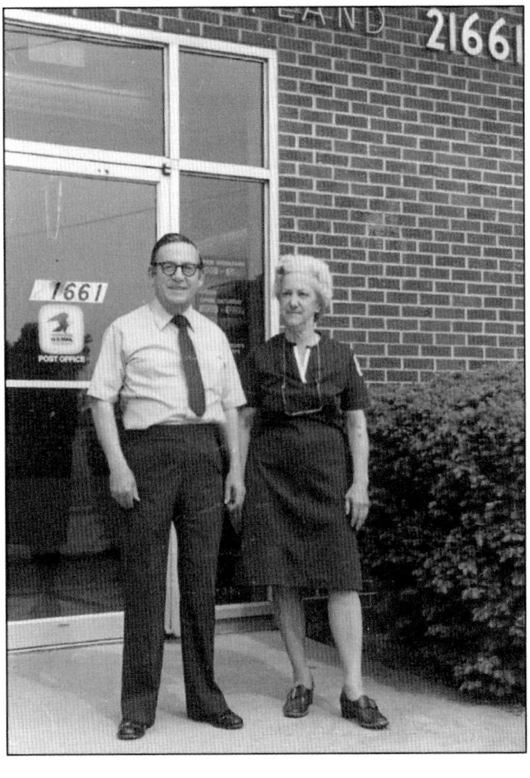

George Parsons, Rock Hall postmaster, is pictured with Hallie Skirven, clerk, in front of Rock Hall's post office on Liberty Street. George's father, Frank, was a Rock Hall postal carrier beginning in the days of the horse and buggy. Frank retired in 1952. (Courtesy of Historical Society of Kent County.)

Pictured here are Olivia Clayton Bringman (left) and Anna Mae Ayres Willson (right), both of Rock Hall. These ladies were teachers in various schools in Kent County, and Anna Mae Ayres Willson taught elementary grades in New Jersey for many years as well. (Courtesy of Joan O. Horsey.)

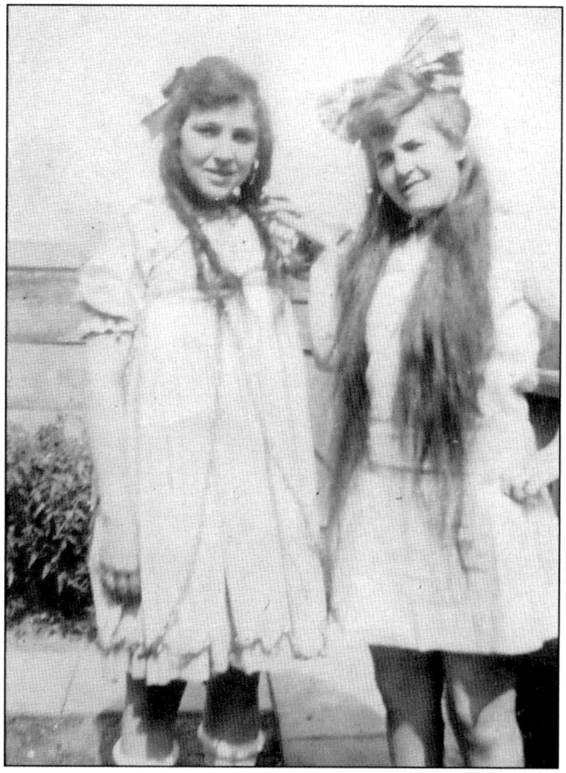

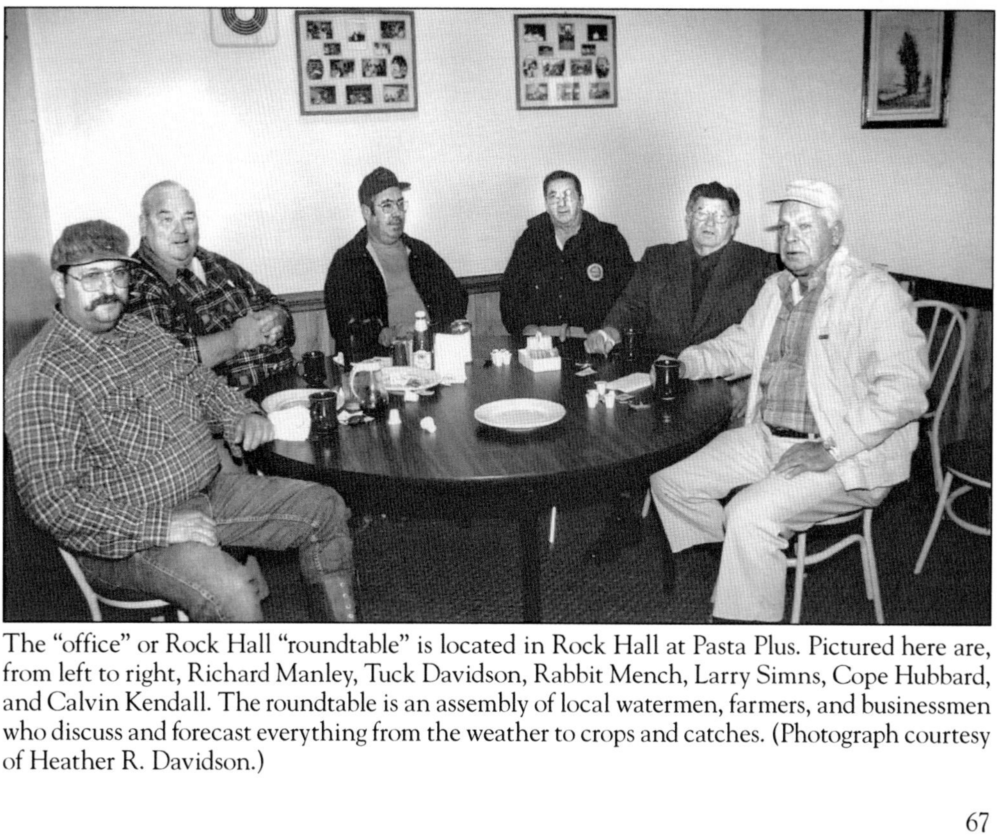

The "office" or Rock Hall "roundtable" is located in Rock Hall at Pasta Plus. Pictured here are, from left to right, Richard Manley, Tuck Davidson, Rabbit Mench, Larry Simns, Cope Hubbard, and Calvin Kendall. The roundtable is an assembly of local watermen, farmers, and businessmen who discuss and forecast everything from the weather to crops and catches. (Photograph courtesy of Heather R. Davidson.)

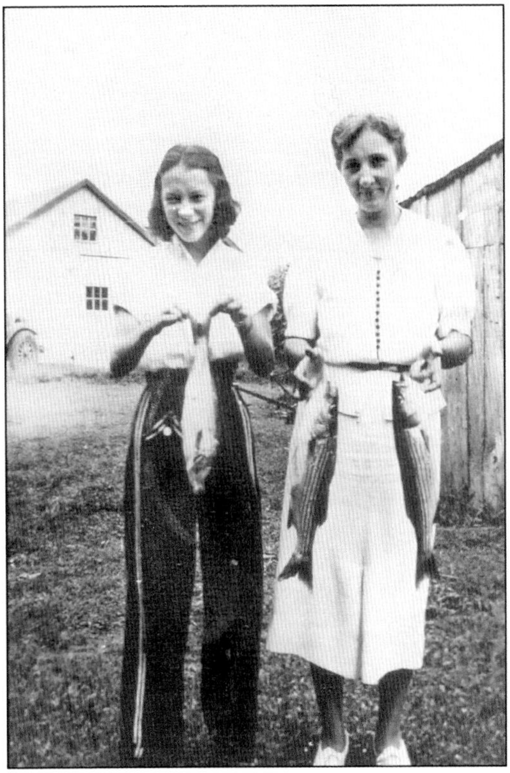

Pictured with a fine catch of rockfish in 1936 are Peg Joiner (left) and Nora Joiner Young of Rock Hall. (Courtesy of Cathy Fisher.)

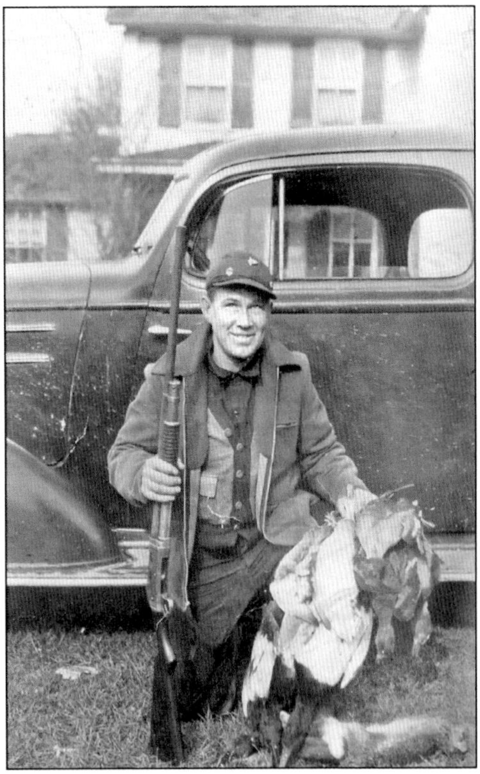

Capt. Maurice Larrimore, oysterman, fisherman, fishing party captain, and hunting guide, is pictured in front of his house on Main Street after rabbit hunting in 1940. Captain Larrimore had a charter boat, the *Hazel A.*, which he kept at the Bud's Seafood wharf. (Courtesy of Clay Larrimore.)

Jean Foreman is pictured in front of the Tolchester Bath House located on the Chesapeake Bay. The bathhouse was located at the popular Tolchester Beach and Park. (Courtesy Jean Foreman.)

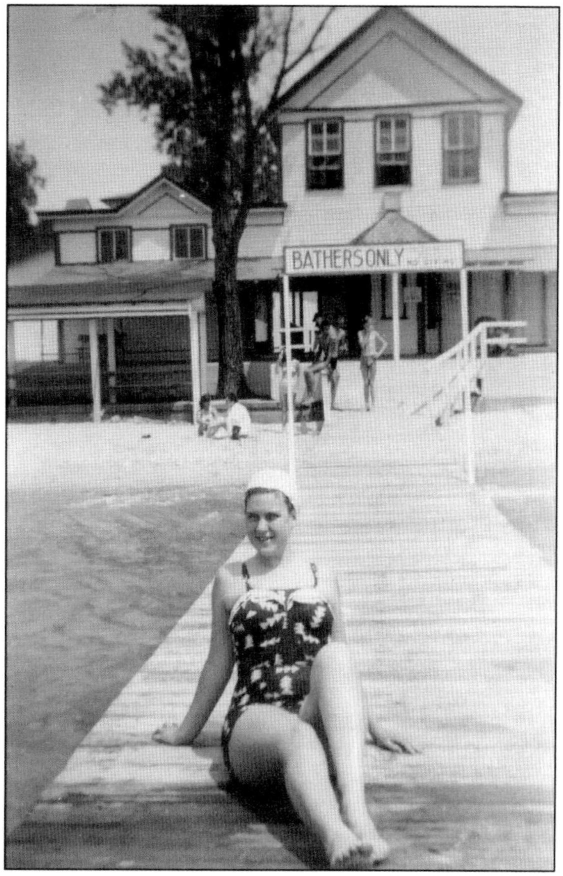

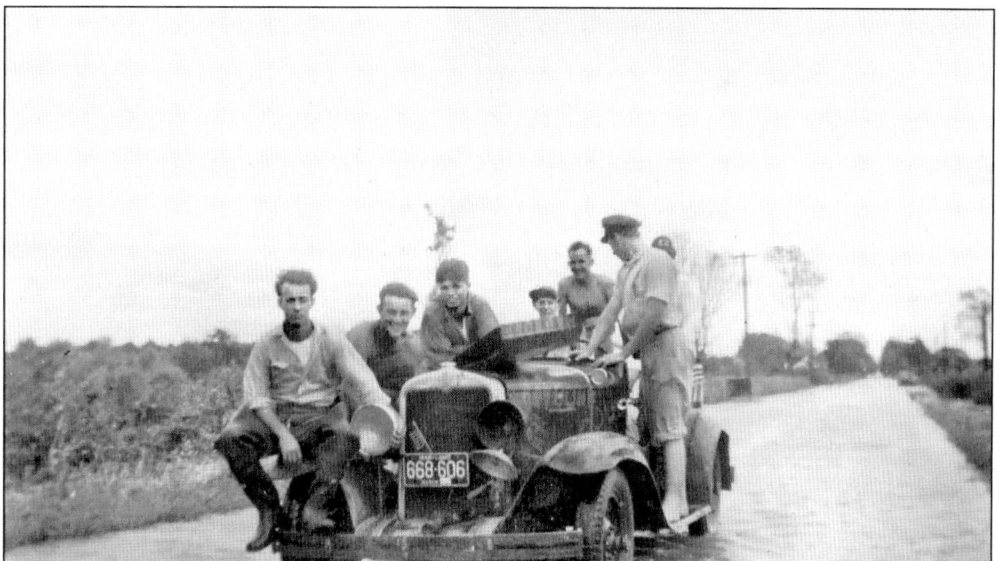

Pictured in this car called "Nellie Belle" are, from left to right, Jack Middletown, Bobby Usilton, Eddie Kuechler, Dale Wood, and Joe Lee Gagalski. This 1952 photograph was taken in the area of Gratitude right after Hurricane Hazel. (Courtesy of Jean Foreman.)

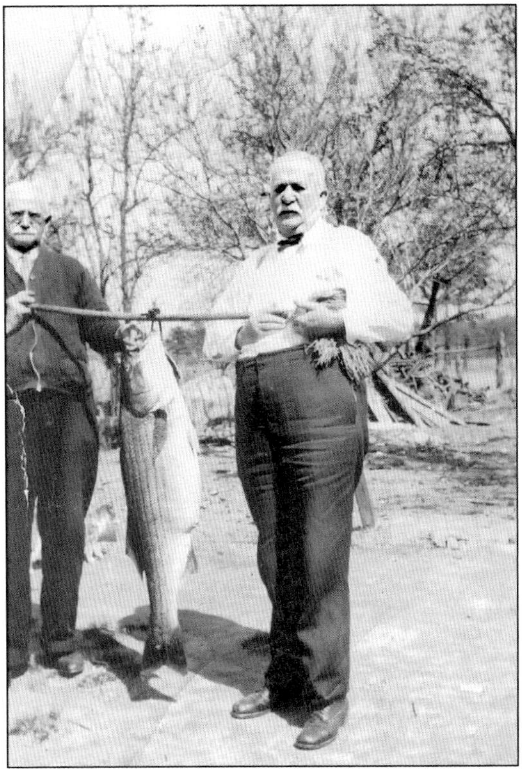

Brothers John E. and Walter H. Hadaway display their rockfish catch close to their home on the Haven, which is now known as Swan Haven Bed and Breakfast. John lived where the Fellows, Helfenbein, and Newman Funeral Home in Rock Hall is located while he was married. (Courtesy of Ida Mae Dulin.)

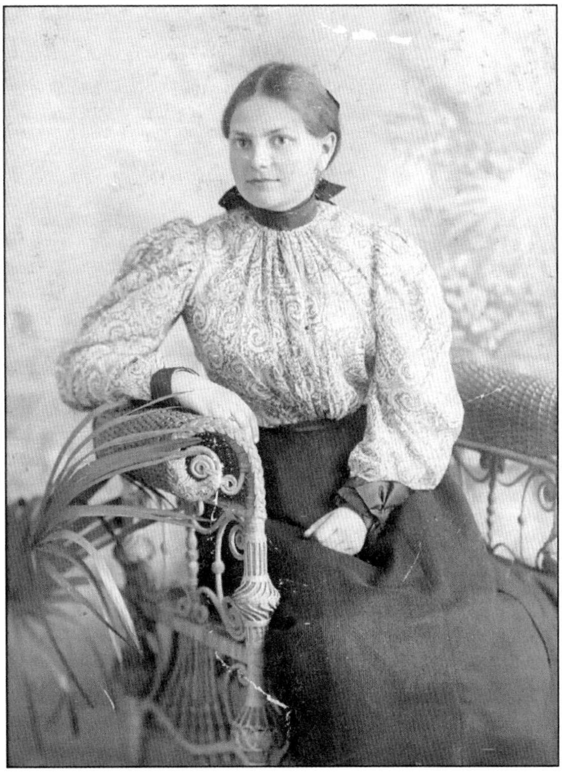

Julia R. Willson Skirven was a descendant of Thomas Smythee of Trumpington, Rock Hall, and Widehall, Chestertown. Her father was Dr. Thomas Bennett Willson. Thomas Smythee was a wealthy immigrant who was a prosperous businessman, landowner, and one of the founding members of St. Paul's Church. (Courtesy of Julie J. Stephens.)

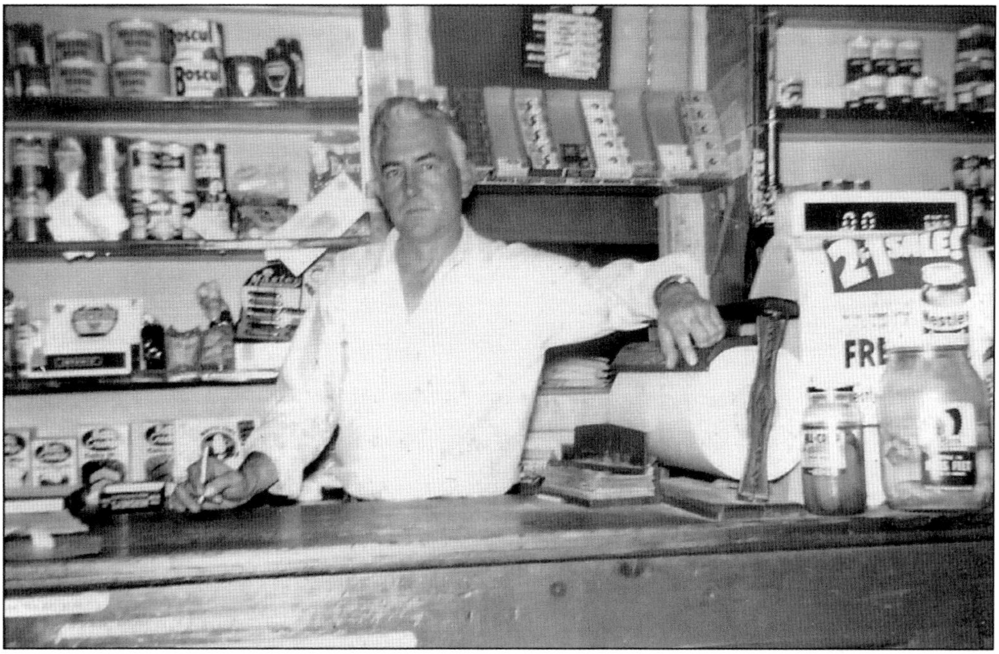

Rock Hall native Medcalf Jacquette is pictured in his general store, Jacquette's, in Edesville, after his father, LeRoy Jacquette, retired. Medcalf also took out fishing parties on the Chesapeake Bay over the years, first in his boat the *Lillian* M. and later in his boat *Bumps*. (Courtesy of Julie J. Stephens.)

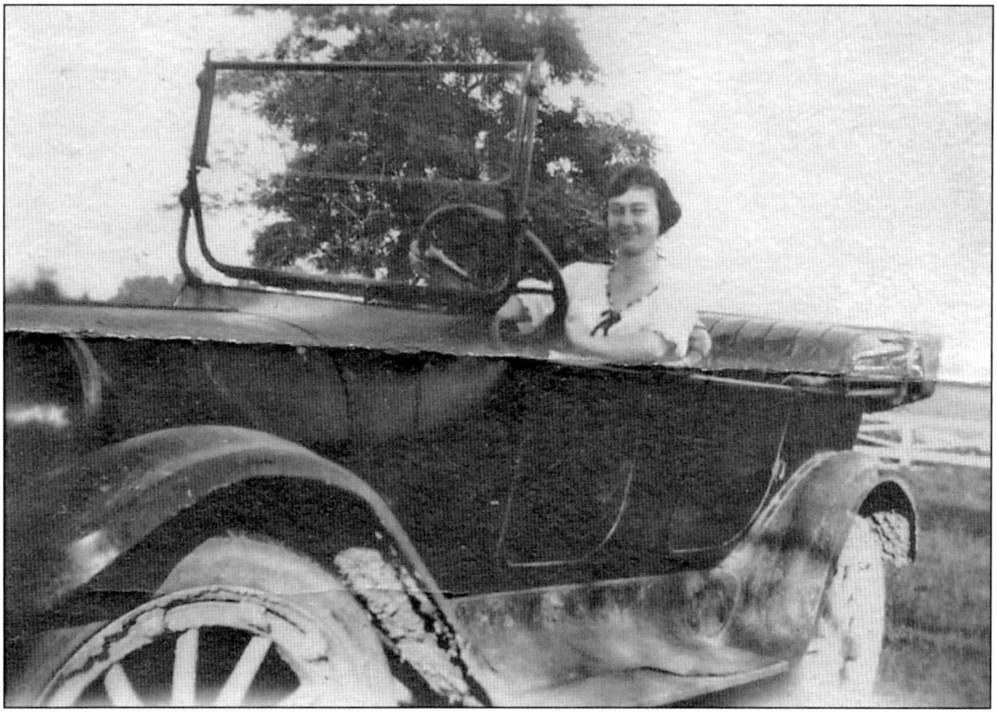

Gertrude Willson Brunt of Rock Hall is pictured in her automobile in the early 1920s. She taught at Swan Creek School. (Courtesy of Anne Willson Grimm McKown.)

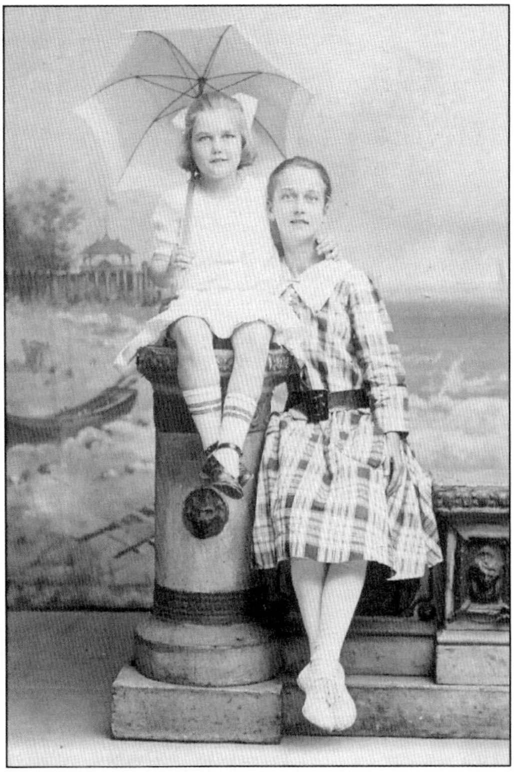

Sisters Isabel Willson Grimm (left) and Gertrude Willson Bunt pose at the photography studio at Tolchester Beach. (Courtesy of Anne Willson Grimm McKown.)

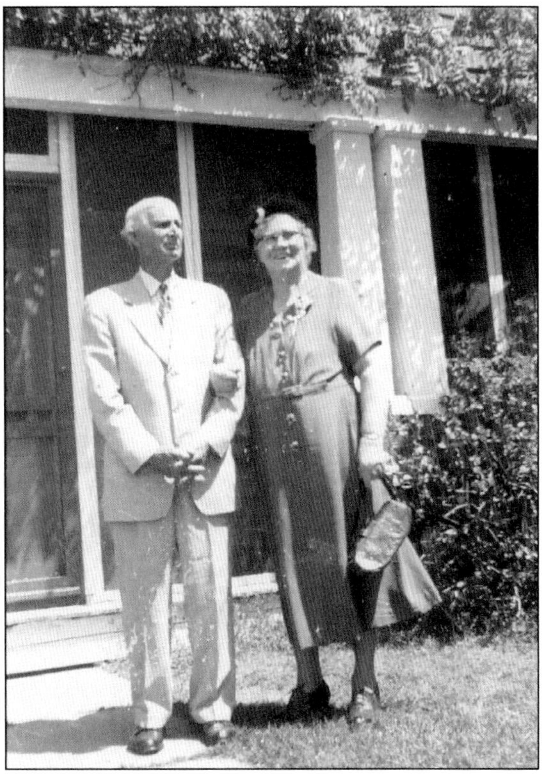

Ella and Capt. Josh Thomas, who is credited with inventing the anchor net, lived at Swan Haven; both were born in the 1880s. Captain Thomas's boat was called the *Comet*. (Courtesy of Judy Hickman.)

Verenita "Neets" Buckheit, a Rock Hall native, poses on Main Street in the 1940s. As a teenager, she worked at the American Store after school. The American Store was located on the site of the present Bayside Foods. In her later years, Neets studied card reading and was known throughout Maryland and Delaware for her card-reading ability. (Courtesy of Judy Hickman.)

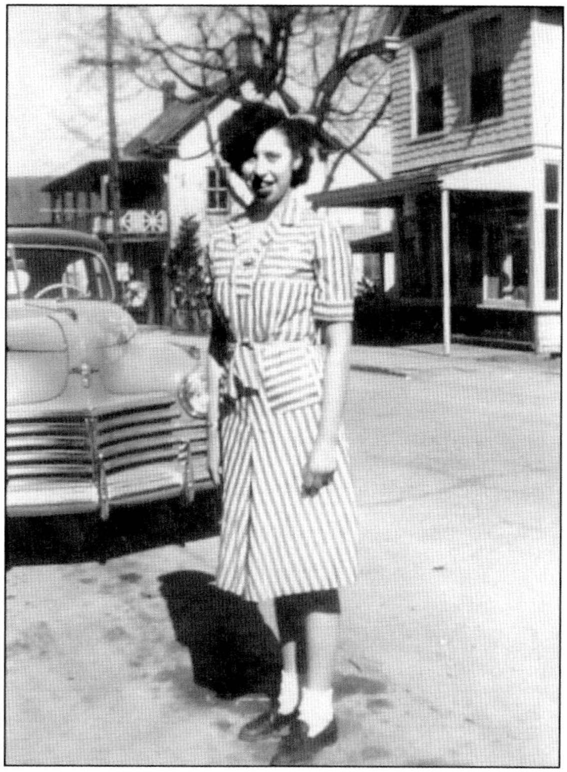

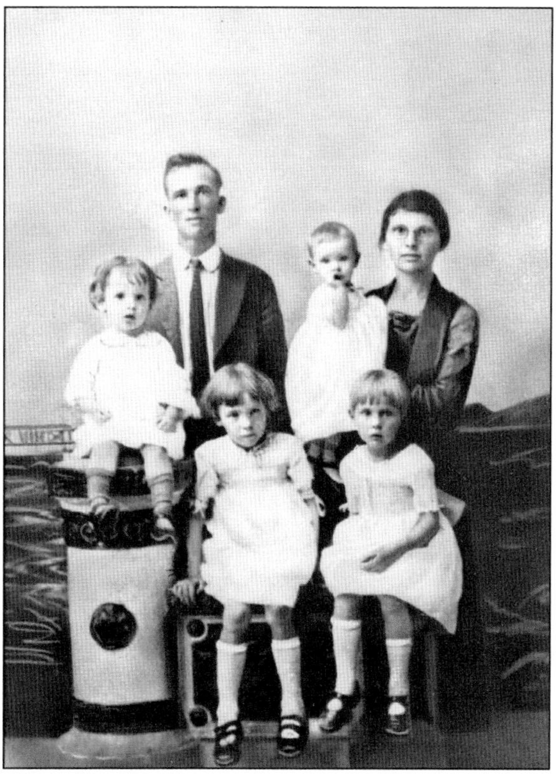

This William and Ella Brooks family photograph was taken at their home on Eastern Neck Road in Rock Hall around 1924. Pictured are William W. Brooks, Ella Nora White, Mary Brooks (left), Martha Cook (in Ella's arms), Helen Brooks (front, center), and Virginia Brooks (creator of Miss Virginia's Crab Cakes). (Courtesy of Joe Dickerson.)

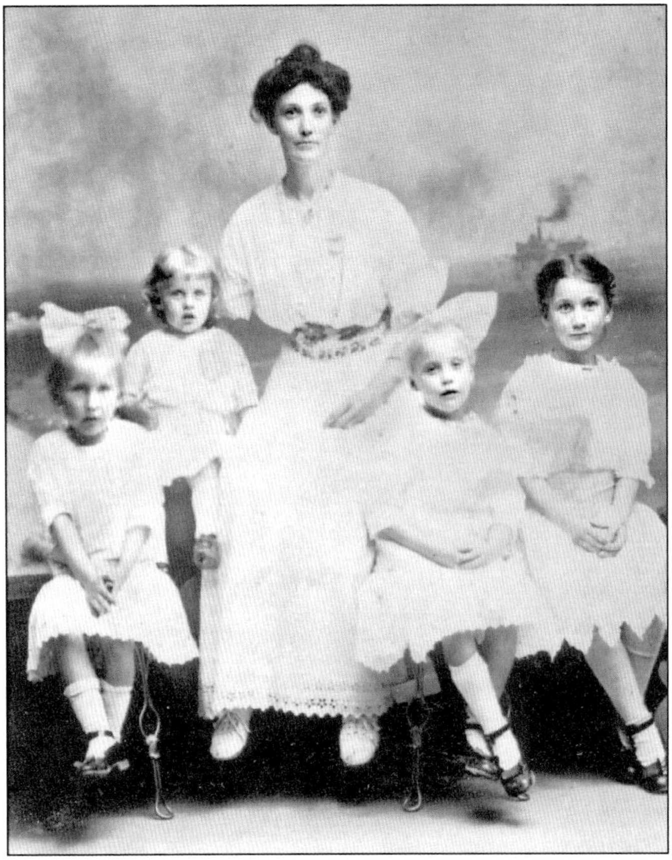

Katie Dickerson Chaires is pictured with her daughters; from left to right, they are Adelaide, Thelma, Gladys, and Evelyn. (Courtesy of Joe Dickerson.)

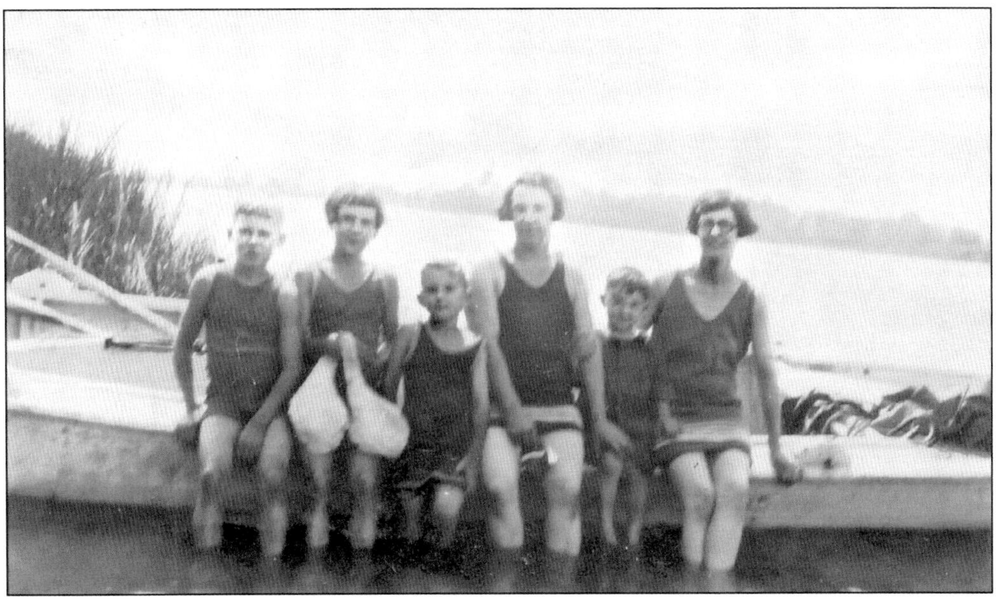

The Dickerson and Walls families enjoy a day at Swan Point Farm in 1928. Pictured are, from left to right, Erdman Walls, Angela Dickerson, Vernon Dickerson, Clara Dickerson, Joseph Dickerson, and Edith Walls Dickerson. (Courtesy of Joe Dickerson.)

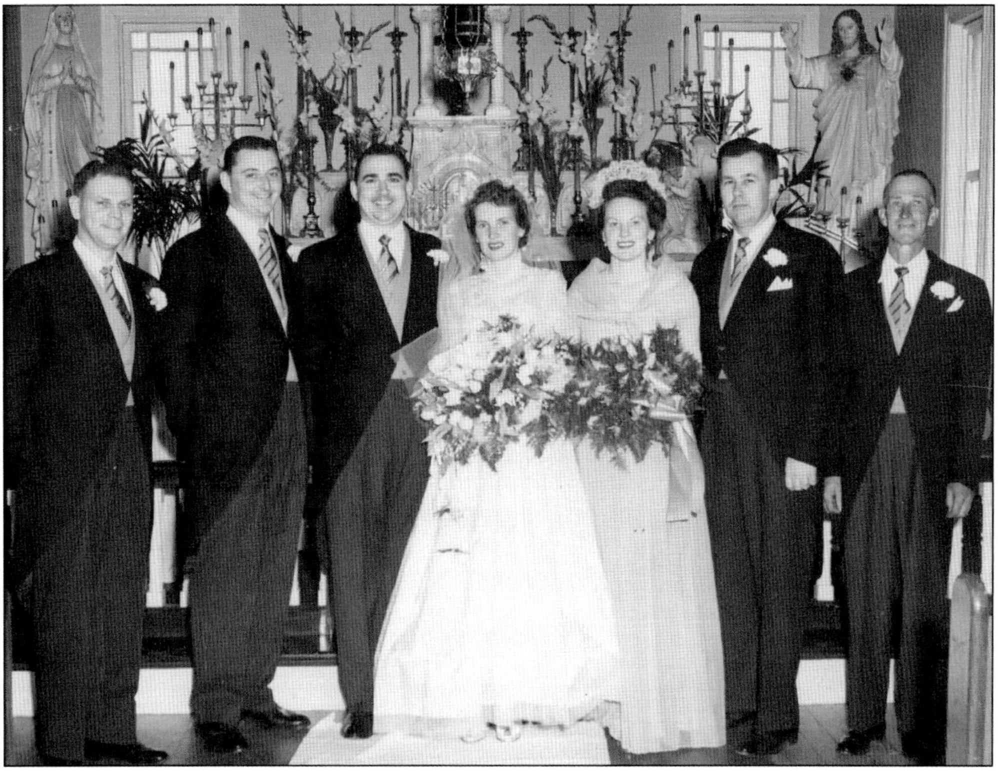

The Dickerson wedding party is pictured here at St. John's Roman Catholic Church in Rock Hall on April 7, 1951. From left to right are Francis X. Wells, Edward Vernon Dickerson (best man), Joseph A. Dickerson (groom), Martha Brooks Dickerson (bride), Helen Brooks Whitney (maid of honor), G. Millard Whitney, and William Webster Brooks (father of the bride). (Courtesy of Joe Dickerson.)

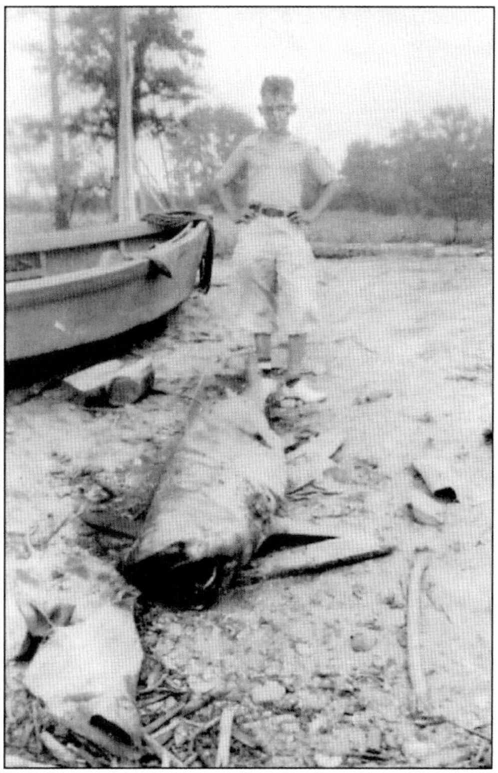

Joe Dickerson looks at the shark caught in a pound net off Tolchester Beach in 1938. The fisherman subdued the shark using Joe's .22 rifle. (Courtesy of Joe Dickerson.)

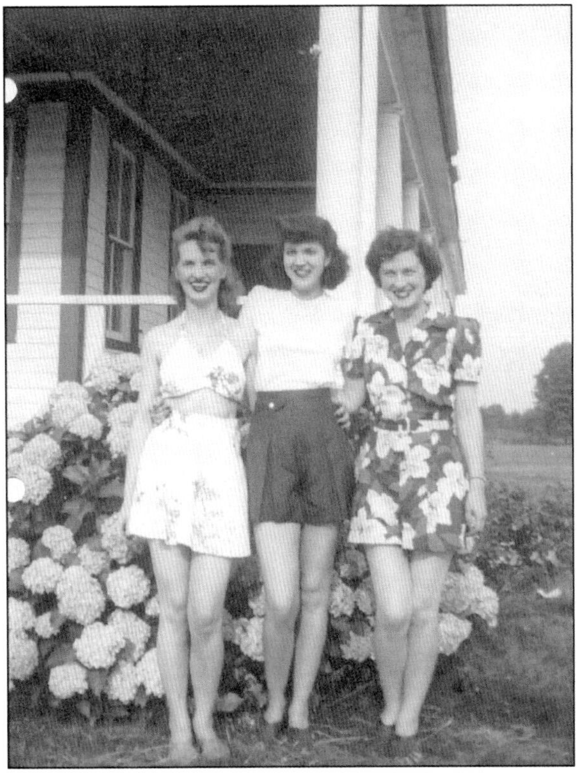

From left to right, Martha Brooks, Betty Smith Stover, and Sue Coleman pose in front of the Rock Hall Yacht Club in 1940. (Courtesy of Joe Dickerson.)

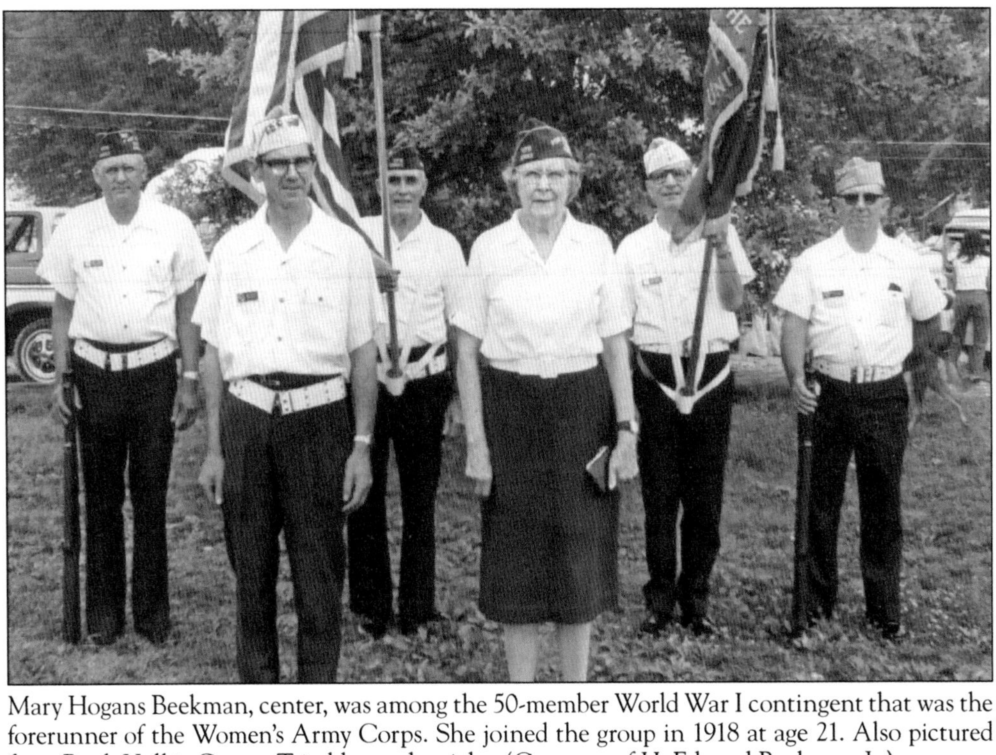

Mary Hogans Beekman, center, was among the 50-member World War I contingent that was the forerunner of the Women's Army Corps. She joined the group in 1918 at age 21. Also pictured from Rock Hall is George Trimble, to the right. (Courtesy of H. Edward Beekman Jr.)

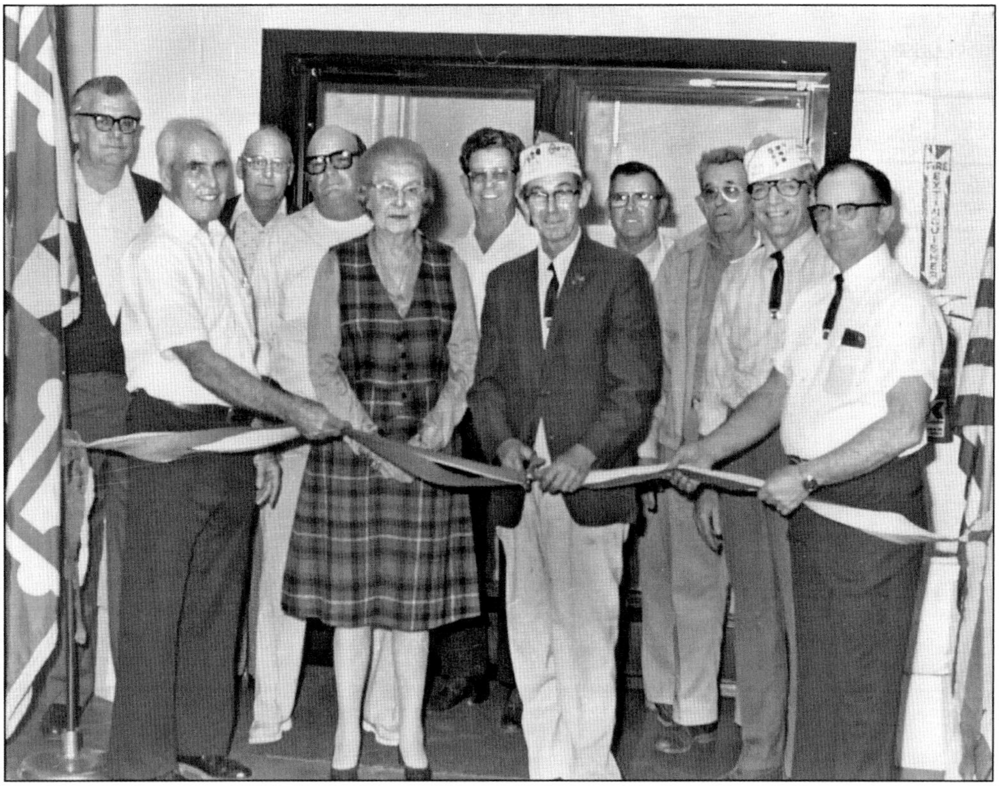

Mary Hogans Beekman, a native of Rock Hall, was the first woman member of the VFW on the Eastern Shore. She is seen here participating in ribbon-cutting ceremonies honoring her acceptance as a member of VFW Post 10063. Seen in this photograph taken by Cliff Simns are, from left to right, Rocky Chaires, Roy Flowers, Urie Younger, Fitzgerald Clayton, Mary Beekman, Robert Edler, Wes Russum (commander), Allen Crouch, Splint Downey, Joe Grosso, and George Trimble. (Courtesy of H. Edward Beekman Jr.)

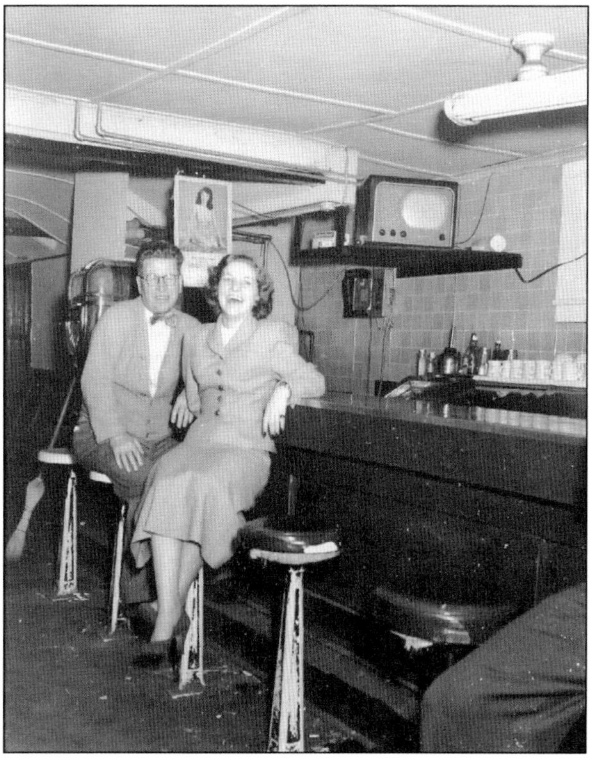

Clifton Simns and daughter Joanne Simns Ransom are shown at Hersch's Bar on Main Street in Rock Hall. Clifton was a well-loved carver, photographer, and barber. (Courtesy of H. Edward Beekman Jr.)

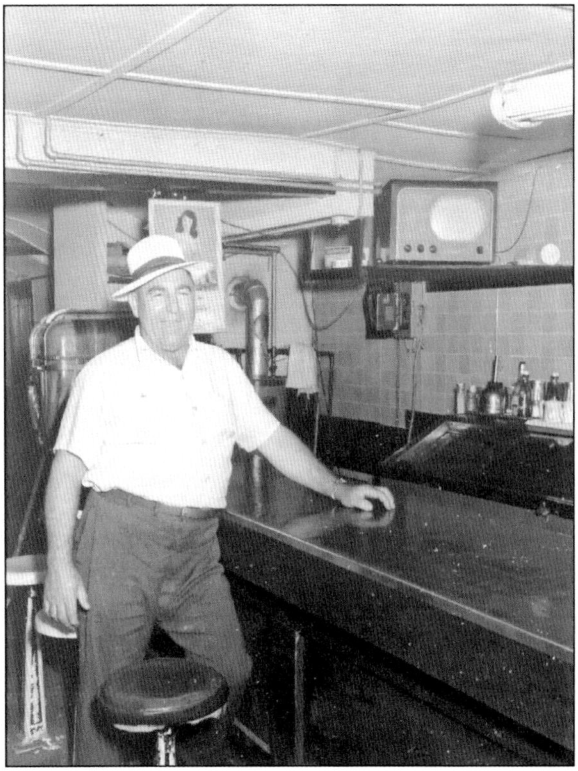

This photograph of Willard "Peaches" Ashley was taken at Hersch's Bar located on the east side of Main Street, Rock Hall. (Courtesy of H. Edward Beekman Jr.)

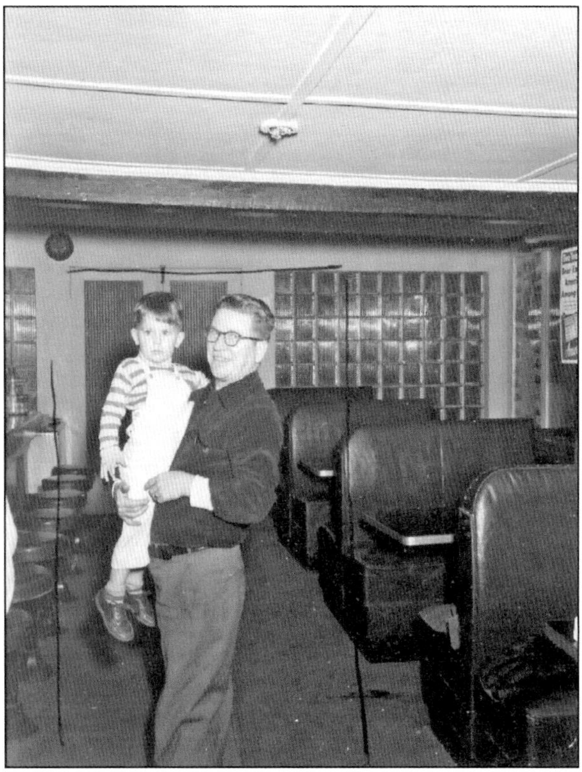

Clifton Simns is pictured with his son, Larry Simns. Larry Simns is the president of the Maryland Waterman's Association. He is a commercial and charter captain and also involved in replenishment and reseeding programs for the Chesapeake Bay. (Courtesy of H. Edward Beekman Jr.)

From left to right, Clifton Simns, Melvin "Trigger" Collyer, and Eddie Buckheit gather around a television in the 1950s. (Courtesy of H. Edward Beekman Jr.)

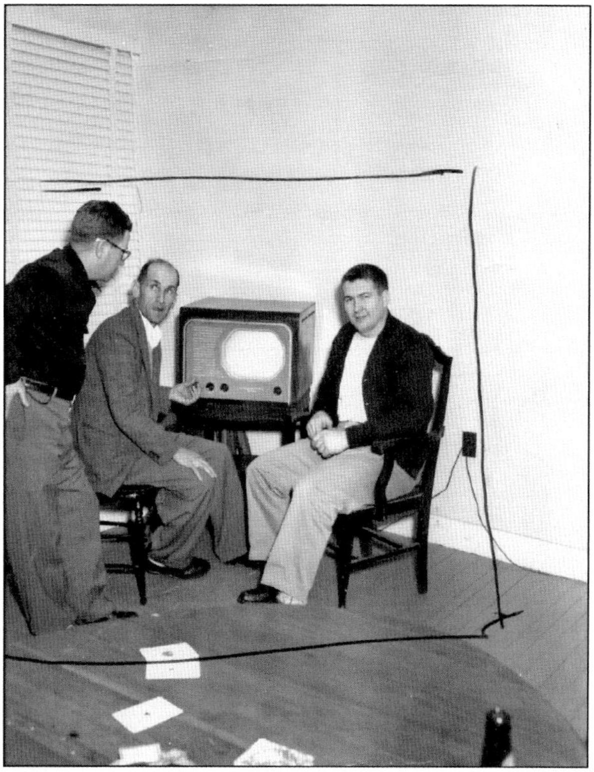

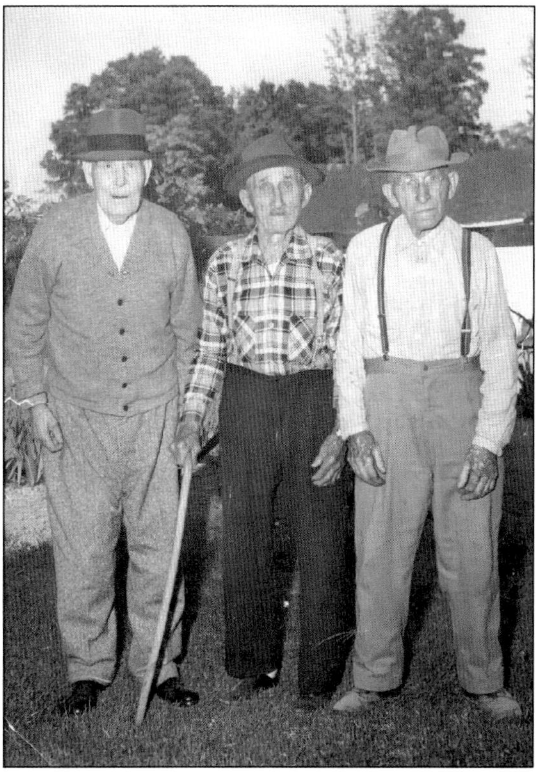

These lifelong Rock Hall residents are, from left to right, Joseph Hogans, William Stevens, and George Downey. (Courtesy of H. Edward Beekman Jr.)

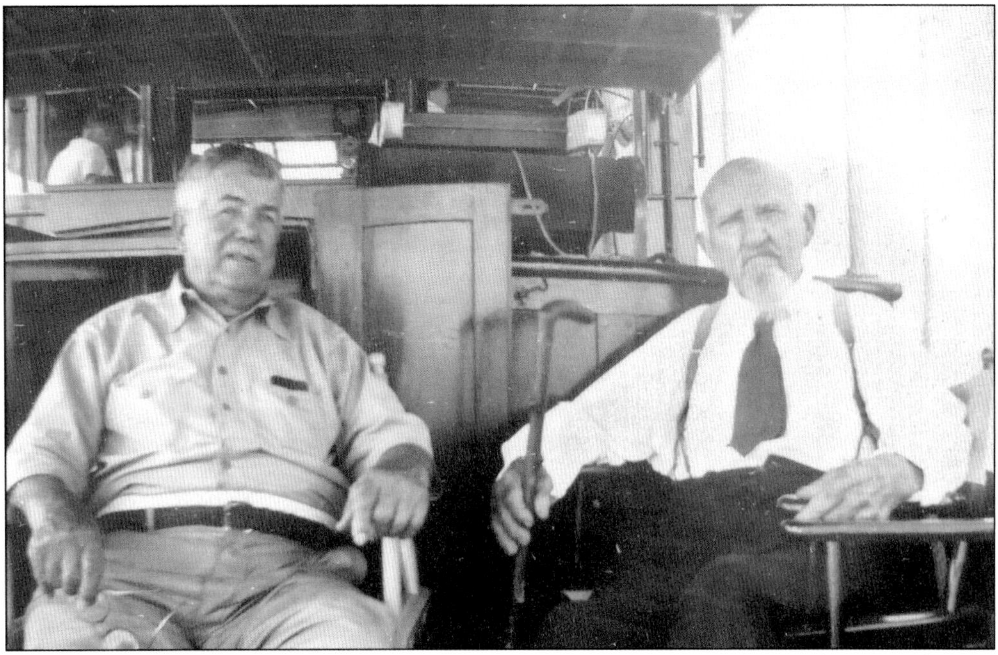

Joseph Hynson, right, takes a boat ride at Rock Hall. Joe fought in the Civil War and was a drummer boy. He was a waterman by trade and lived to be 102 in Rock Hall. He is probably 100 in this image. (Courtesy of H. Edward Beekman Jr.)

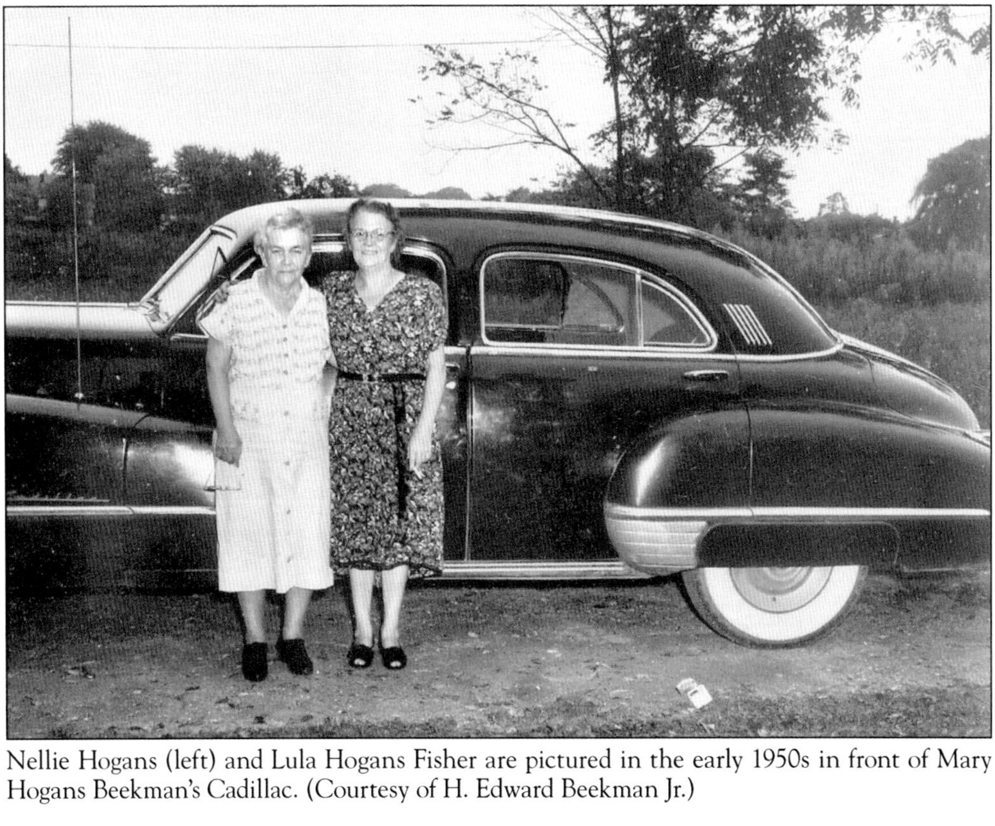

Nellie Hogans (left) and Lula Hogans Fisher are pictured in the early 1950s in front of Mary Hogans Beekman's Cadillac. (Courtesy of H. Edward Beekman Jr.)

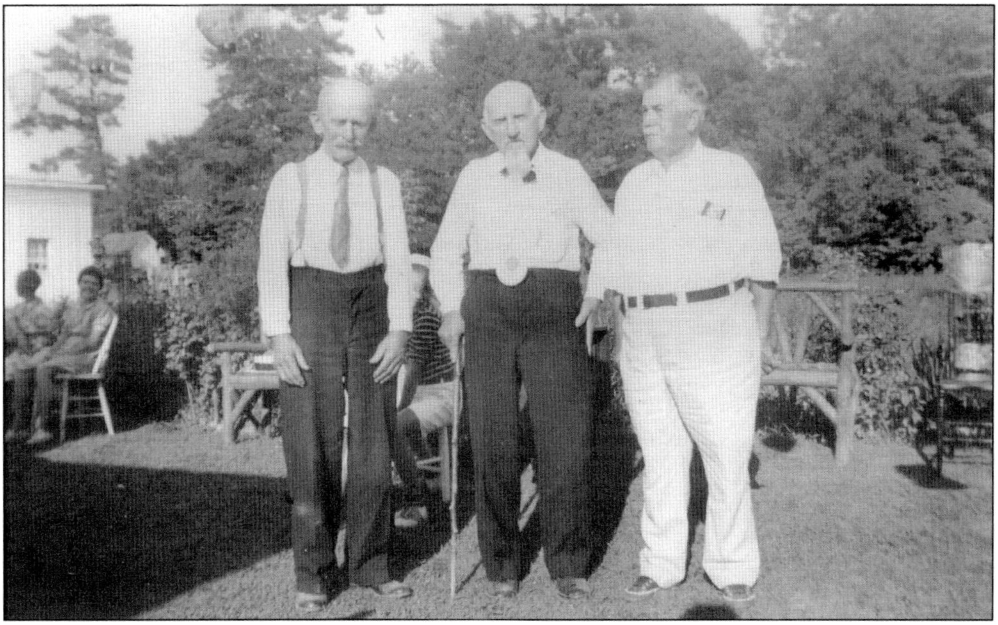

Daniel Ayres (left) and Joseph Hynson (center) are seen here during the 100th birthday celebration of Joseph Hynson at his home on the Haven, Rock Hall. (Courtesy of H. Edward Beekman Jr.)

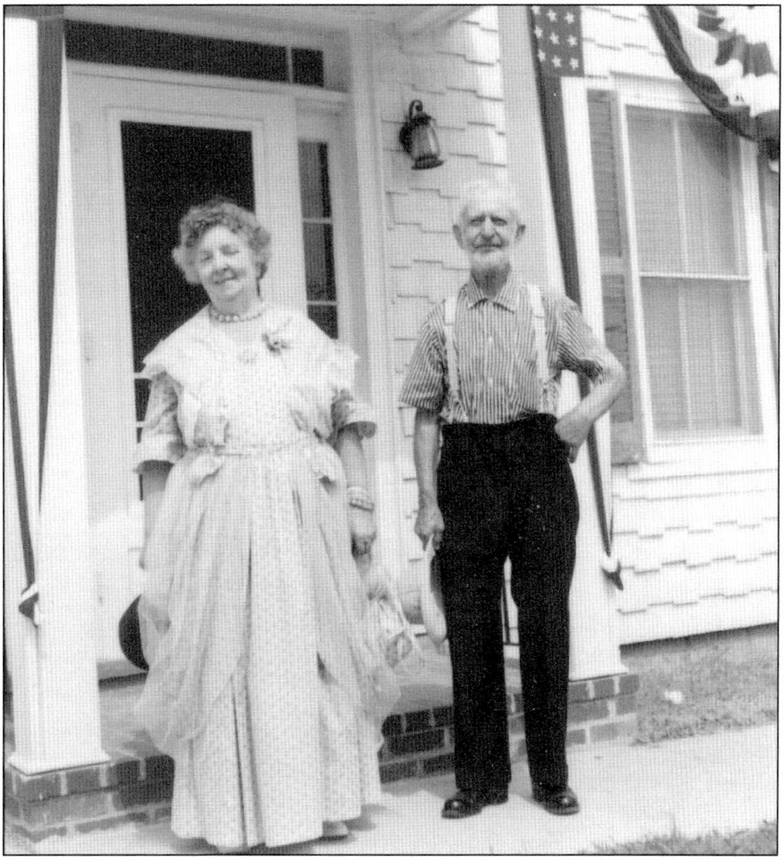

Ida Hynson Straff and her brother, William Hynson (children of Joseph Hynson), are ready for the Fourth of July celebration in the early 1940s. This photograph was taken at the Haven, Rock Hall. The Haven was considered a section of town along the road that runs to Haven Creek. (Courtesy of H. Edward Beekman Jr.)

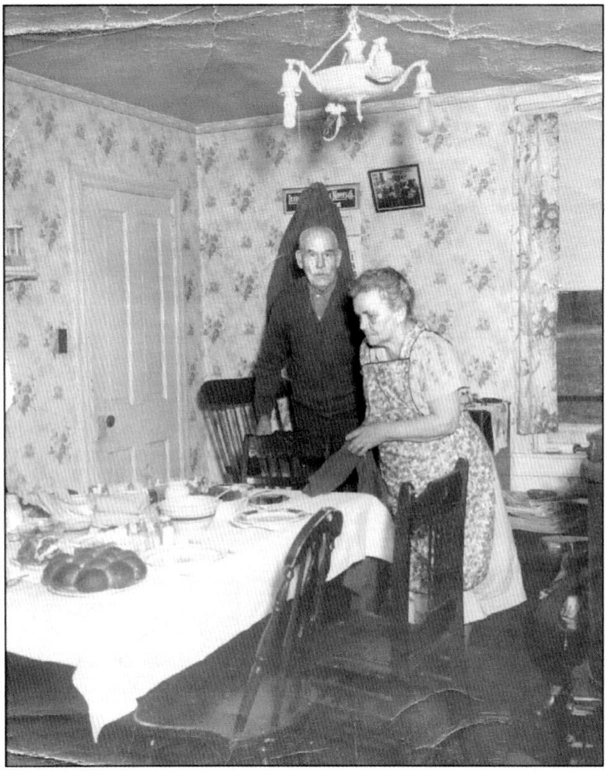

Nellie Lloyd Ayres Hogans and Joseph Hogans have prepared a family dinner, including beaten biscuits, at their home on the Haven in 1940. At the time the photograph was taken, the Hoganses' home had no electricity, no indoor plumbing, and no telephone. (Courtesy of H. Edward Beekman Jr.)

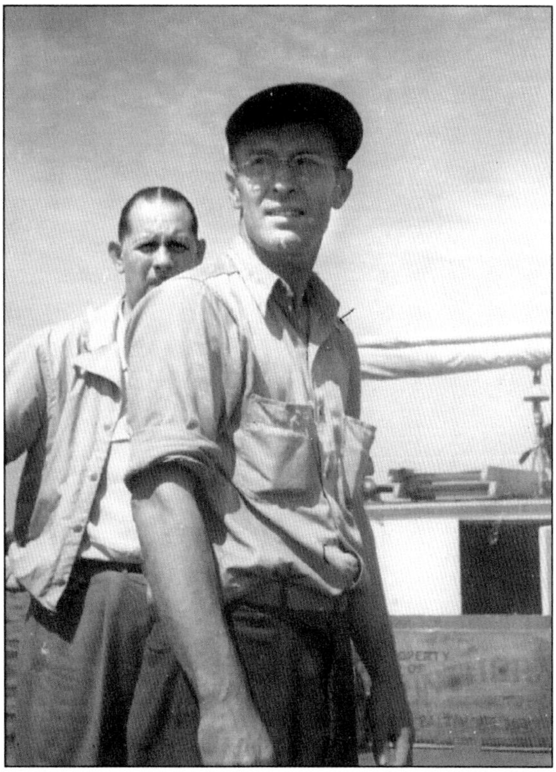

Randolph "Pete" Burgess of Rock Hall served as Kent County Register of Wills for many years. He was also a funeral director and a farmer. (Courtesy of H. Edward Beekman Jr.)

Bob Lewis had a big truck that was referred to as "Store at Your Door." The truck carried meats, canned goods, and food to Rock Hall residents and those who lived in the "Necks." He owned a slaughterhouse with John Dowling, Casey Dowling's father, in the area near where Oyster Court is now located. The Necks are the outlying areas on the river and creek sides known as Skinners Neck, Piney Neck, and Eastern Neck. (Courtesy of H. Edward Beekman Jr.)

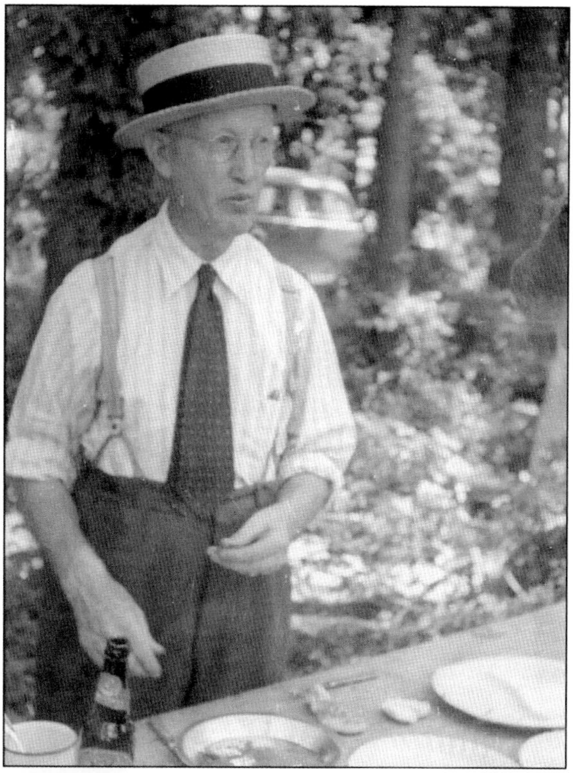

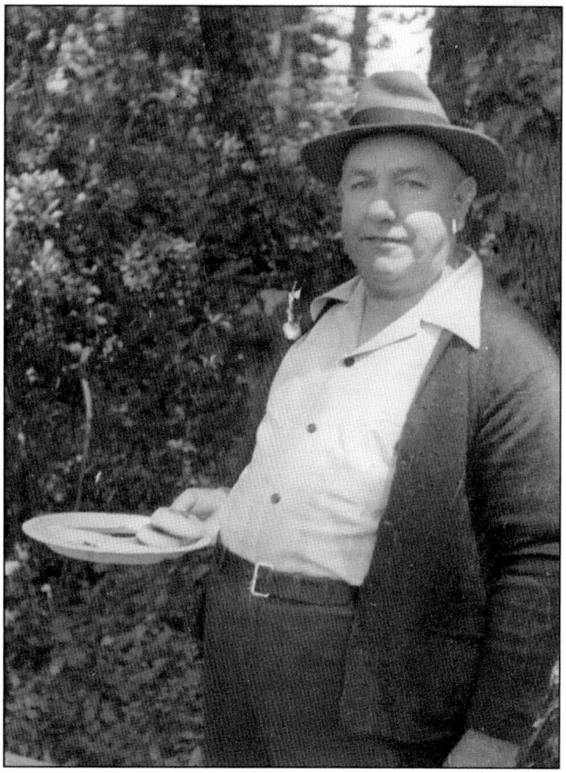

Frank Kline owned Kline's Store, boasting that it was the "Big Store with Little Prices." The store was a favorite shopping spot, especially during the Christmas season. (Courtesy of H. Edward Beekman Jr.)

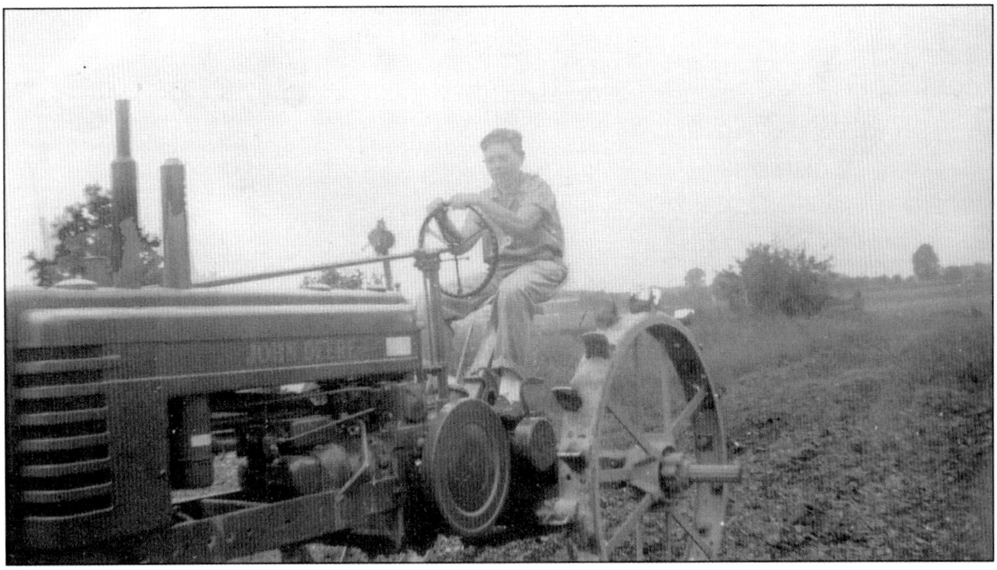

Ed Beekman Jr. is pictured on a John Deere tractor in the 1940s at his farm in Skinners Neck, which was once known as the Dierker farm. (Courtesy of H. Edward Beekman Jr.)

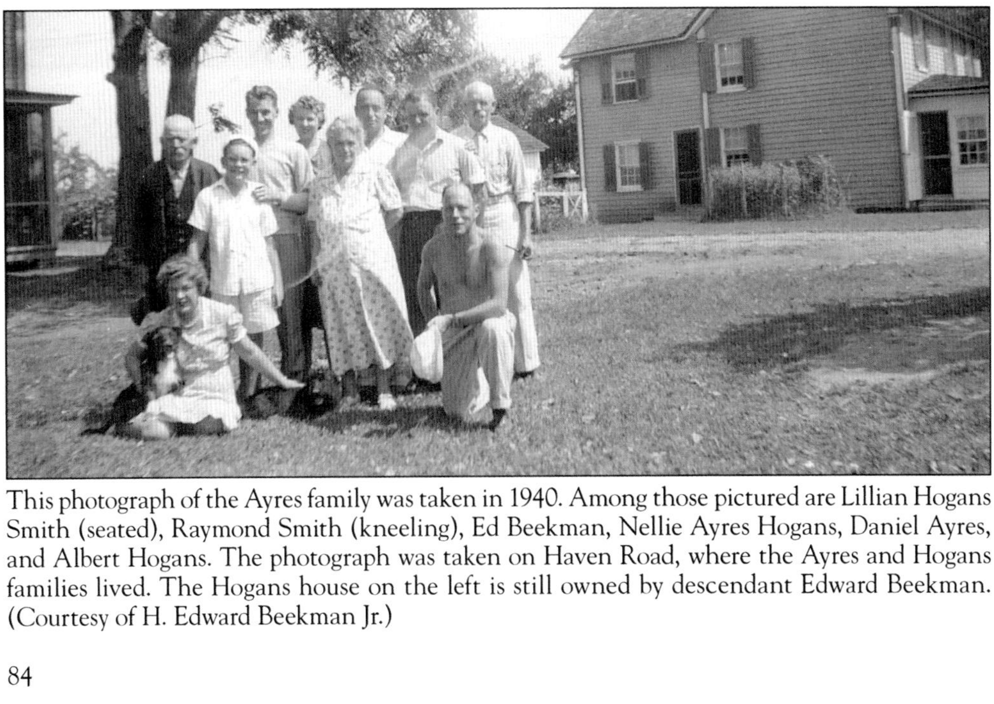

This photograph of the Ayres family was taken in 1940. Among those pictured are Lillian Hogans Smith (seated), Raymond Smith (kneeling), Ed Beekman, Nellie Ayres Hogans, Daniel Ayres, and Albert Hogans. The photograph was taken on Haven Road, where the Ayres and Hogans families lived. The Hogans house on the left is still owned by descendant Edward Beekman. (Courtesy of H. Edward Beekman Jr.)

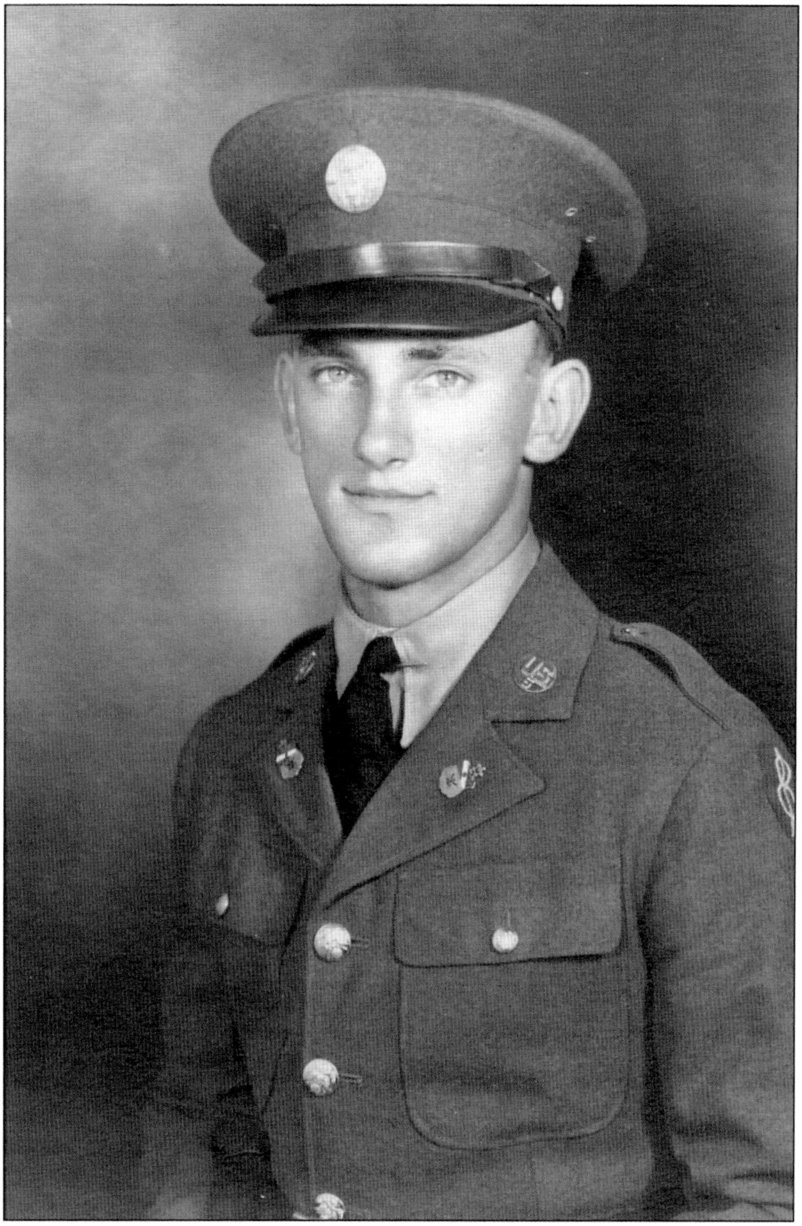

Sgt. Preston Ashley was born in 1919 on the Ashley family farm in Piney Neck. He was one of 10 children of Joseph Columbus Ashley and Augusta (Miss Gussie) Crouch Ashley. He enlisted in the U.S. Army, Engineer Company 427, at age 19 in 1938. He served in England, Northern Ireland, the seaport of Oran, Algeria, and North Africa. On May 10, 1943, Sergeant Ashley was wounded in battle and died at age 23 at the 1st Mobile British Military Hospital in Sousse, Tunisia, North Africa. He was laid to rest in the North Africa American Cemetery. A bronze marker was erected at the Ashley family plot at Wesley Chapel Cemetery in Rock Hall. American Legion Post No. 228 is named after Preston Ashley. The post formed in 1948 and remains active today with full membership. Many events are held at the post, as well as fund-raisers that provide money to assist veterans and members of the community. (Courtesy of Pat Reihl and Sgt. Preston Ashley American Legion Post 228, Rock Hall, Maryland.)

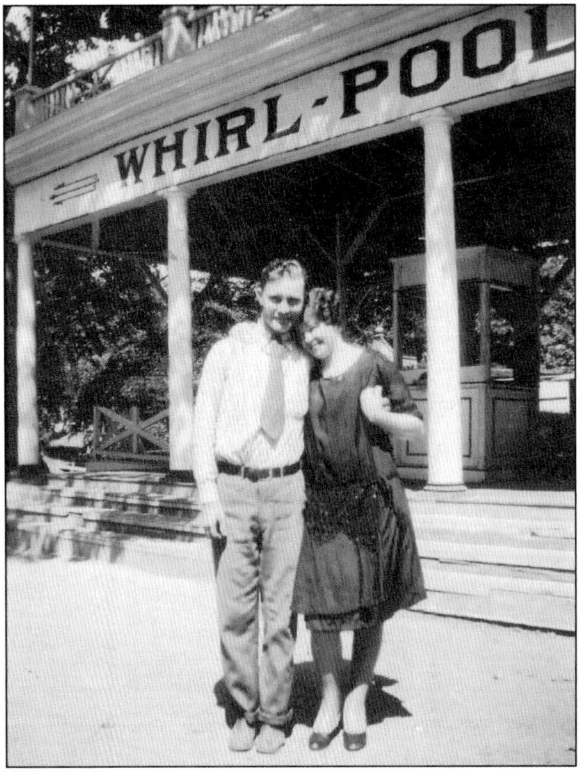

Wilson and Mary Hudson Ward pose in front of the Whirl-Pool Dip ride at Tolchester Park, located near Rock Hall. (Courtesy of Jane and Carroll Thompson.)

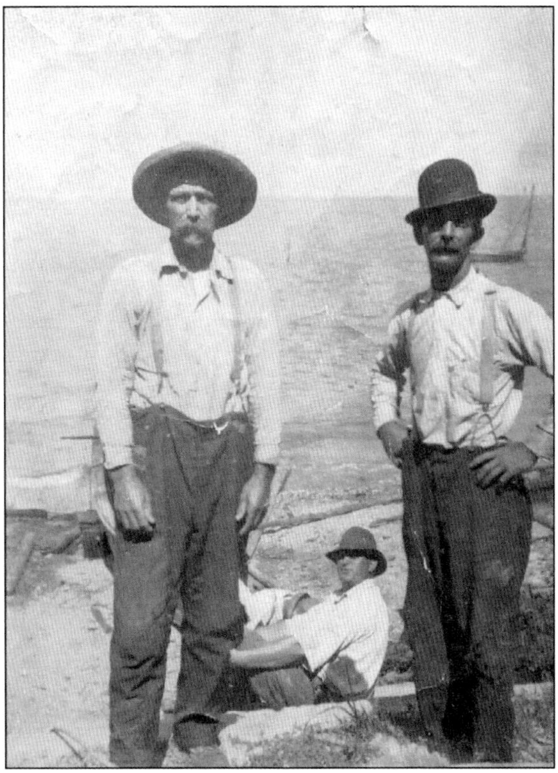

This photograph shows Joseph Hynson (left) and Abe Kendall (right). It was taken at Tolchester Beach along the shores of the Chesapeake Bay. (Courtesy of Jane and Carroll Thompson.)

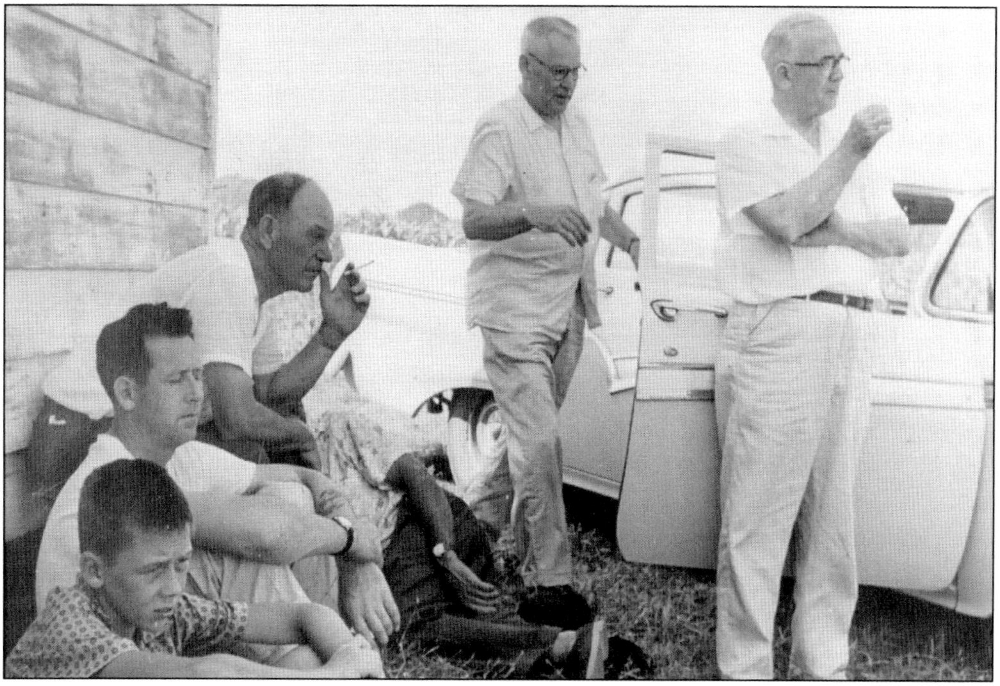

Pictured from left to right are Carroll Thompson, John Cavender Thompson, Chap Willis, "Runt" Boulter (lying down), Lewin Deputy, and Jewell Thompson, all members of the Swan Point Gun Club. They are planning a hunting season at Swan Point and Little Neck Island, Rock Hall, in the 1950s. (Courtesy of Jane and Carroll Thompson.)

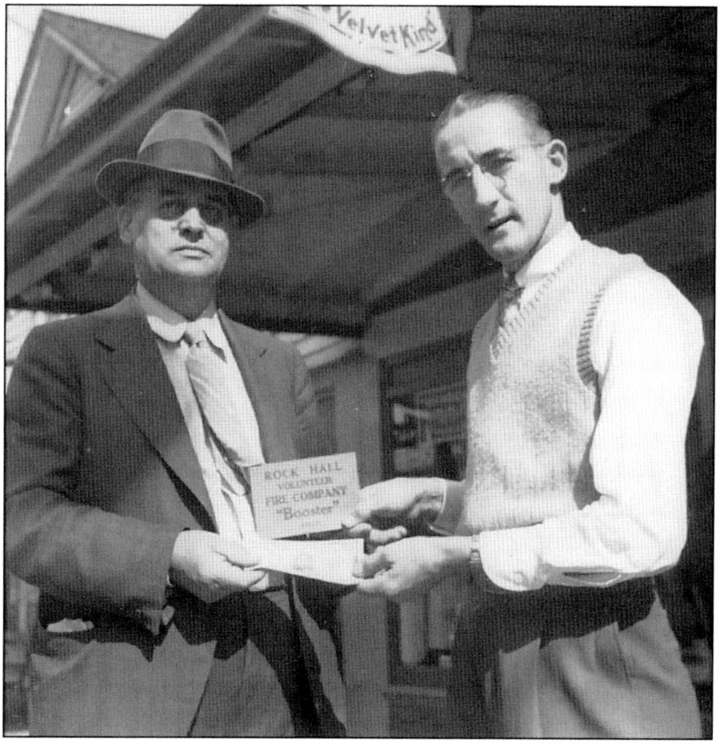

Frank "Doc" Smith Jr. (right) presents a donation to the Rock Hall Volunteer Fire Company (RHVFC) and becomes a Rock Hall Volunteer Fire Company booster in the 1940s. The first officers for the RHVFC were Herbert Urie, president; B. Trew Durding, vice president; Allen Urie, secretary; Walter H. Coleman, assistant secretary; Joseph Downey Jr., treasurer; B. Trew Durding, chief; Walter H. Coleman, first assistant chief; and J. Purnell, second assistant chief. (Courtesy of Patricia Joan O. Horsey.)

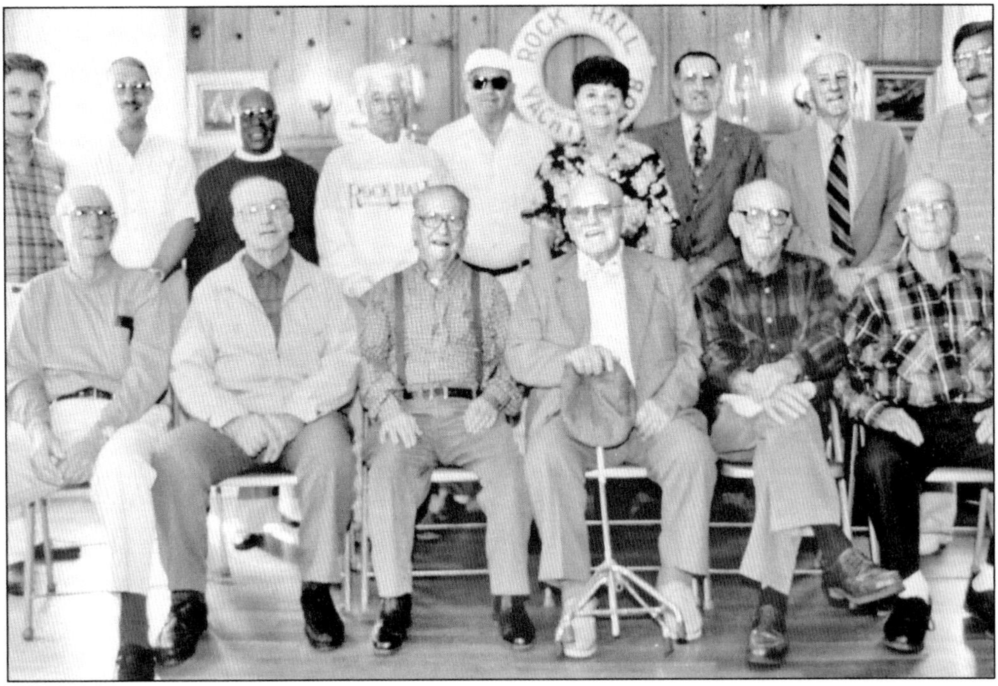

At the 1994 Waterman's Appreciation Day at Rock Hall Yacht Club are, from left to right, (first row) Emory "Pie" Edwards, Roby Cornelius, Clifton Simns, Harry Carter, Franklin Edwards, and John C. Edwards; (second row) Charlie Higgs, Wayne Brady, Clarence "Turtle" Hicks, Jimmy Bryden, Billy Creighton, Patsy Glenn Higgs, Billy Collyer, Hilton Crouch, and John D. Edwards. (Courtesy of Emory "Pie" Edwards.)

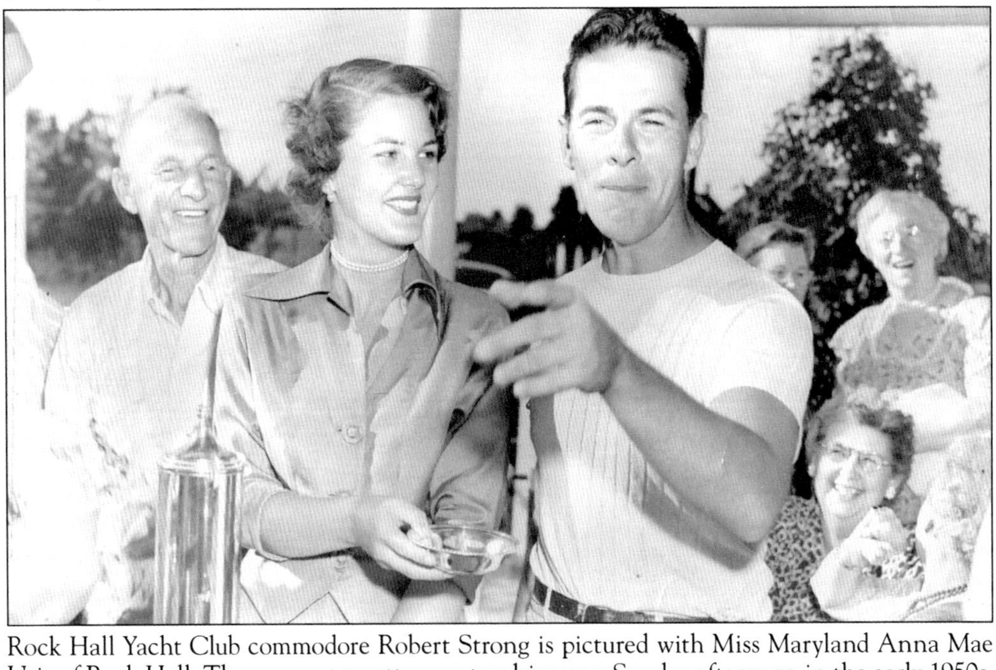

Rock Hall Yacht Club commodore Robert Strong is pictured with Miss Maryland Anna Mae Urie of Rock Hall. They present regatta race trophies on a Sunday afternoon in the early 1950s. (Courtesy of Patsy Reihl.)

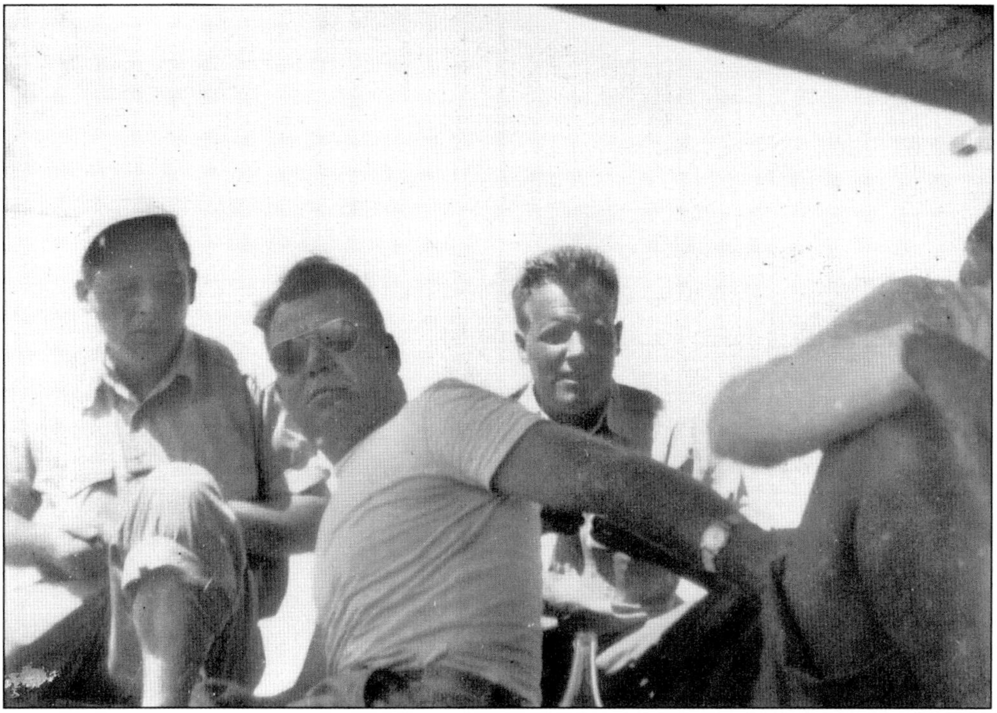

From left to right are Cordray Wood, Harold Hill, and Albert "Snooks" Strong during a Rock Hall Yacht Club Regatta. Chesapeake 20 racing was popular at the time. (Courtesy of Robin Wood Kurowski.)

Harry Green is pictured here with his Chesapeake Bay retriever, Chief, while at a dove shoot. Green retired to Yarmouth, a farm located just outside of Rock Hall on Eastern Neck Road that he had owned since 1945, after working as a stockbroker in New York City. He lived to be 100 years old. (Courtesy of Julie J. Stephens.)

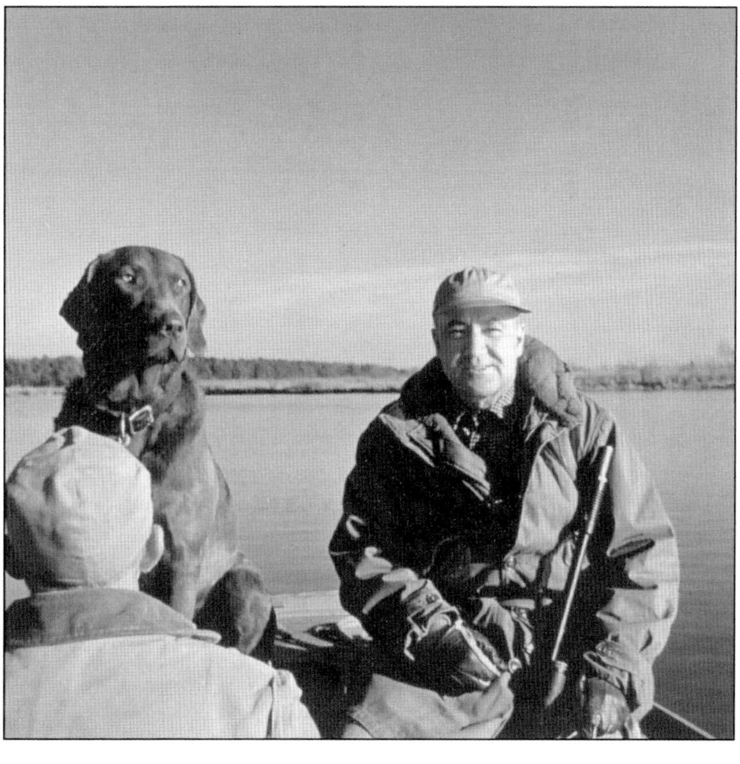

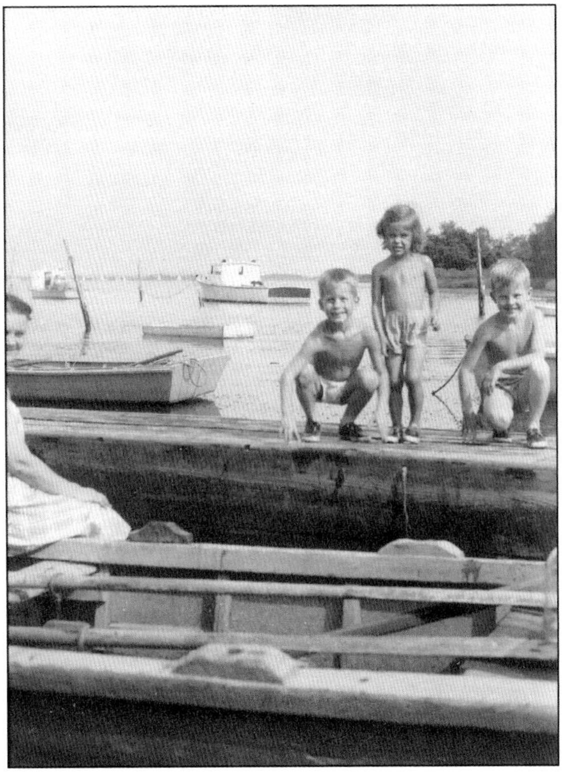

Pictured here at Long Cove in Piney Neck are, from left to right, Edith Lamakis, George Lamakis, Janie Hudson Thompson, and Corey Jones. (Courtesy of Jane and Carroll Thompson.)

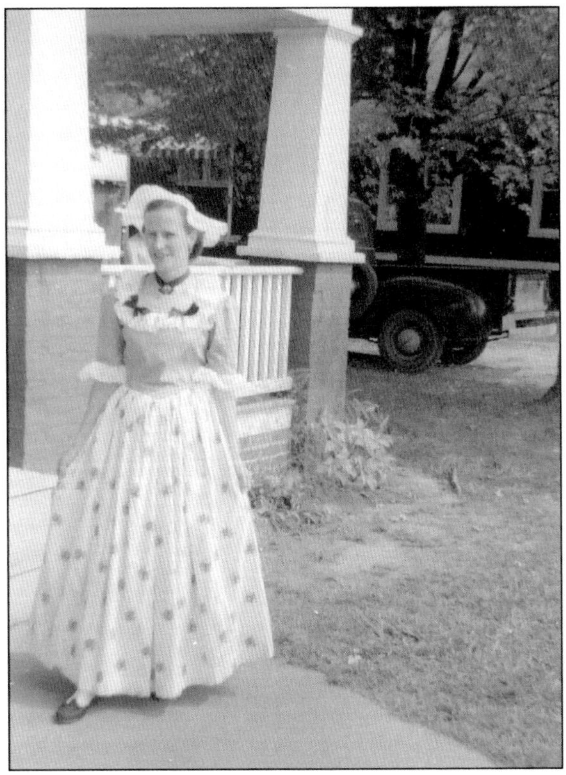

Bertha Dowling Jacquette participates in Rock Hall's 250th anniversary parade in 1957. Blanche Dlugoborski, her sister, made the dress. Blanche and her family watched the 2007 birthday parade and celebration from this same family homestead. (Courtesy of Harriett Creighton and Blanche Dlugoborski.)

Glady Wilson is pictured in her dress made especially for Rock Hall's 250th anniversary parade in 1957. (Courtesy of Harriett Creighton and Blanche Dlugoborski.)

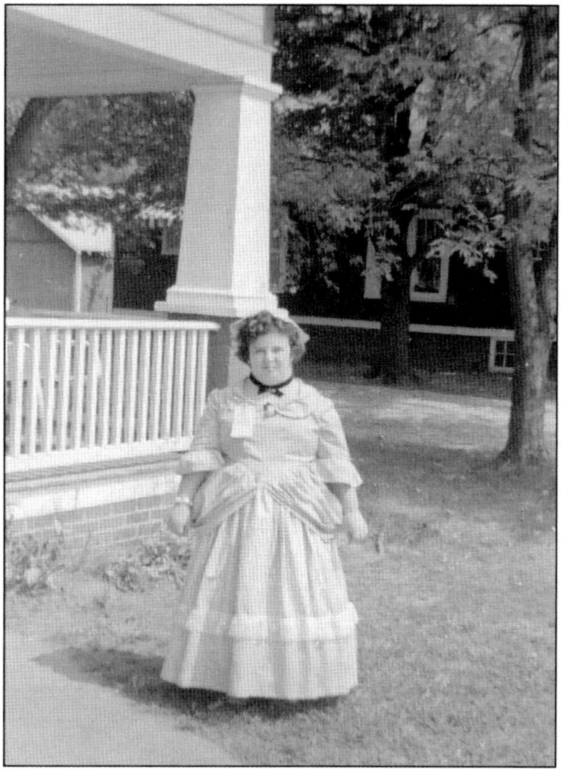

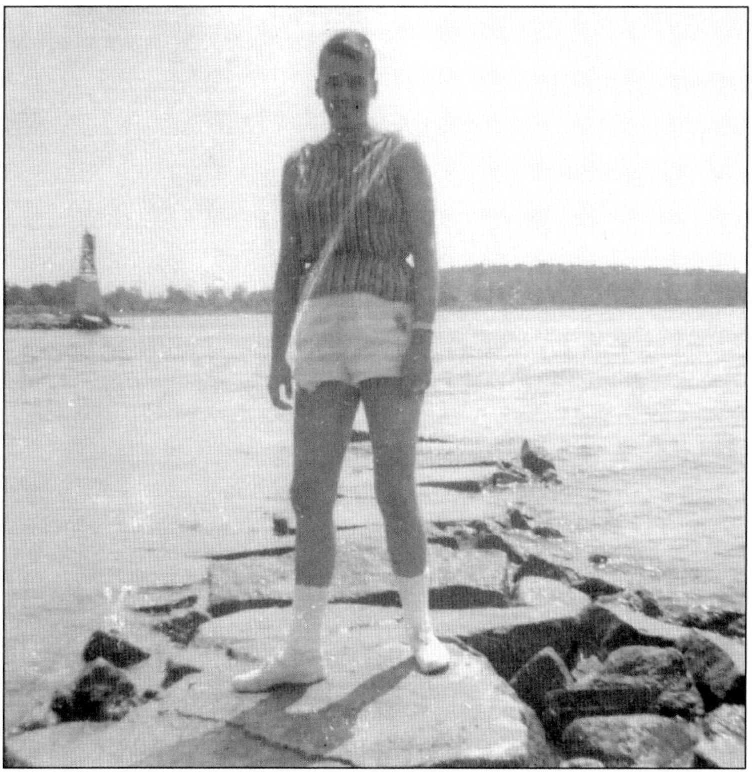

Madelyn Cornelius stands on the jetty constructed at Rock Hall Harbor in 1956. (Courtesy of Madelyn Cornelius.)

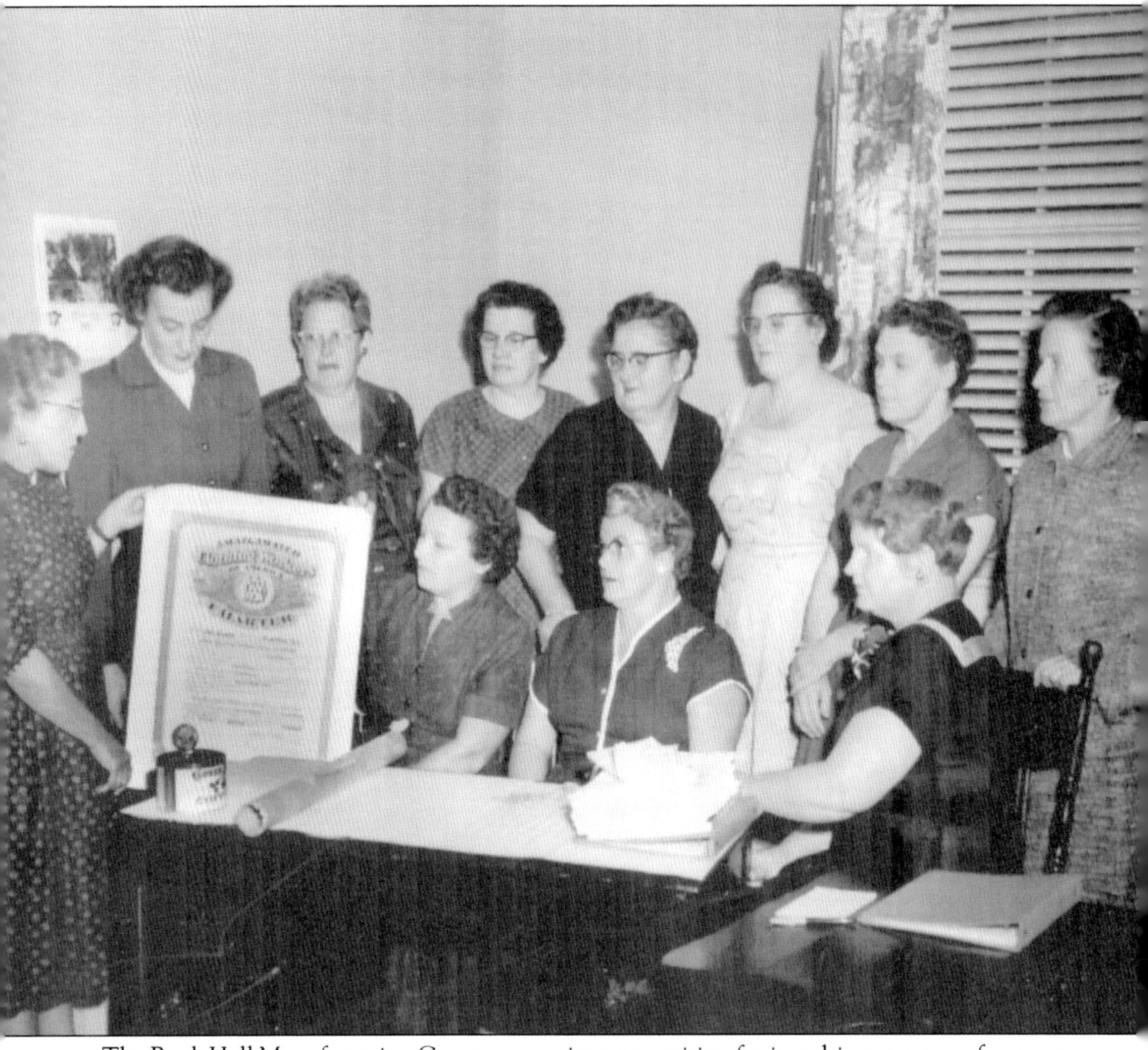

The Rock Hall Manufacturing Company receives recognition for its achievement, performance, and quality. The company, owned by the Purnell Elbourn family, produced various lines of clothing for national distribution. Pictured with the certificate are employees and management. (Courtesy of the Elbourn family.)

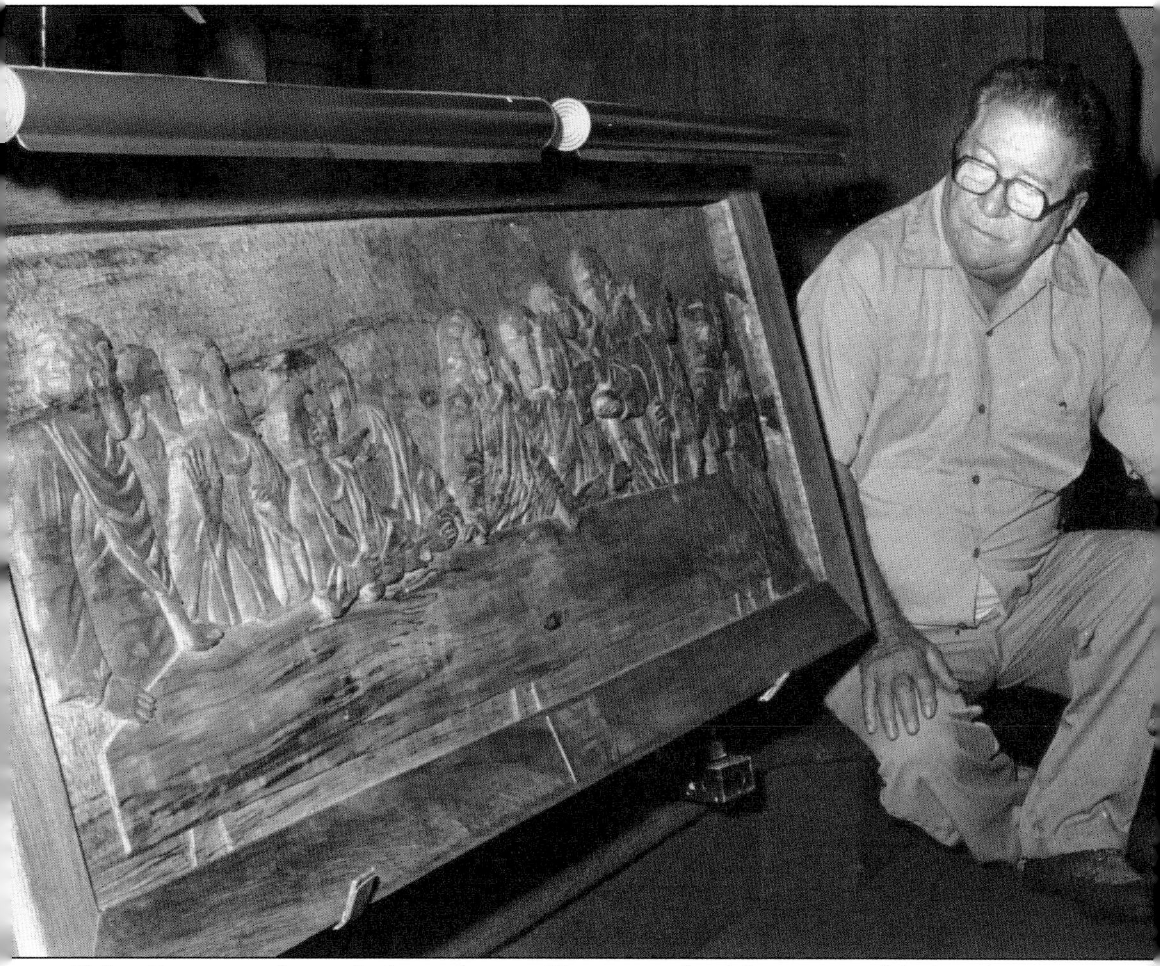

Clifton Simns was a famous barber and carver. He is pictured with his carving of the Last Supper, which he created for the Rock Hall Seventh-Day Adventist Church. The carving hangs in the church today. (Courtesy of Larry Simns and Madelyn Cornelius.)

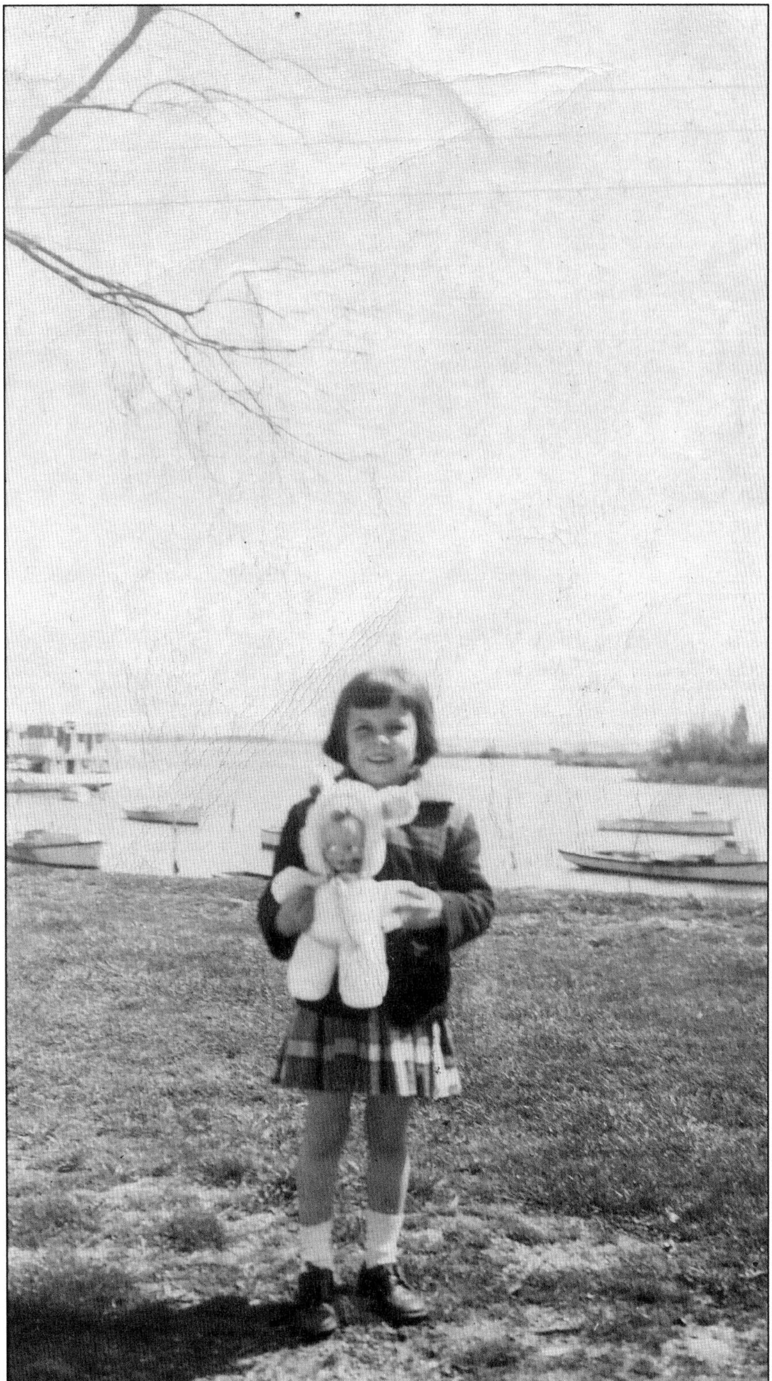

Honey Wood is pictured at her grandfather's seafood business, C. H. Ashley and Son, on Long Cove in Piney Neck. It was common for the Ashley grandchildren to spend summer days at the seafood business. When all the work was done, they would take the family boat out and anchor off Gray's Inn Point to swim. Captain Ashley taught the grandchildren how to do the watermelon roll off the stern of his boat. (Courtesy of Robin Wood Kurowski.)

Five

PLACES

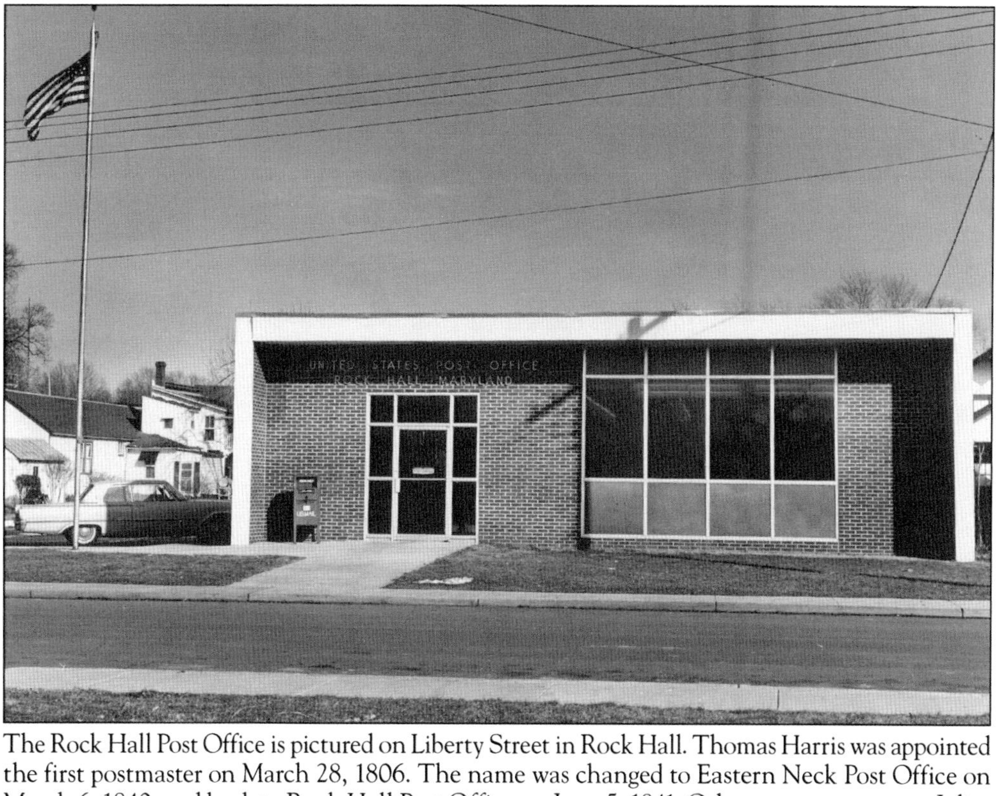

The Rock Hall Post Office is pictured on Liberty Street in Rock Hall. Thomas Harris was appointed the first postmaster on March 28, 1806. The name was changed to Eastern Neck Post Office on March 6, 1840, and back to Rock Hall Post Office on June 5, 1841. Other postmasters were Juliet Harris, Isaiah Ashley, Stephen Kendall, Joseph Harris, James D. Ashley, John Downey, Simon G. Swart, Thomas Burgess, Samuel A. J. Wickes, Wesley Stevens, Joseph Downey, Samuel I. Wickes, John W. Downey, Benjamin R. Durding, John W. Downey, Ida M. Hynson, Charles Judefind, Allan Urie, Harry R. Price, George Parsons, James Nicewarner, and Holly Johnson. Kay Barnes is the present postmistress. (Courtesy of Historical Society of Kent County.)

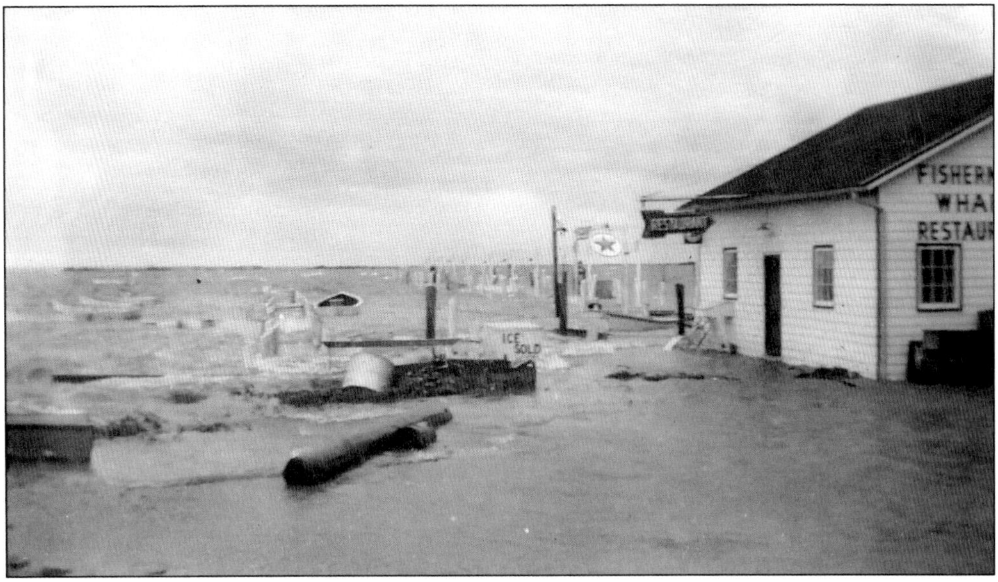

This is the end of Rock Hall Avenue (also known as Route 20). Fisherman's Wharf Restaurant no longer exists. The pier is now part of Gratitude Marina and the bulkhead. Tilghman's Landing condominiums are also located in this area. (Courtesy of Jean Foreman.)

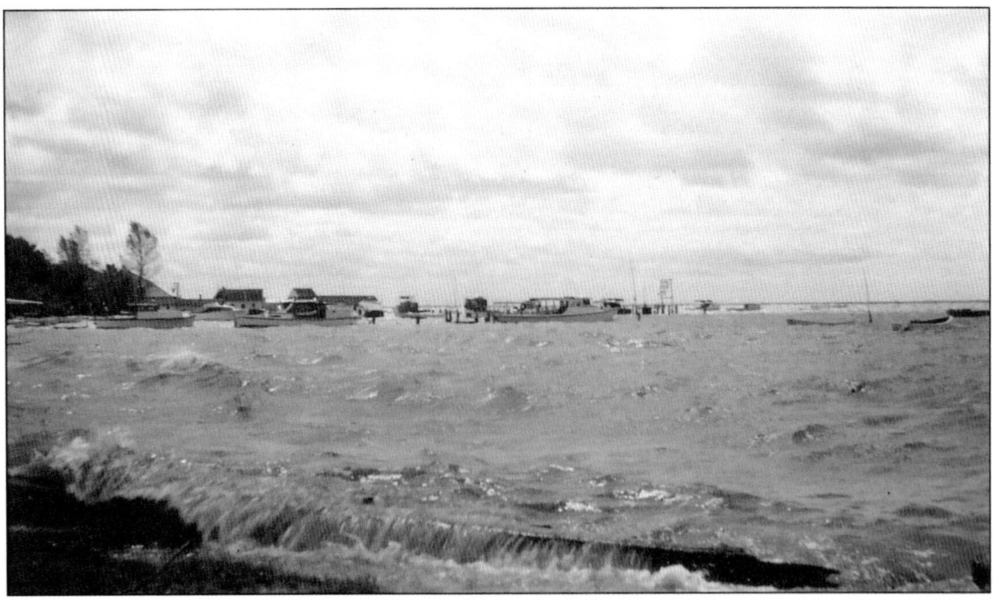

This view from Thomas's Pier shows Gratitude harbor with the original pier, which has been replaced by Gratitude Marina and a bulkhead. The pier no longer exists. (Courtesy of Jean Foreman.)

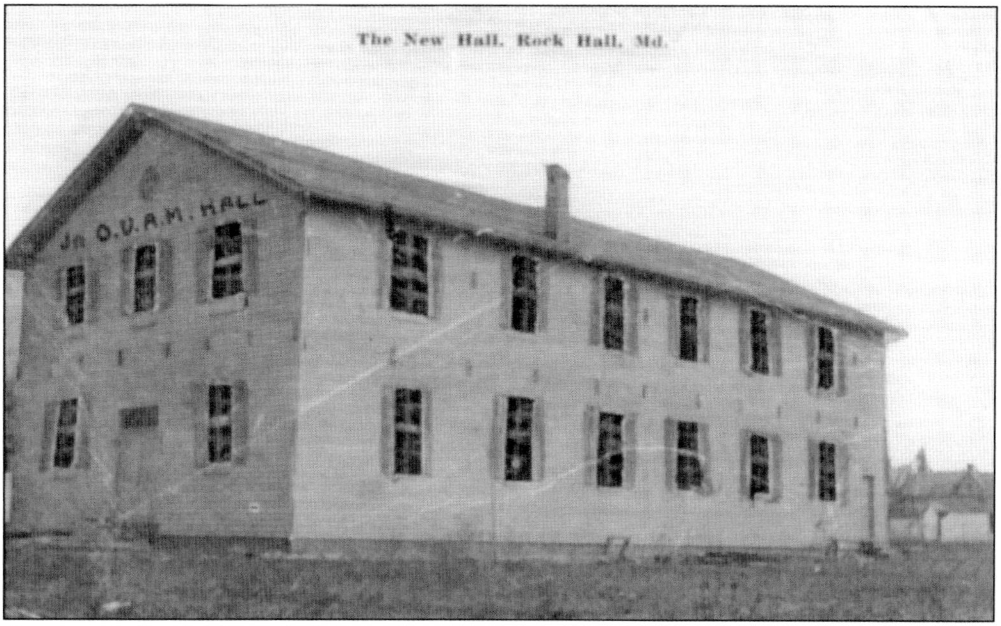

The initials on the side of this building stand for Junior Order United American Mechanics. The structure was also known as the New Hall. Organized in 1896, the second story of this building was used as a community hall for banquets, dances, and other events. Movies were started in the hall in 1905, with sound added in 1930 and a large Cinemascope screen in 1957. It has also been used as a dress factory. (Courtesy of Ida Mae Dulin.)

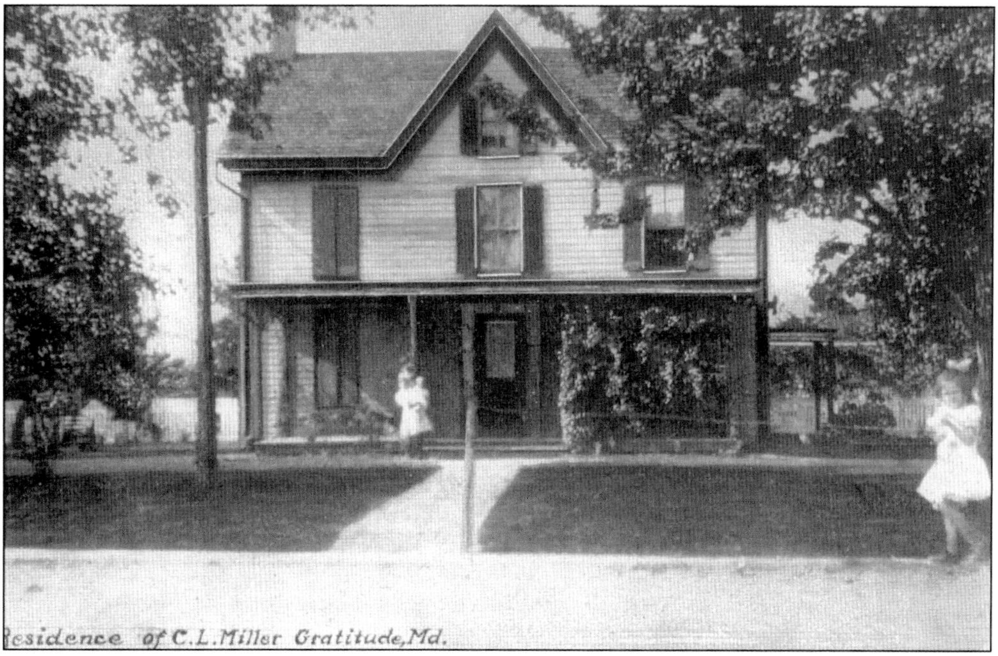

The Miller residence on Lawton Avenue was owned by Charles "Charlie" L. Miller, the brother of the Miller's Store owner, Marion T. "Manny" Miller. Charlie Miller worked on the waterfront and docks in Gratitude. The Miller residence later became Eulah Williams's Shady Rest; it is now the Moonlight Bay Marina and Inn. (Courtesy of Ida Mae Dulin.)

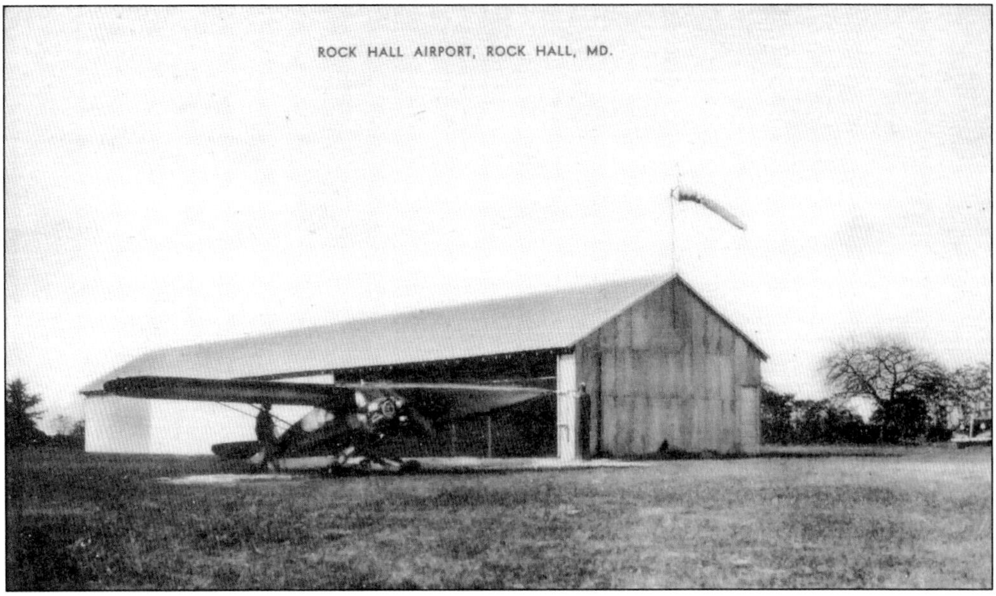

The original Rock Hall Airport was on the left side of Route 445 across from Boxley Farm and was owned by Oscar and Ralph McGinnes. (Courtesy Judy Hickman.)

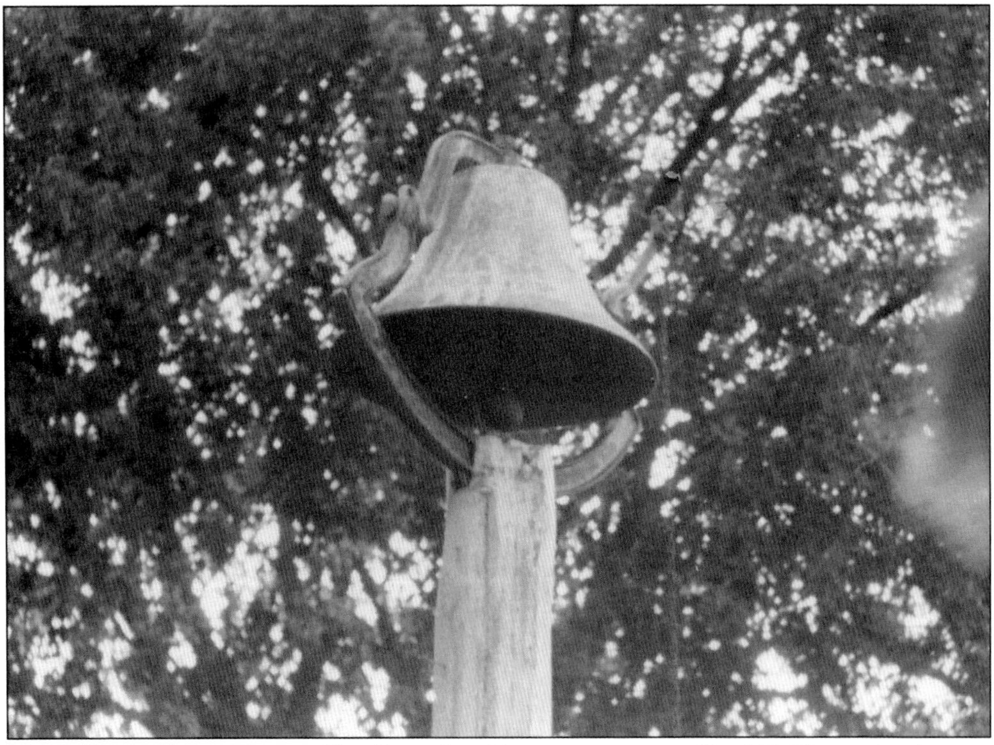

This bell, more than 100 years old, still stands at Trumpington, one of Rock Hall's grandest historic homes, built in 1723 by Thomas Smythee. An earlier house burned down and was replaced by the present structure. An old millstone serves as a stepping-stone at the front of the house. At one time, the bell rang at noon to call the farm help in from the fields for a middle-of-the-day dinner. (Courtesy of Anne Willson Grim McKown.)

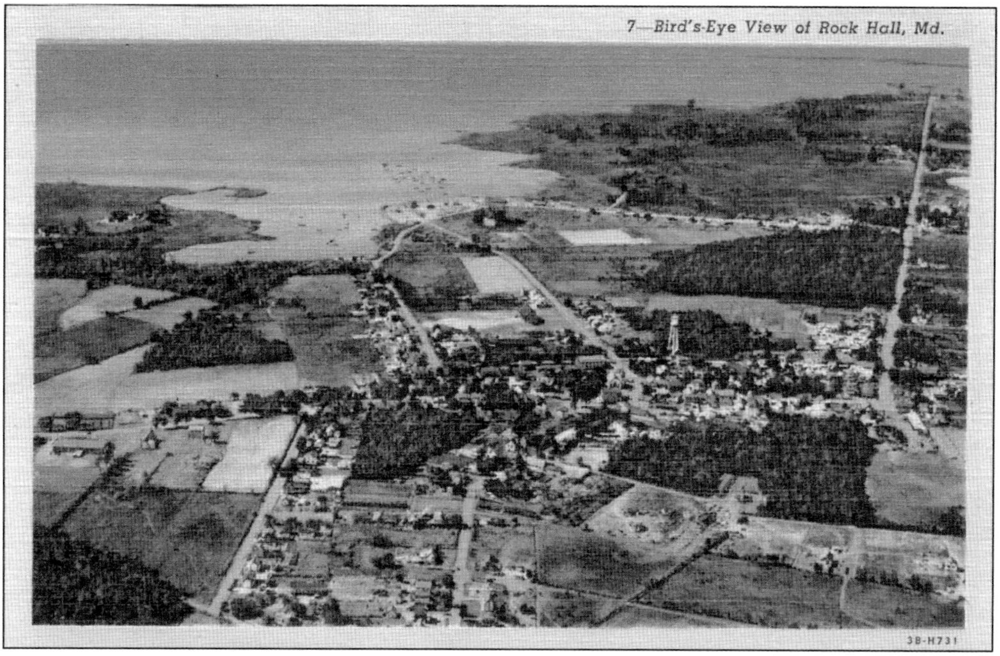

This "Birds Eye View of Rock Hall" was taken before the Rock Hall harbor jetty was built in the early 1950s. The jetty was built for harbor protection and originally had a sounding beacon on it. The original jetty has since been repaired and fortified. (Courtesy of Ida Mae Dulin.)

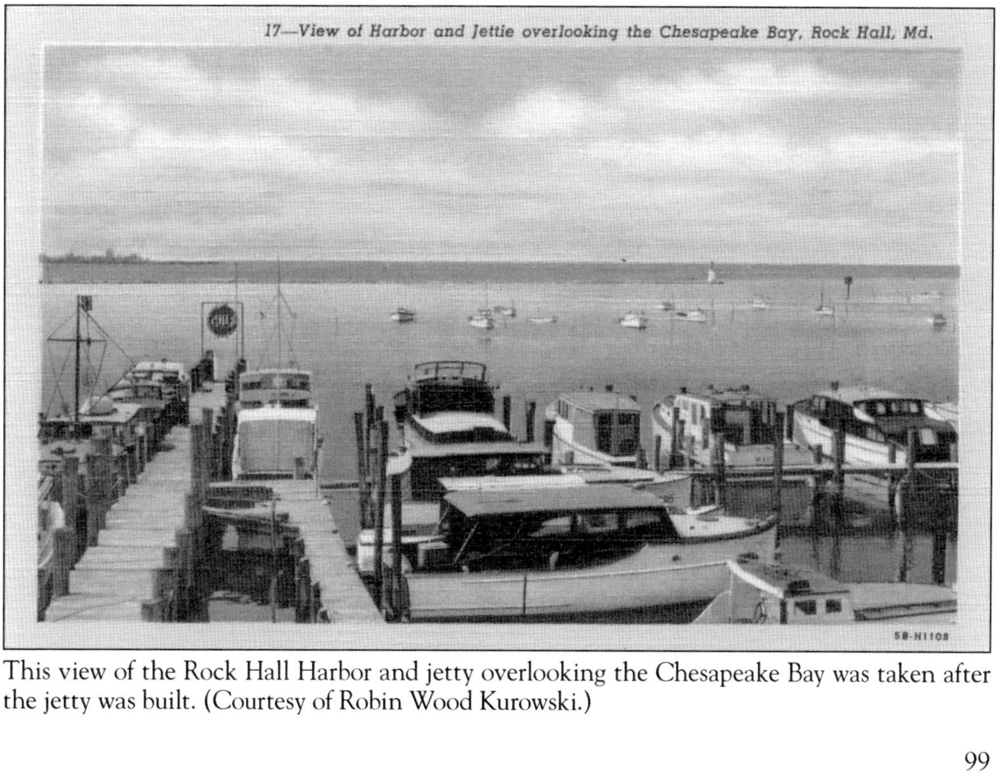

This view of the Rock Hall Harbor and jetty overlooking the Chesapeake Bay was taken after the jetty was built. (Courtesy of Robin Wood Kurowski.)

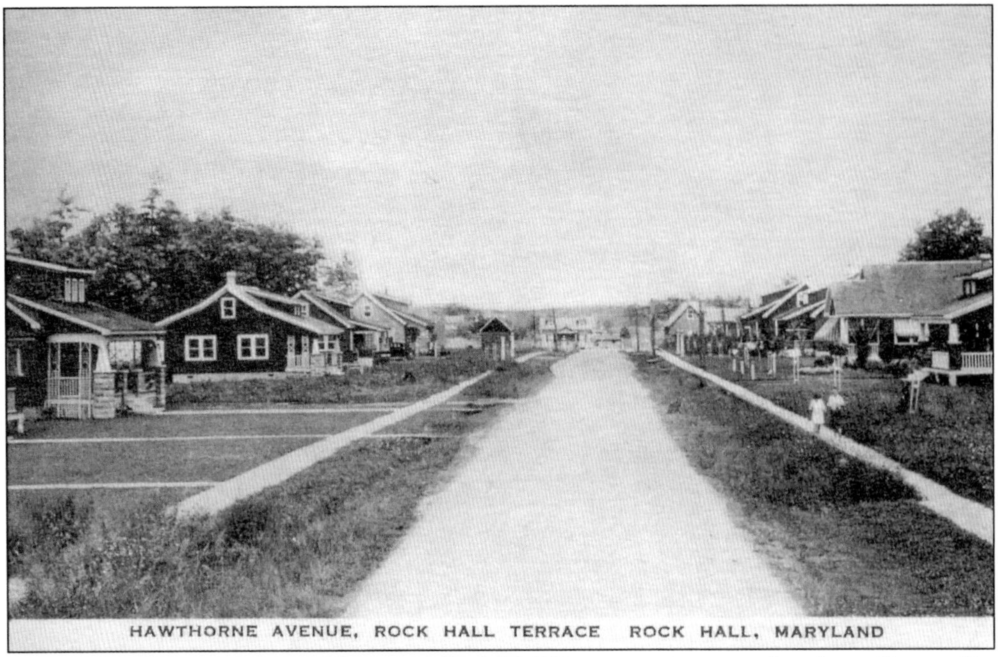

In 1951, Hawthorne Avenue was known as Rock Hall Terrace; today it is referred to as Puppeville, named after Frank Puppe, who built most of the houses on this street. Many of the houses remain today. (Courtesy of Ida Mae Dulin and Dorothy McKinney.)

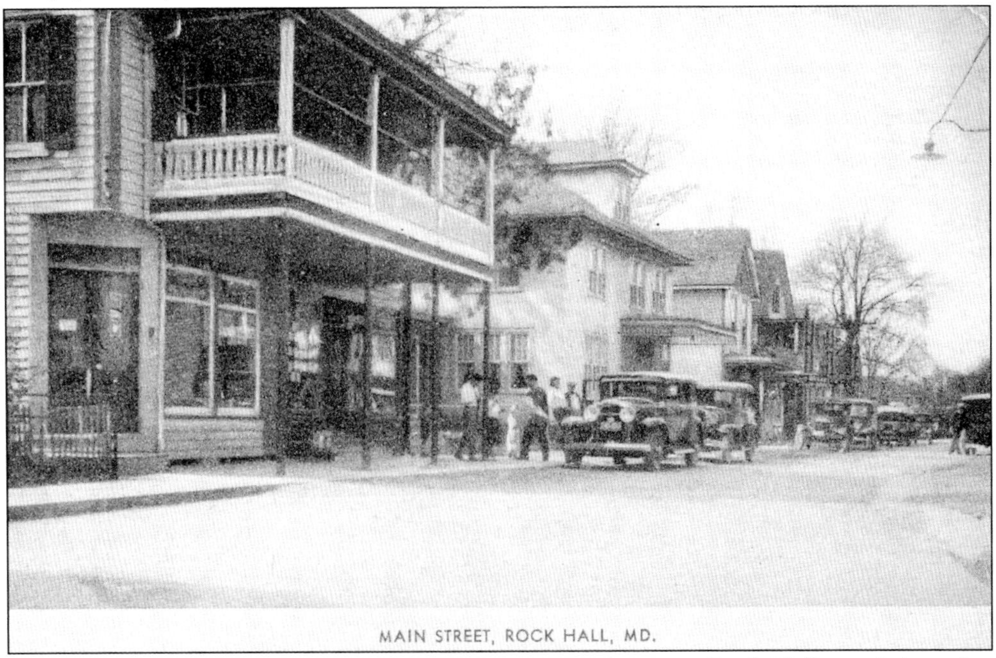

Casey Dowling's retail meat and grocery store on Main Street in Rock Hall is at left in this photograph. Abe Casey established the business in the period after the Civil War. Also on the left is Henry's Five Cents to Five Dollar store. Henry's was established in October 1932 and prominently promoted itself as "the home of Endicott Johnson Shoes for men and boys." (Courtesy of Ida Mae Dulin.)

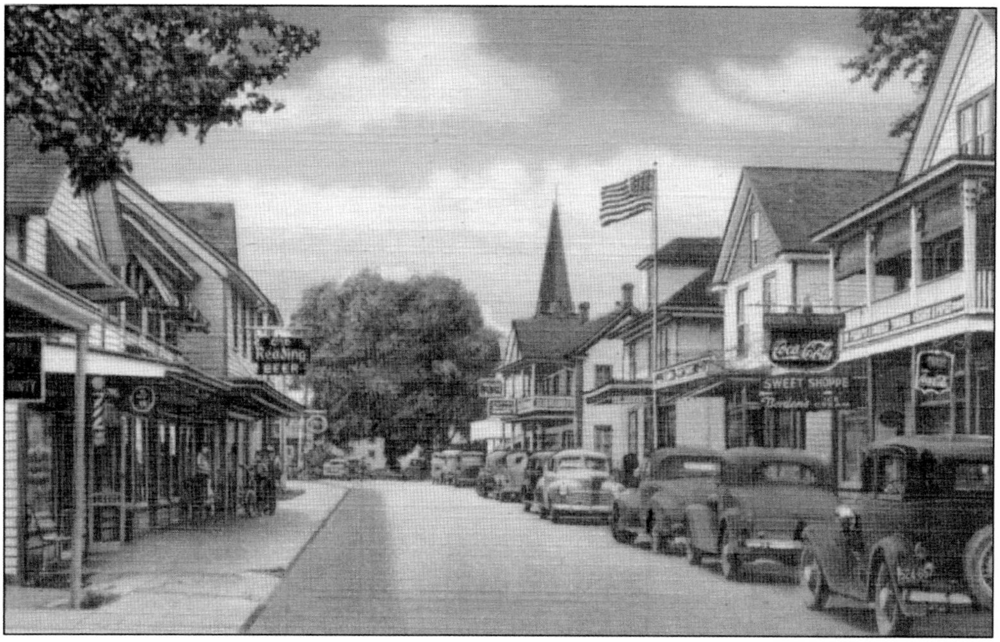

Rock Hall's Main Street, looking south, shows a thriving downtown. The steeple from the Rock Hall Methodist Church can be seen in the background. (Courtesy of Ida Mae Dulin and Dorothy McKinney.)

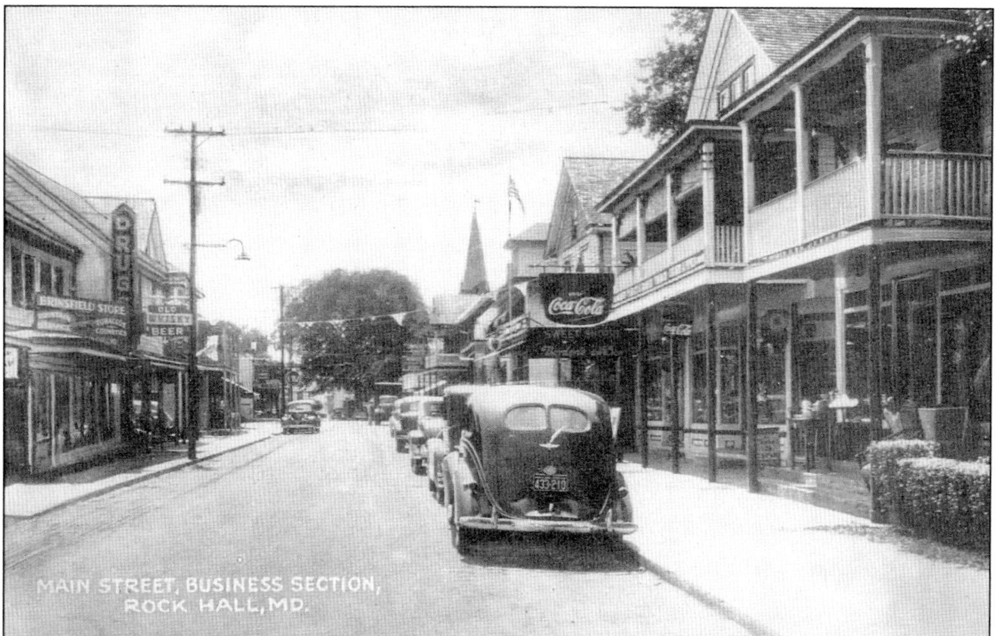

This photograph of Rock Hall's Main Street business section shows Brinsfield's Drug Store on the left. This business no longer exists. (Courtesy of Ida Mae Dulin and Dorothy McKinney.)

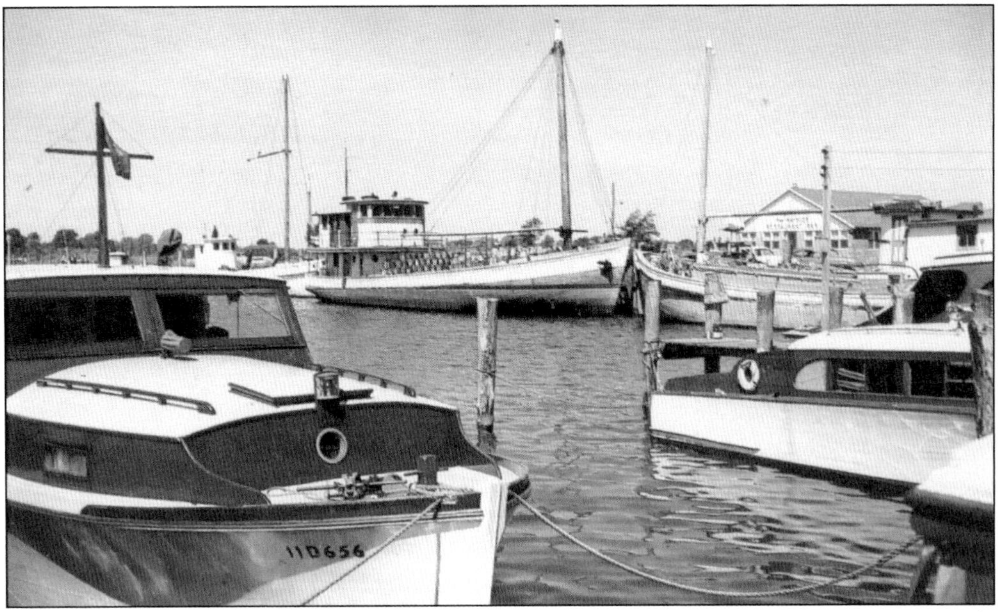

This photograph, taken from the Leary's Rock Hall Marine Railway property, shows the Bayside Restaurant and Bar at the Rock Hall harbor, owned by Gertrude and Lloyd Stevens, at right. This restaurant was later known as Someplace Else, Paradise, and Mason's Crabs and Ribs. The building remains today. Also pictured is a buy boat at the Rock Hall Harbor bulkhead bayside. (Courtesy of Ida Mae Dulin and Dorothy McKinney.)

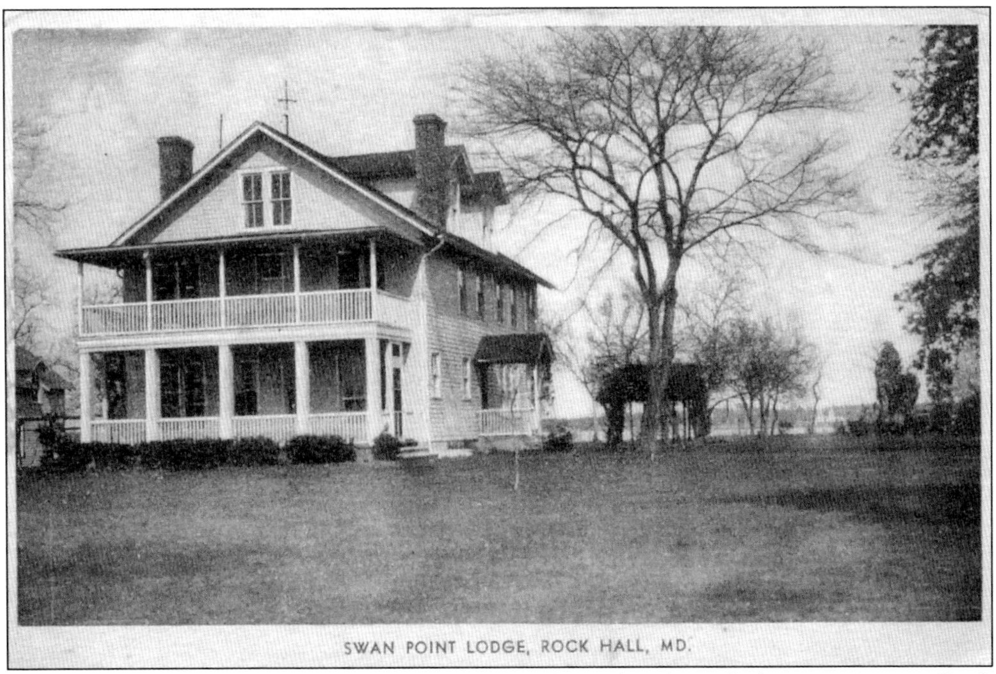

Swan Point Lodge is now called Deep Landing and is located at the end of Lawton Avenue, Rock Hall. It is a private residence. (Courtesy of Ida Mae Dulin and Dorothy McKinney.)

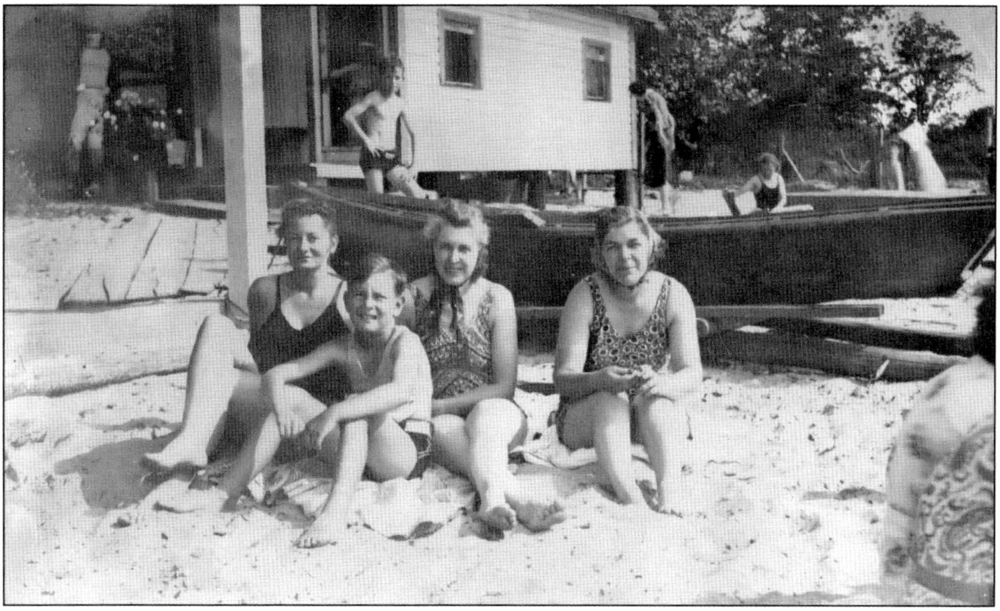

Sitting in the sand at Tolchester Beach in front of the Tolchester Bath House and a lifesaving rescue boat are, from left to right, Jane Beekman Pickard, Ed Beekman, Mary Hogans Beekman, and Lillian Hogans Smith. (Courtesy of H. Edward Beekman Jr.)

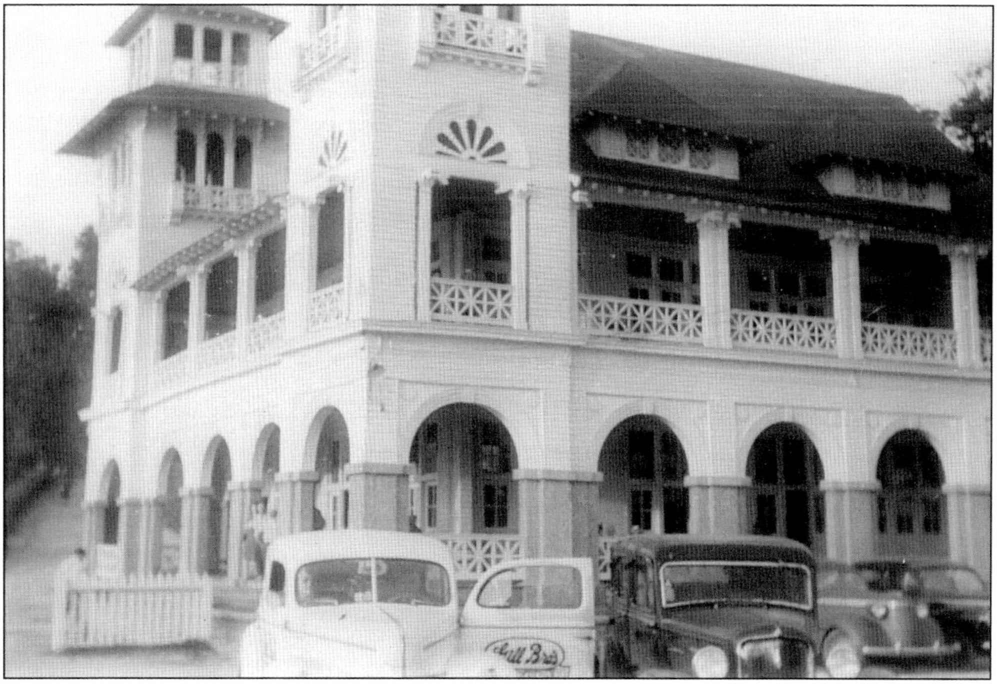

Pictured here is the Tolchester main building, which housed the Lower Dairy Bar on the first floor. (Courtesy of H. Edward Beekman Jr.)

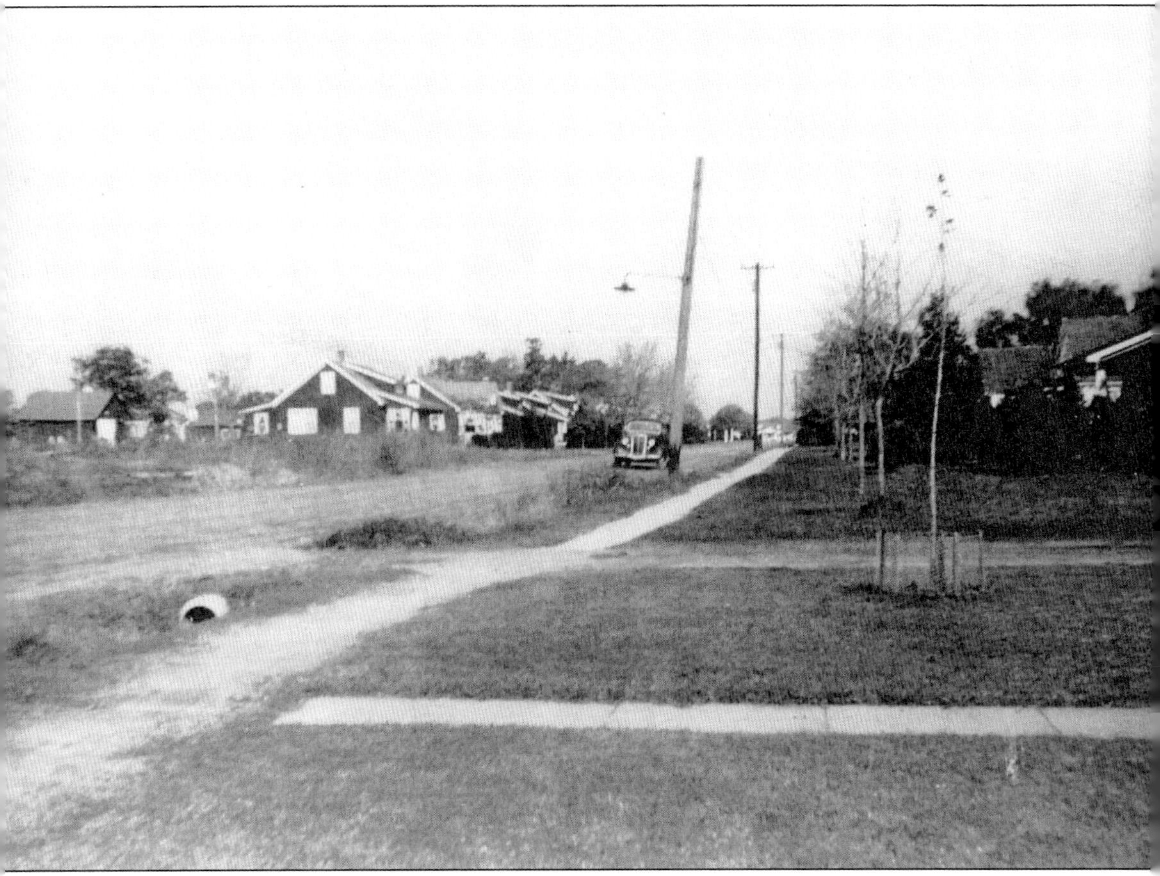

Hawthorne Avenue, also known as Puppeville, is show prior to paving. The homes built by the Frank Puppe family still line this serene street. (Courtesy of H. Edward Beekman Jr.)

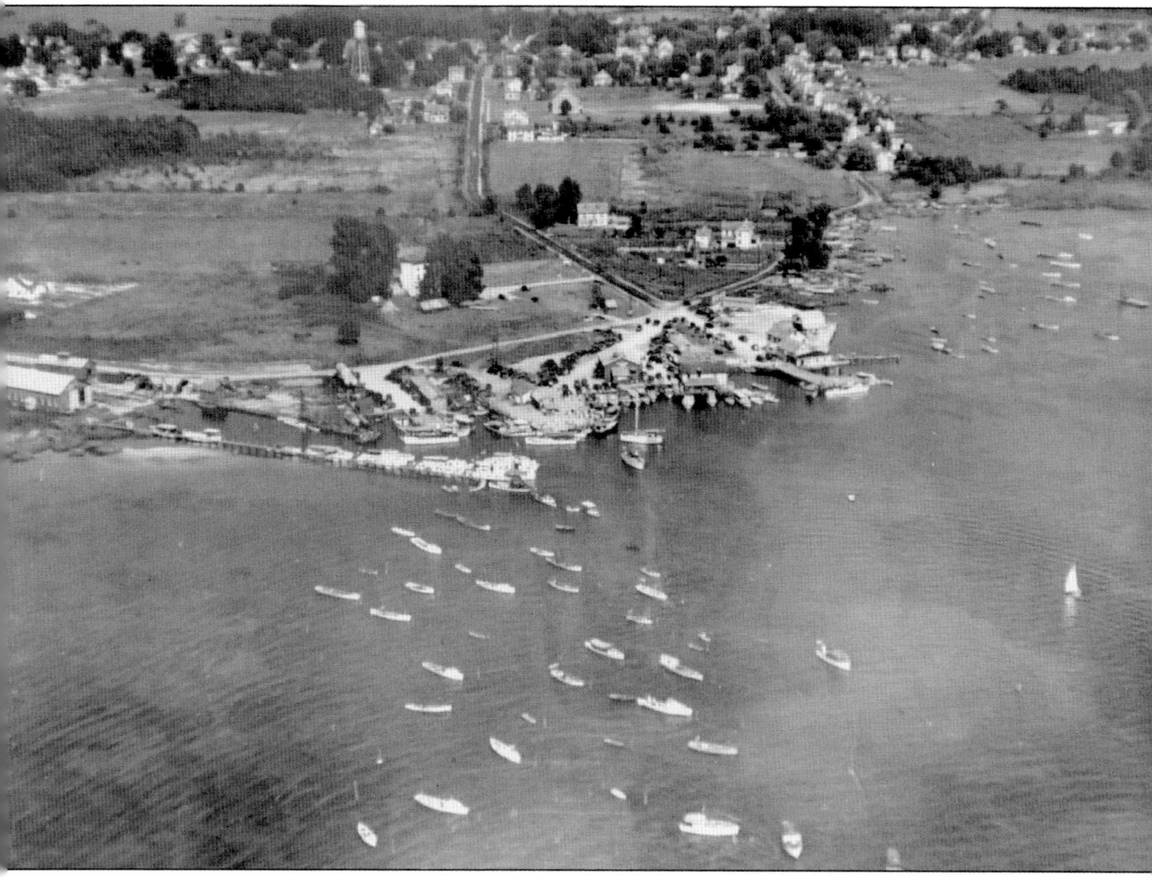

This photograph shows Rock Hall Creek (today known as Rock Hall Harbor). The Rock Hall Marine Railway property can be seen, as well as Mansion House, which was constructed by the Sharp family. The Sharp Street Wharf, where Rock Hall Seafood was once located, is now Waterman's Crab House. The property's owners have included the Scoons family, Paul Shirk, Roy Evans, Ernie Coleman, Wayne Brady, Harry Bissell, and Bill Weldon. Hubbard's Pier and Seafood is also pictured. This property was torn down, and Rock Hall Landing Marina is located there today. (Courtesy of H. Edward Beekman Jr.)

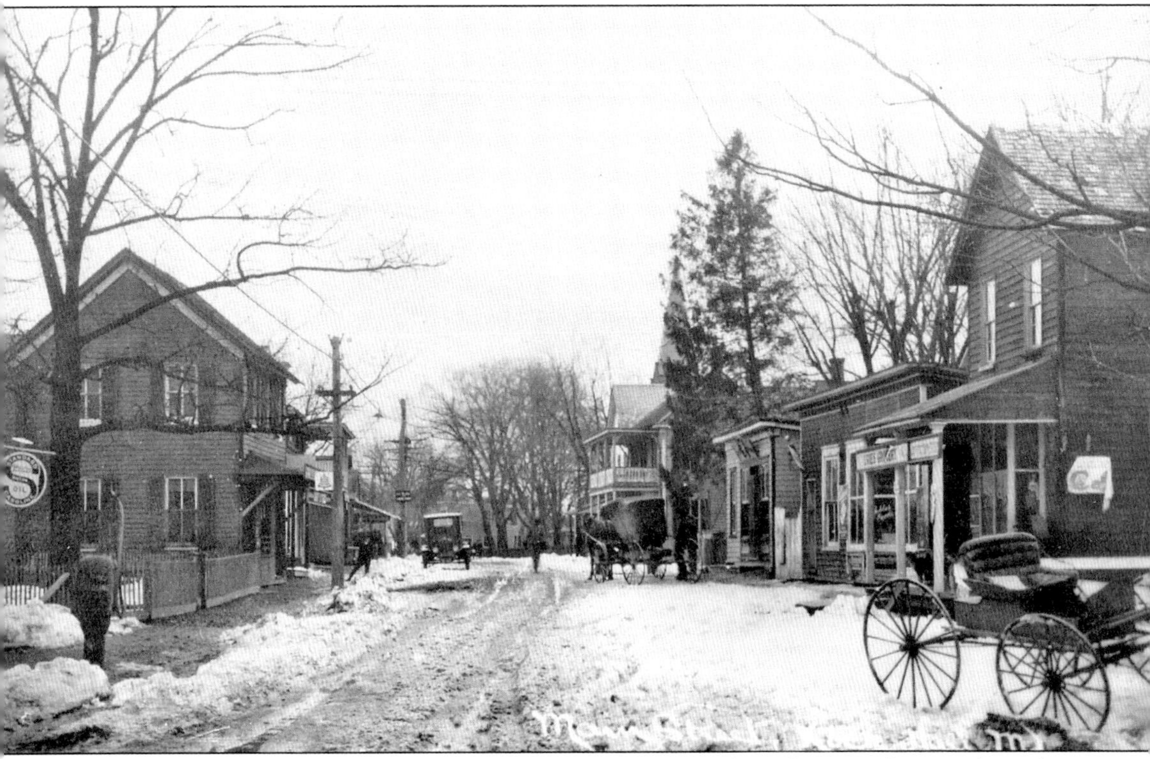

This photograph of Rock Hall's Main Street shows the Rock Hall Post Office on the right, a gasoline and oil business on the left, and Durding's Store just past the post office. The steeple from the Rock Hall Methodist Church can be seen in the background. (Courtesy of Robin Wood Kurowski.)

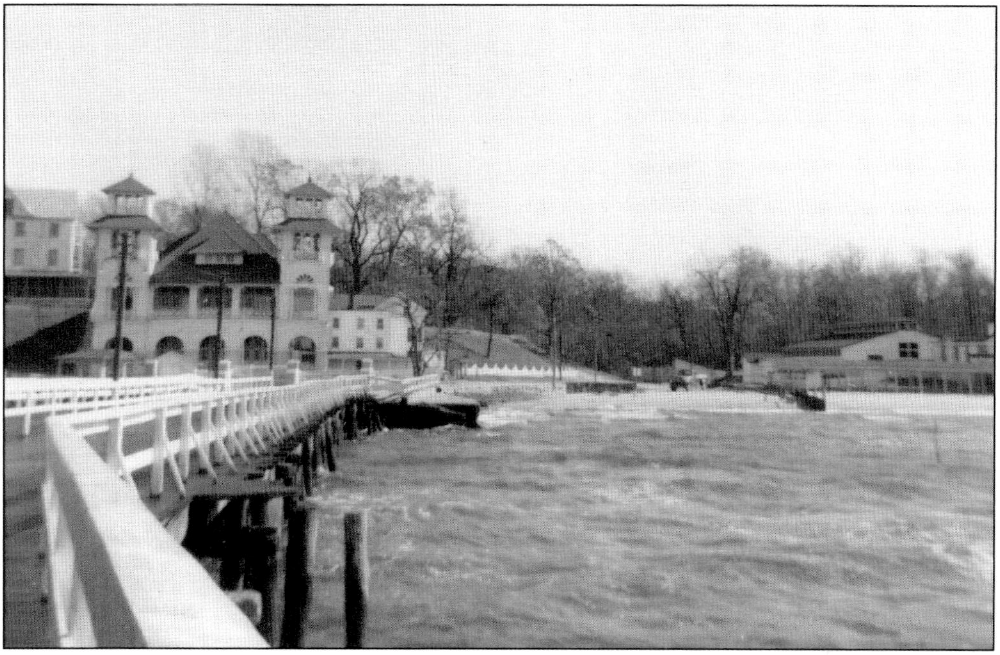

The Tolchester Pier and Tolchester casino building are pictured during the winter months. The closeness of the Tolchester Amusement Park to Rock Hall made it a popular place for church and family picnics, and it provided summer jobs to Rock Hall residents. Many learned to swim at Tolchester Beach on the Chesapeake Bay. (Courtesy of Carroll Thompson.)

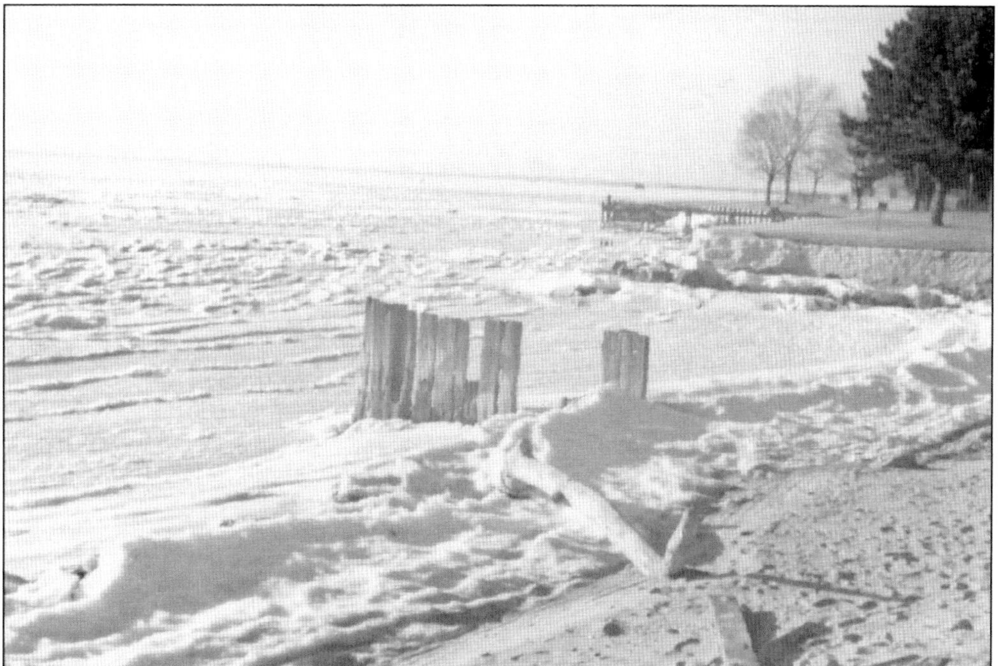

The view from the old Ferry Park Pier located on Beach Road, Rock Hall (now the Rock Hall Public Beach), is pictured during the winter months. This is a popular spot to view sunsets and catch a glimpse of the Chesapeake Bay Bridge. (Courtesy of Madelyn Cornelius.)

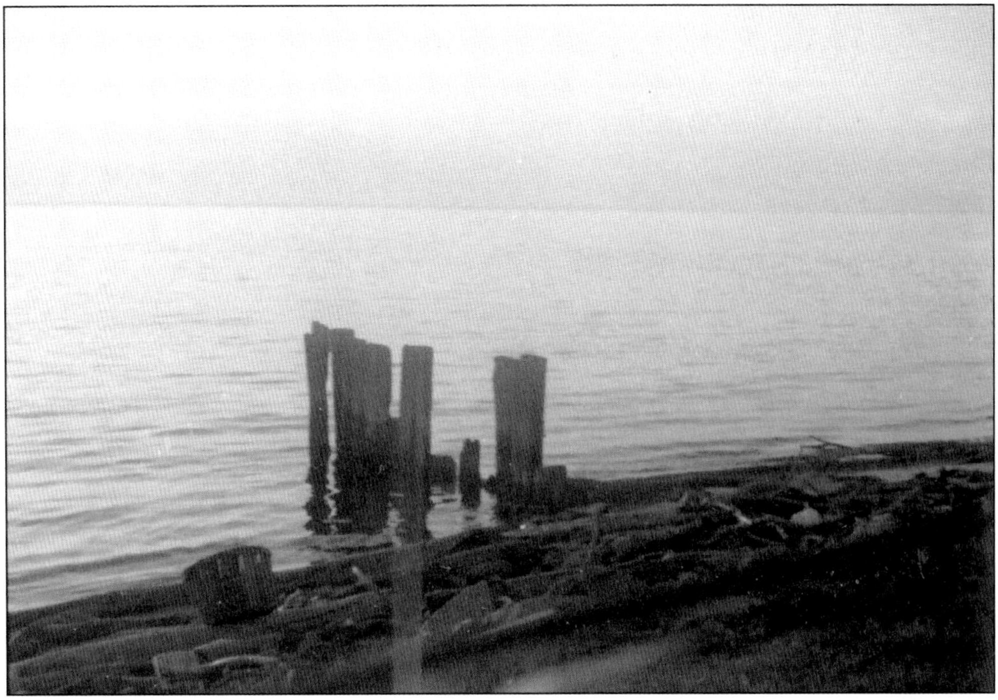

Located on Beach Road, Rock Hall (now the Rock Hall Public Beach), Old Ferry Park Pier is pictured here during the summer months. Those visiting the beach today look forward to a local ice-cream truck stopping by with treats. (Courtesy of Madelyn Cornelius.)

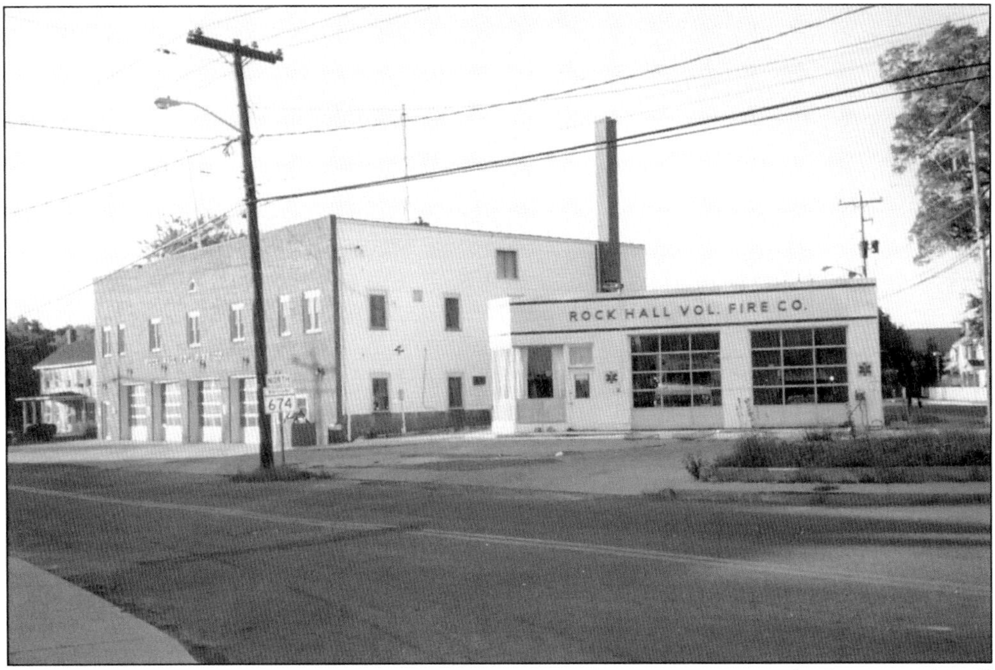

The Rock Hall Fire and Ambulance building is located on Sharp Street next to the former Rock Hall Volunteer Fire Company building and is now the location of Java Rock. A new Rock Hall Volunteer Fire Company building is now located on Route 20. (Courtesy of Madelyn Cornelius.)

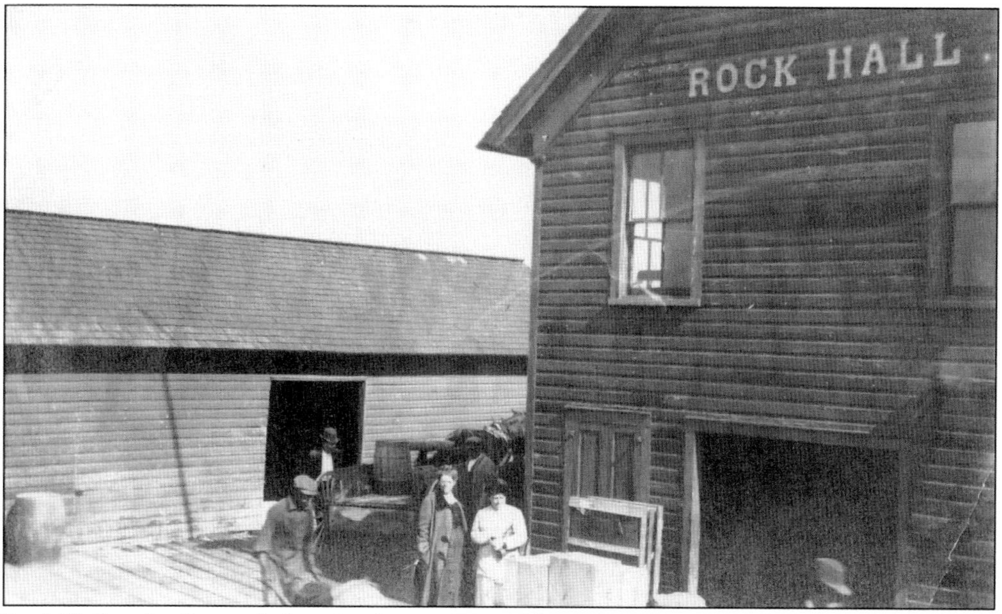

Rock Hall at the Gratitude ferry landing is pictured from the side. Passengers and cargo assembled here while waiting for a steamer such as the *Gratitude*. (Courtesy of H. Edward Beekman Jr.)

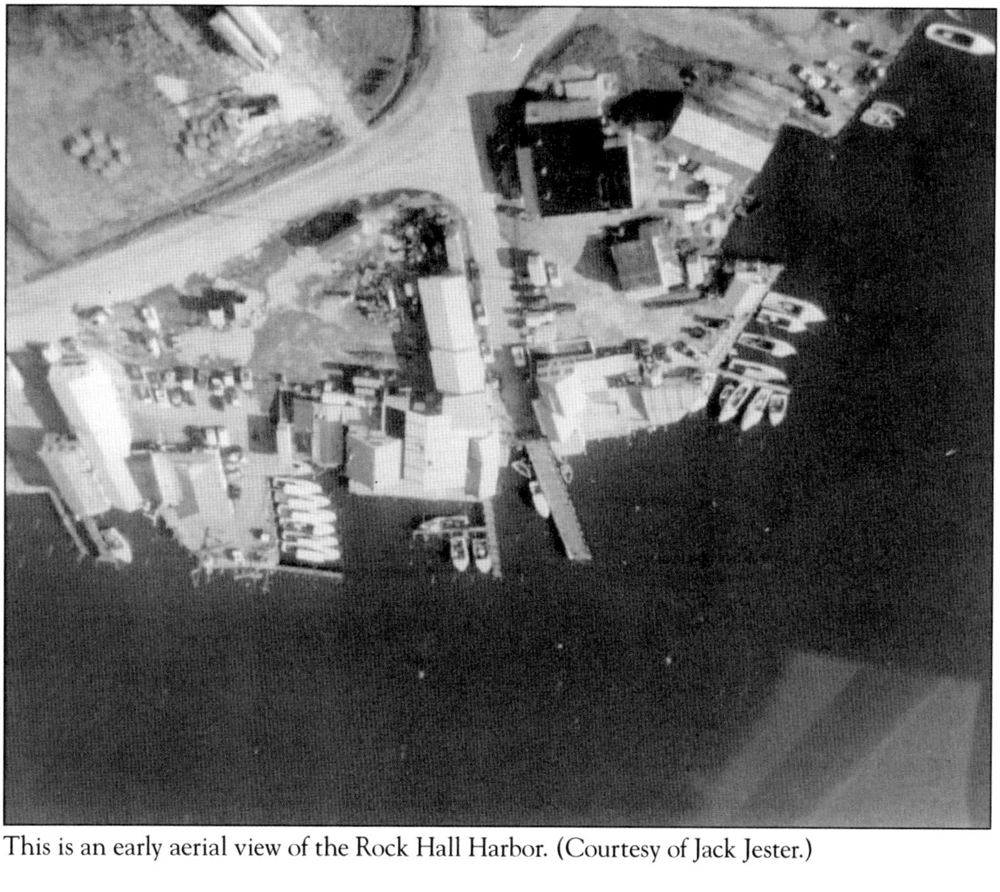

This is an early aerial view of the Rock Hall Harbor. (Courtesy of Jack Jester.)

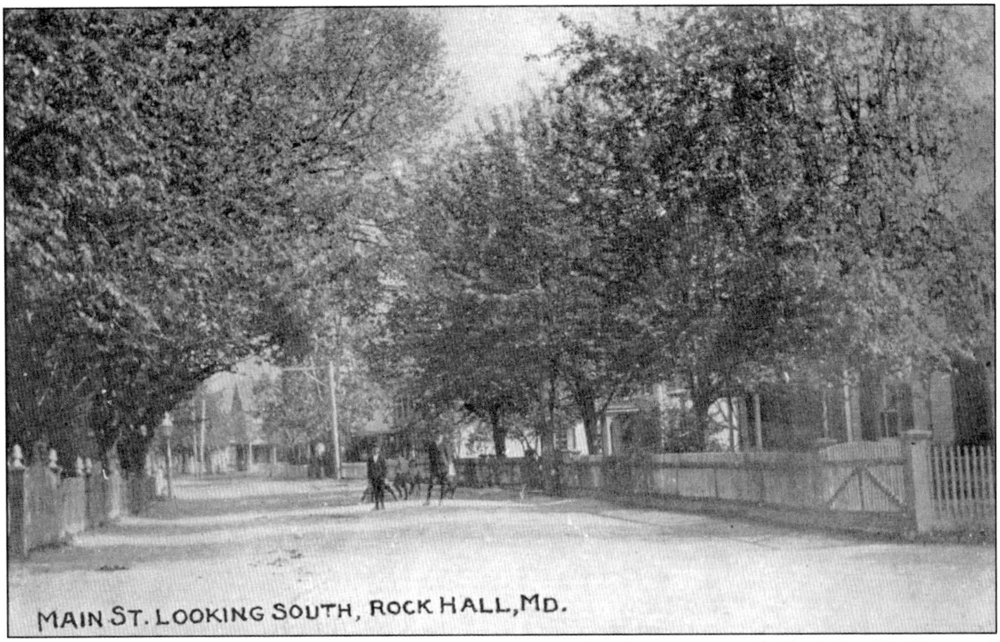

This is a photograph of Main Street looking south. (Courtesy of Ida Mae Dulin and Dorothy McKinney.)

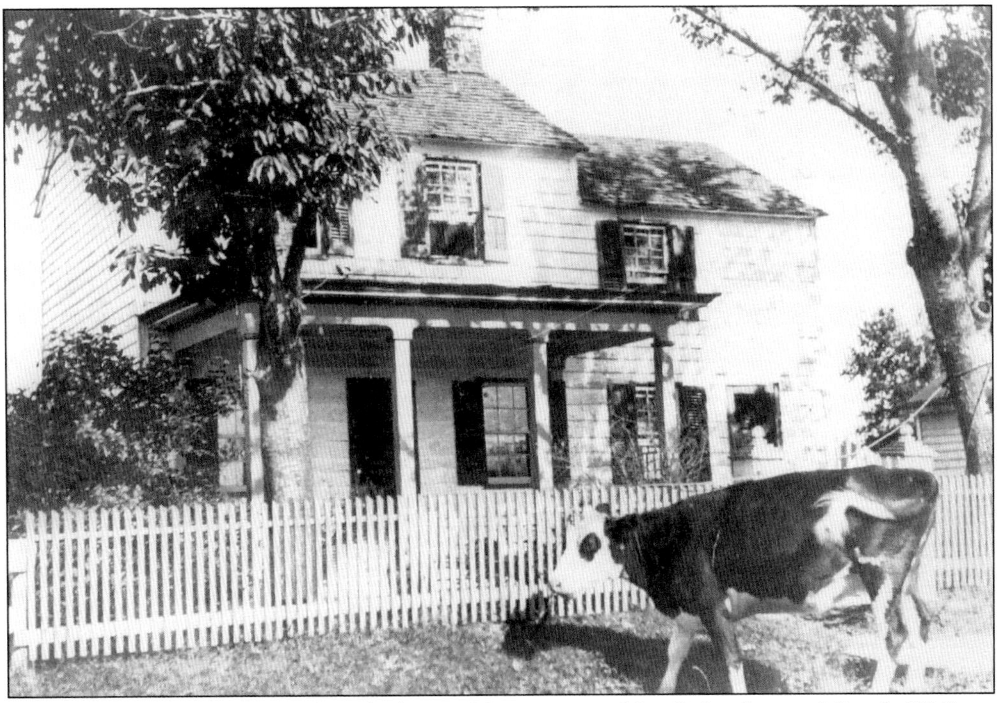

Pictured here around 1895, the Blackiston House, owned by Columbus and Sarah Walbert Blackiston, was located across from the Rock Hall Lumber Company. Columbus Blackiston was a waterman, and his father, John J. Blackiston, was a shoemaker. At one time, this house was a grocery store. The house no longer exists. (Courtesy of Jean Foreman.)

Six

Assorted Images of Rock Hall

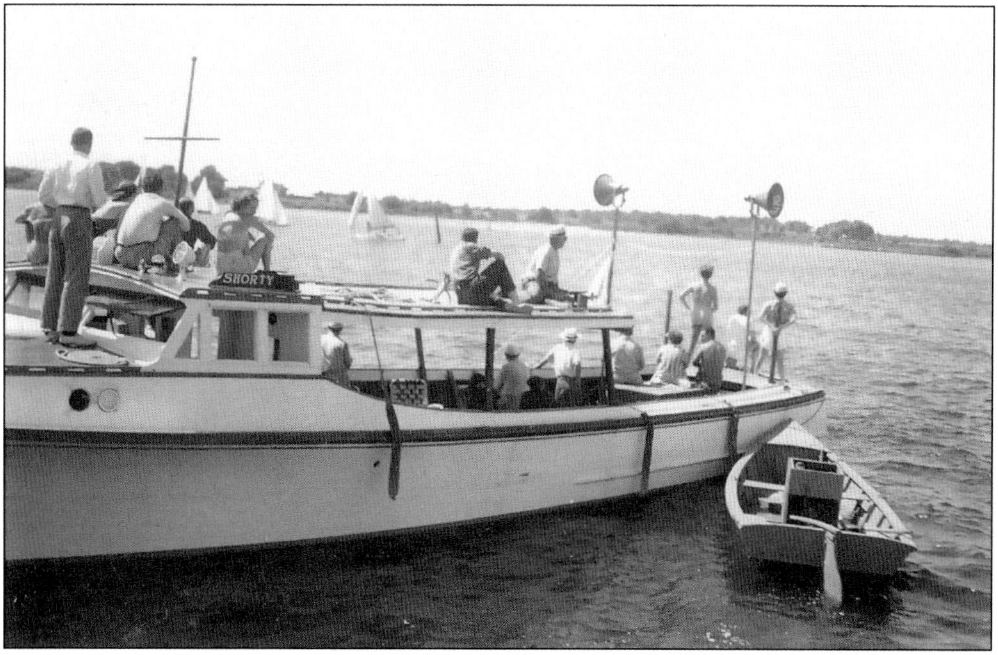

The sailing regatta committee boat, shown with its speakers, monitors the races sponsored by the Rock Hall Yacht Club, which is celebrating its 70th year in 2007. The club was founded and officially accepted into the Chesapeake Bay Yacht Racing Association in October 1937. It hosted the Chesapeake Fishing Fair in 1938, and its first regatta was held in 1938 with 80 entries. In 1950, Miss Maryland, Ann Urie of Rock Hall, presented a Rock Hall Regatta Race trophy to Brian Kane of Chestertown. Over the years, many types of events, including skeet-shooting tournaments, have taken place at the Rock Hall Yacht Club. (Courtesy of Honey Wood.)

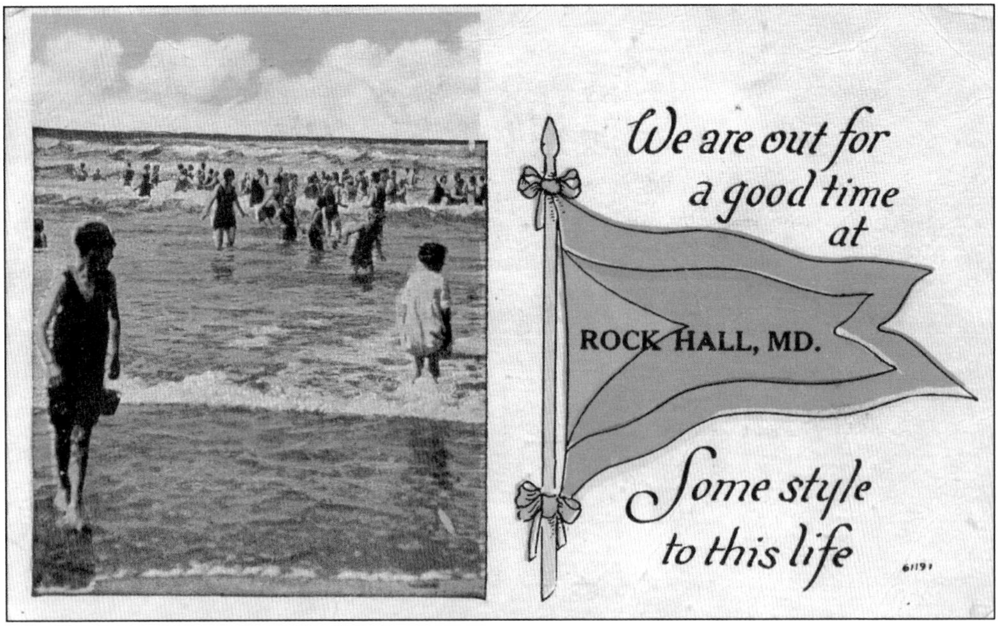

This Rock Hall postcard still holds true to this day. (Courtesy of Robin Wood Kurowski.)

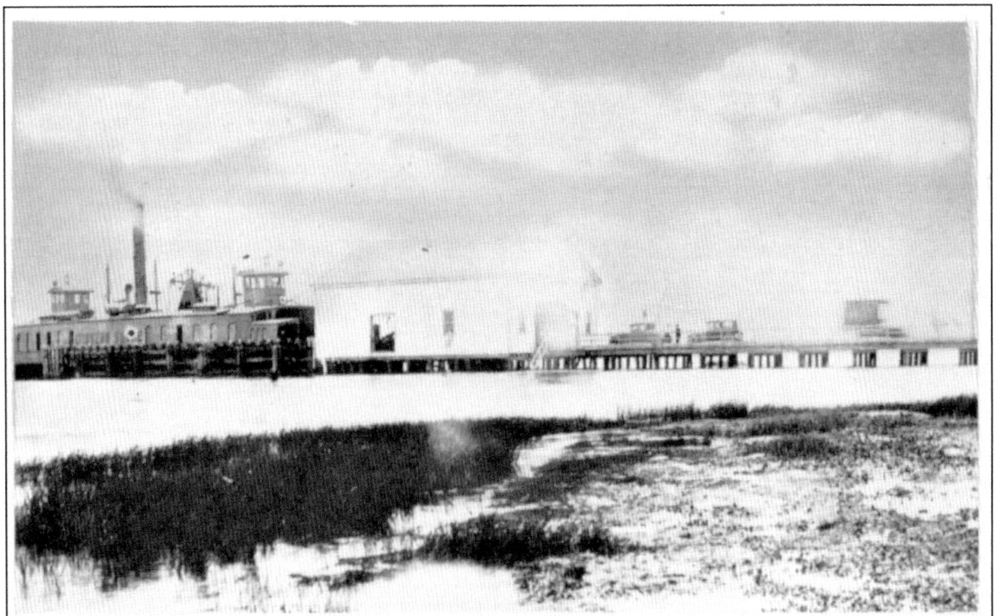

The Eastern Shore Ferry at Rock Hall provides a view to the past in terms of transportation and bustling trade. Passengers, produce, and seafood were all transported. Before the rail and better road systems, ferry boats and their management companies were essential to travel and shipping on the Chesapeake Bay and its rivers. (Courtesy of Ida Mae Dullin and Dorothy McKenney.)

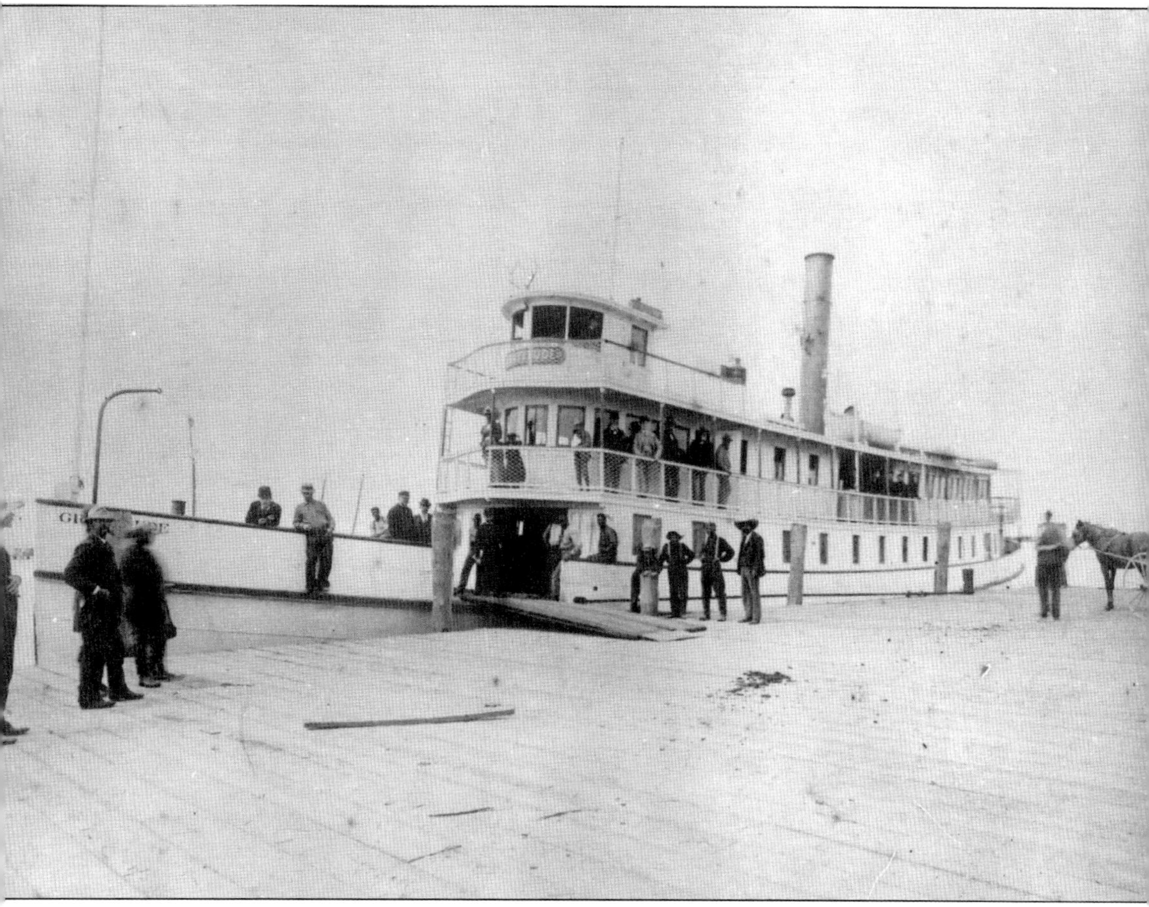

The steamer *Grattitude* (*Gratitude*) is pictured in midwinter at Rock Hall. The SS *Gratitude* was built in 1880 in Philadelphia and ran there until sold and renamed *Captain Miller* in 1882 for New Orleans–Pensacola and Chester River routes. After burning, she was reconstructed and again renamed *Gratitude*, running from Baltimore to Rock Hall and on the Chester River until 1914, when she sank in a collision in Eastern Bay. After repair, she was sold and then acquired by the U.S. Navy in 1918 for a year's service in Virginia under the name USS *Gratitude*. She was returned in 1919 and served in Virginia until 1926, when she was purchased, taken to Cuba (possibly Havana), and renamed *Cuba*. The section of Rock Hall referred to as Gratitude received its name from this special steamship and its landing. (Courtesy of Robin Wood Kurowski.)

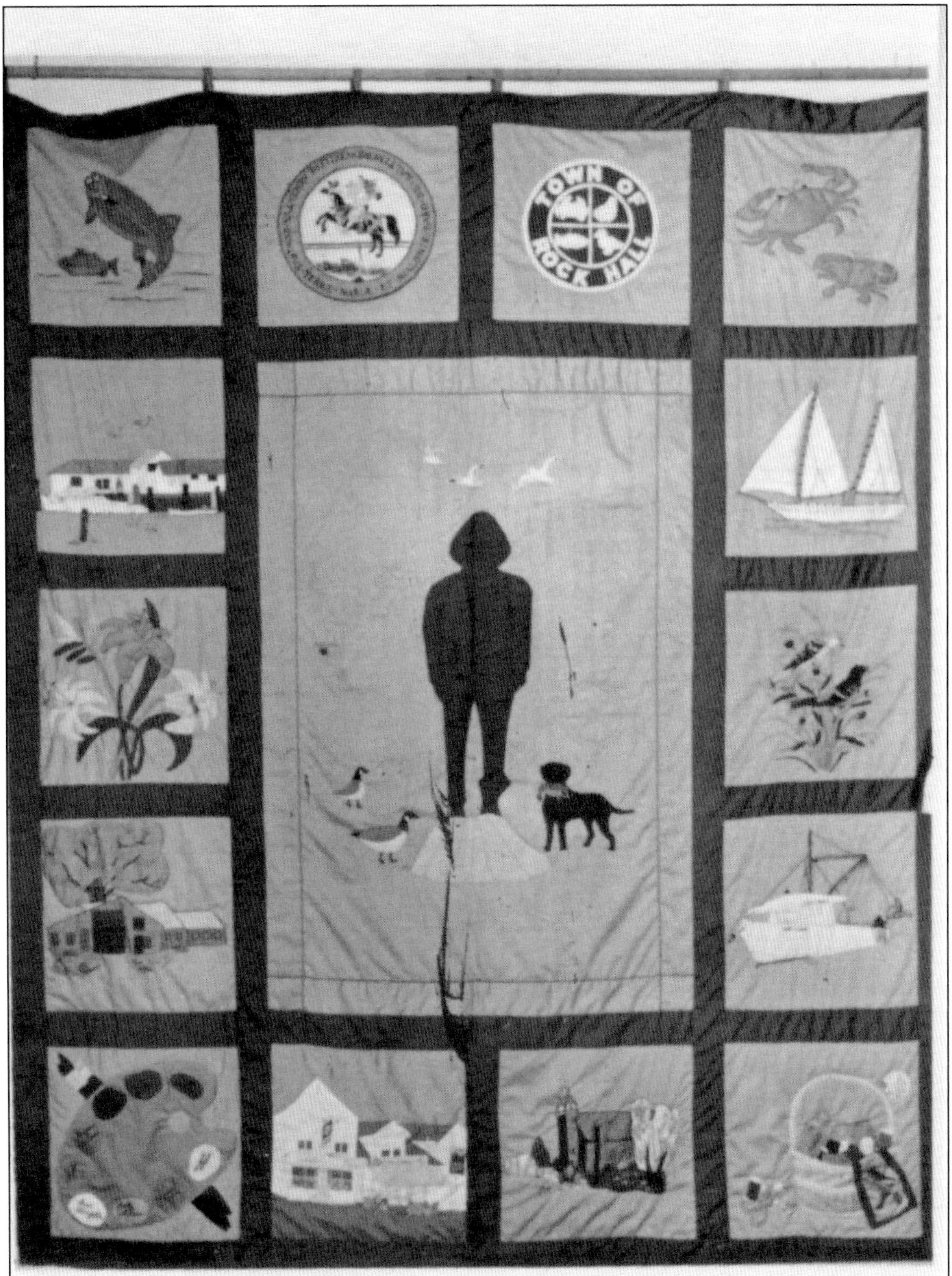

The Friendly Crafters of Rock Hall created a Rock Hall Heritage Quilt in 1982. Resident artists submitted sketches for the quilt that most symbolized Rock Hall. The artistry and crafting of quilts has long been practiced and is part of the Rock Hall heritage in Kent County. The Rock Hall Heritage Quilt is on display at the Rock Hall Museum and Municipal Building. (Courtesy of Dorothy McKenney.)

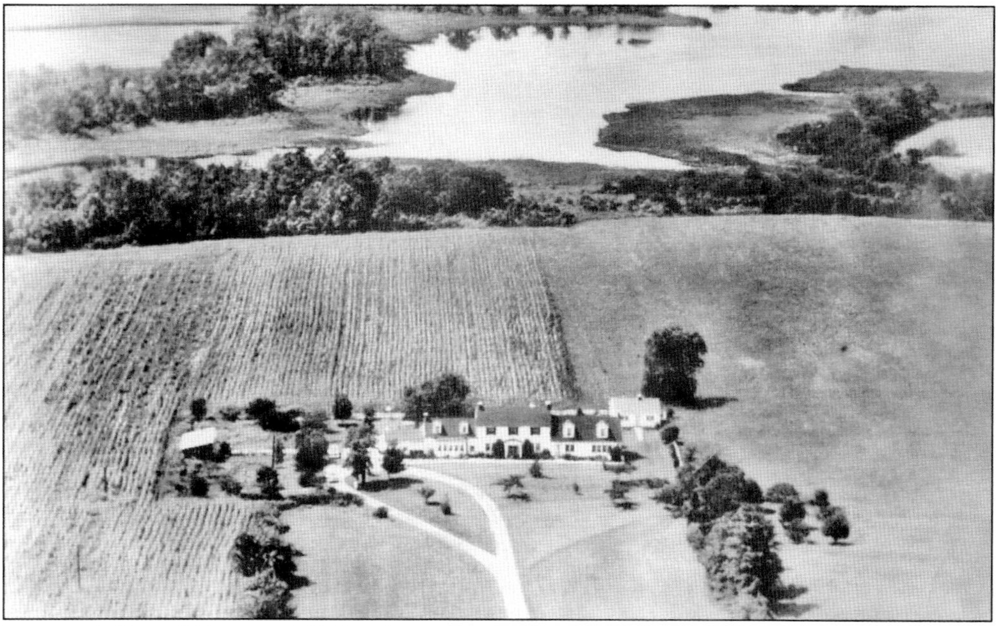

Huntingfield and Huntingfield Creek are pictured in 1966. Native Americans were the first to live at this land. It truly must have been a hunting ground, as many Native American weapons are found here. A patent of 1,200 acres was granted to Col. Thomas Ringgold by Lord Baltimore on January 4, 1659. The land has been farmed and hunted. It was known at one point as Feather Dusters when it served as a gunning club. It was renovated to operate as a bed and breakfast by the Starken family. It is still operated as such today by Jim and Joanne Rich. (Courtesy of Jim and Joanne Rich.)

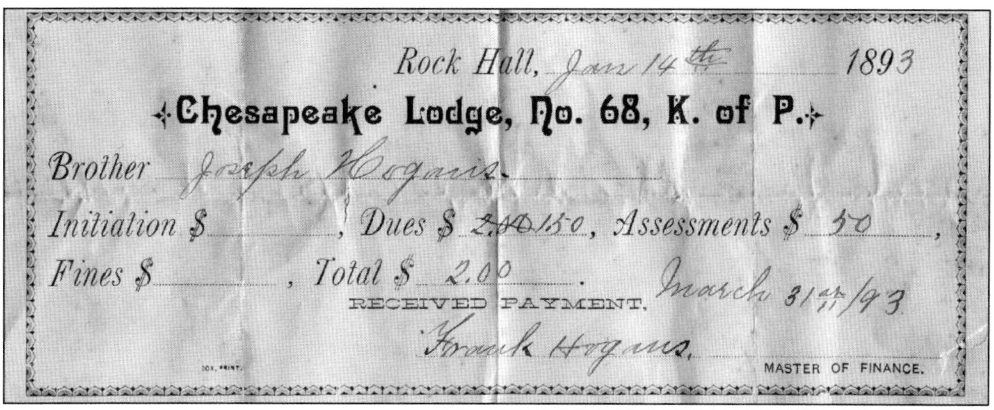

Rock Hall, Jan 14th 1893

Chesapeake Lodge, No. 68, K. of P.

Brother Joseph Hogans

Initiation $, Dues $ 1.50, Assessments $ .50,

Fines $, Total $ 2.00.

RECEIVED PAYMENT, March 31st/93

Frank Hogans, MASTER OF FINANCE.

"Brother" Joseph Hogans pays his dues to Chesapeake Lodge No. 68, Knights of Pythias, Rock Hall, in 1893. Frank Hogans was the master of finance. (Courtesy of H. Edward Beekman Jr.)

NOTED FOR FINE FISHING

ARRANGEMENTS FOR

Fishing Guides and Parties

ROOMS MEALS DANCING

ALL MODERN CONVENIENCES

History Of The

Mansion House

Overlooking Chesapeake Bay at the mouth of the Chester River, The Mansion House was constructed in 1884 by Dr. A. P. Sharp, of Baltimore, on the site of the original building which was known as "Rock Hall". This structure, according to tradition, was so named because it stood on a ledge of rock. And, as the town grew up around it, the name was given to the surrounding community. The original house was known by travelers in colonial times as a place of rest and relaxation while waiting for the packet.

DAY AND NIGHT SERVICE

Capt. Eldridge M. Glenn

PHONE 75

EASTERN SHORE DINNERS, SEAFOODS A SPECIALTY

This was an advertisement for Capt. Eldridge Glenn's guide and party services. Note the description of the history of the Mansion House. It indicates the Rock Hall received its name from a ledge of rock. There are three popular name theories: that Rock Hall received its name from a ledge of rock; that Rock Hall was named after a famous estate in England; and that Rock Hall was named for its popular rockfishing or rock hauling. (Courtesy of Jack Jester.)

Pictured here are Mildred Thomas (left) and Florence "Shug" Parsons Thomas (right). This was a barge located at Capt. Joseph Hynson's home. Captain Hynson also owned a buy boat. (Courtesy of H. Edward Beekman Jr.)

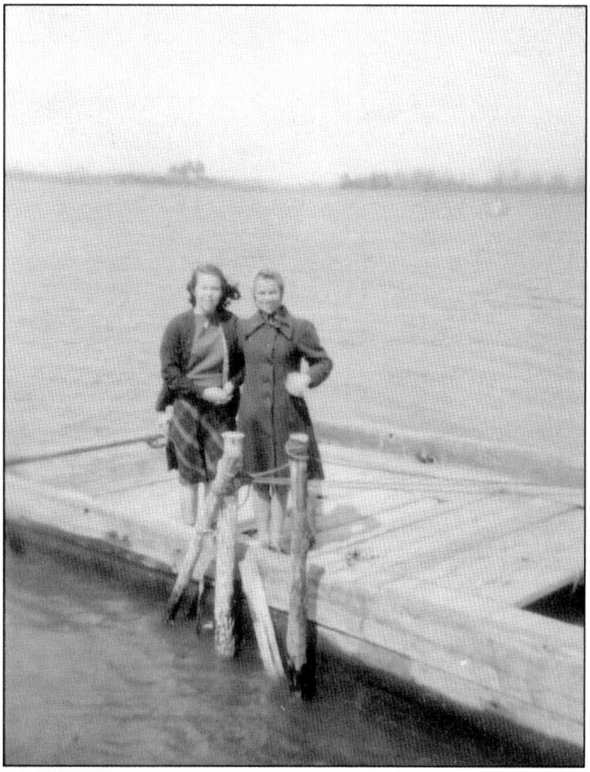

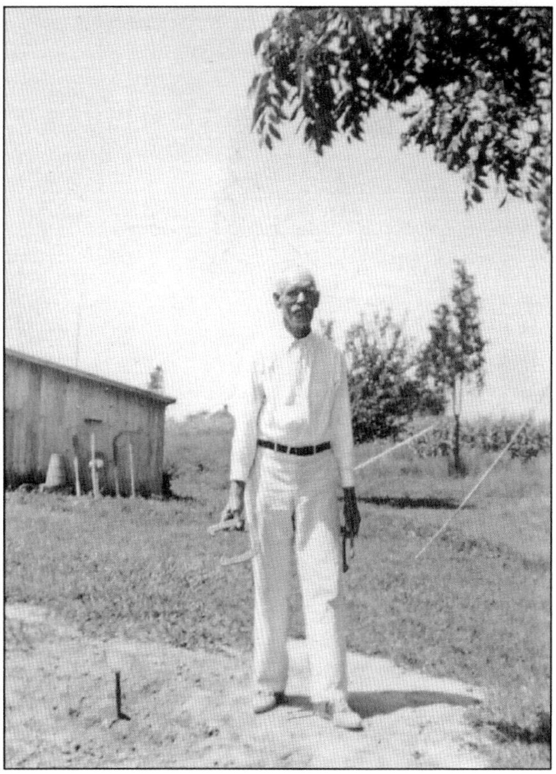

Joseph Hogans enjoys playing horseshoes at his home on Haven Road in Rock Hall. (Courtesy of H. Edward Beekman Jr.)

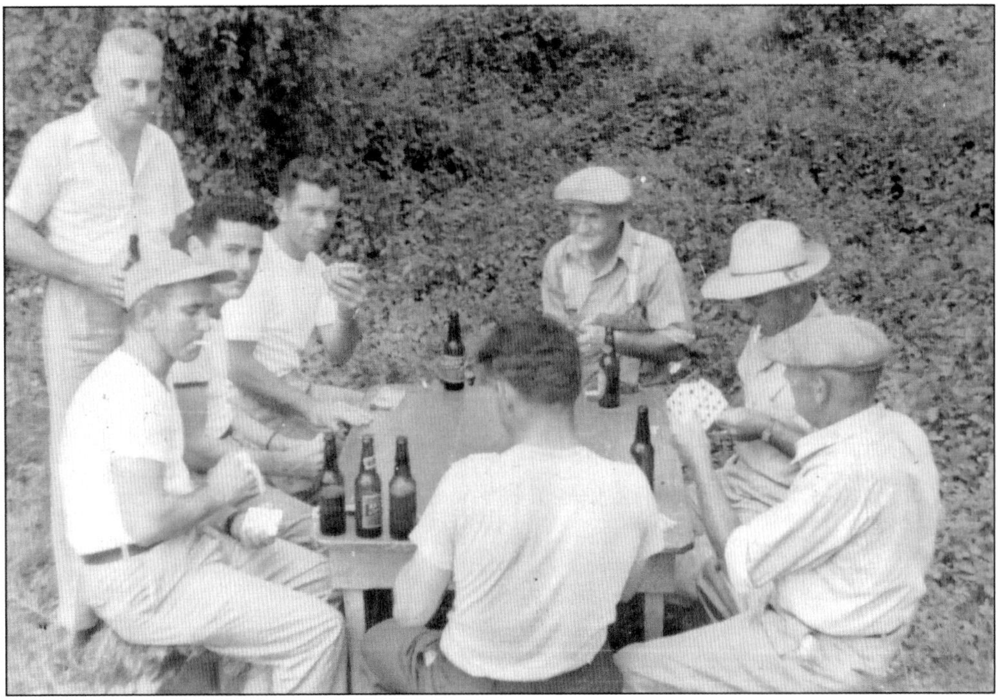

Playing card games such as pitch and poker has always been a favorite pastime of residents in Rock Hall. Horseshoe matches are another favorite activity. Among those pictured are Frank Jester (standing), Ernest Hepbron (third from left), and Medford Carr (with white cap). (Courtesy of H. Edward Beekman Jr.)

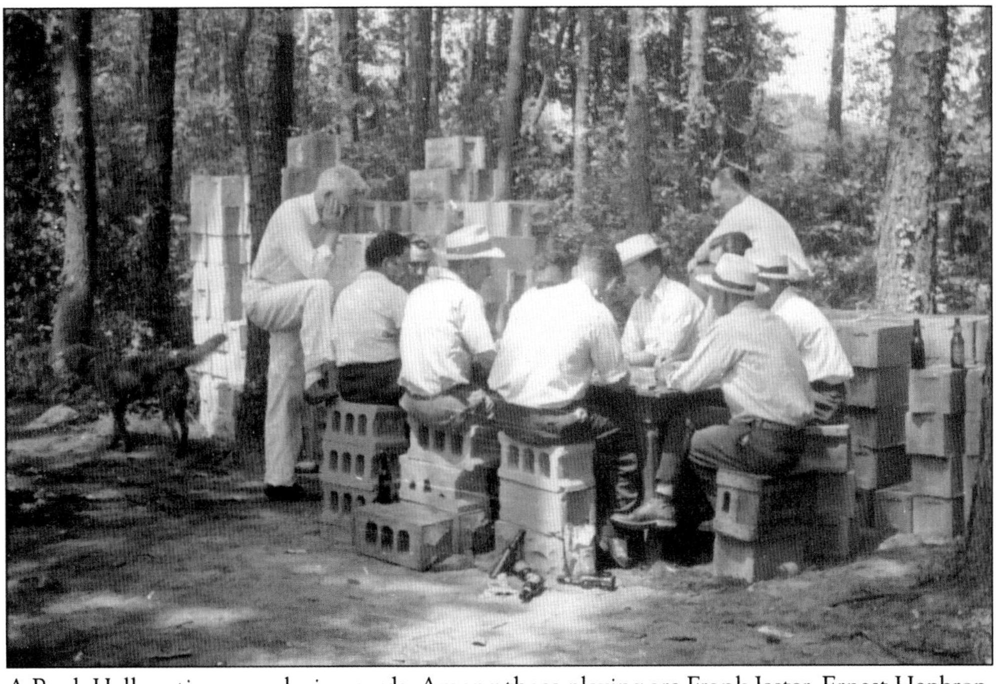

A Rock Hall pastime was playing cards. Among those playing are Frank Jester, Ernest Hepbron, Doc Smith, and Melvin "Trigger" Collier. (Courtesy of H. Edward Beekman Jr.)

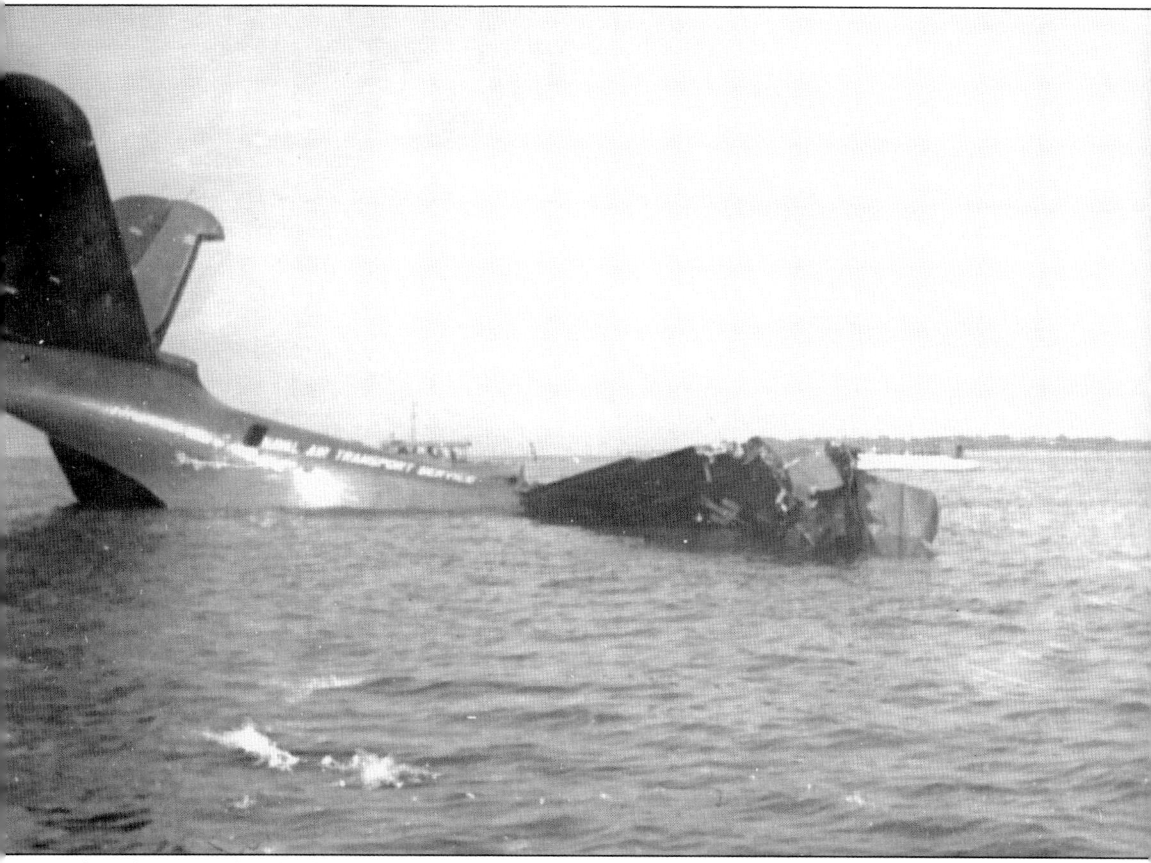

This plane is said to be the *Hawaii Mars*, which was still undergoing tests at the Glenn L. Martin Aircraft Company in Baltimore when she sank in the Chesapeake Bay off Swan Point and Gratitude near Rock Hall after a rough landing ripped her hull in early August 1945. She was fished out of the bay and returned to the Martin plant. The plane was the first of 20 supercargo carriers built for the navy, she it had not yet been commissioned. Glenn L. Martin owned the lands known as Broadnox, later purchased by the Remington-DuPont Group. (Courtesy of H. Edward Beekman Jr.)

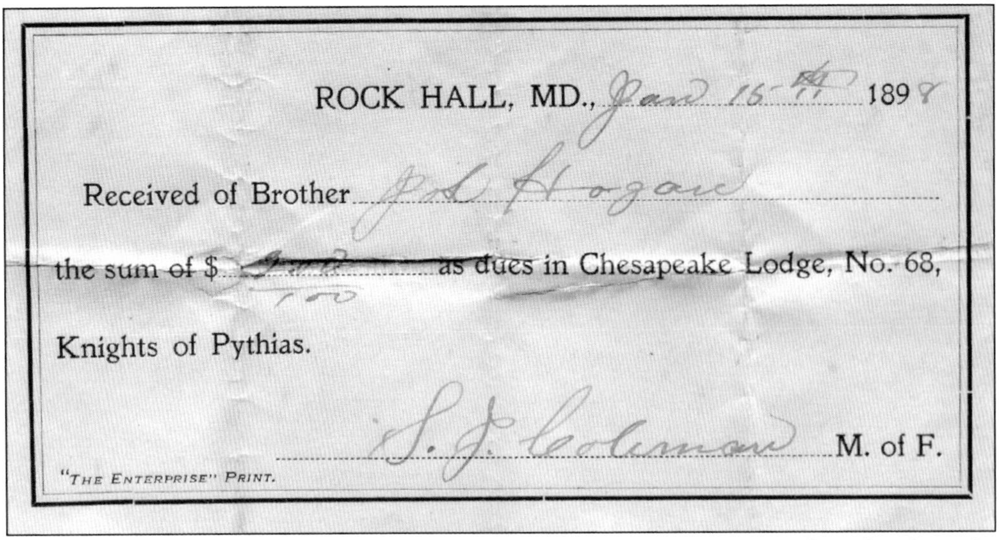
ROCK HALL, MD., Jan 15th 1898

Received of Brother J. L. Hogan

the sum of $ 1.00 as dues in Chesapeake Lodge, No. 68,

Knights of Pythias.

S. J. Coleman M. of F.

"THE ENTERPRISE" PRINT.

Pictured is a membership dues receipt from Chesapeake Lodge No. 68, Knights of Pythias, for dues paid by "Brother" Joseph Hogans in January 1898. (Courtesy of H. Edward Beekman Jr.)

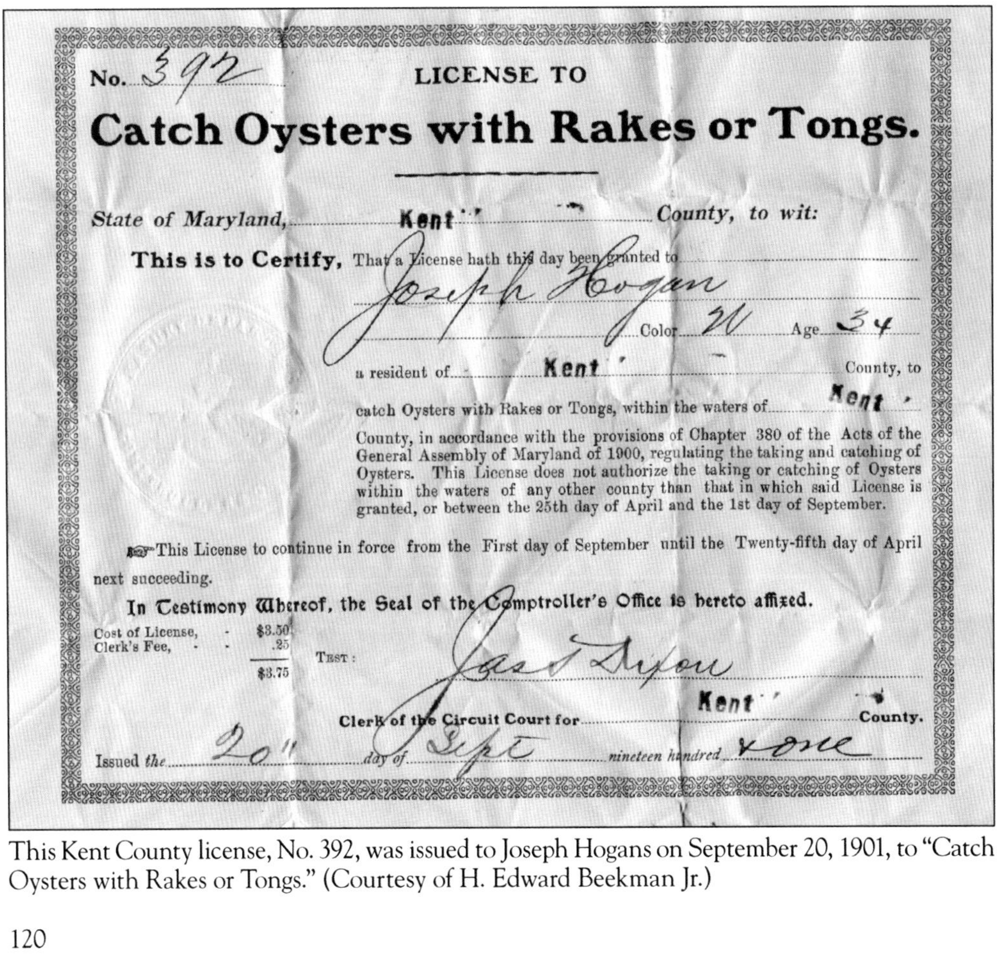
No. 392 LICENSE TO

Catch Oysters with Rakes or Tongs.

State of Maryland, Kent *County, to wit:*

This is to Certify, That a License hath this day been granted to Joseph Hogan Color W Age 34

a resident of Kent County, to catch Oysters with Rakes or Tongs, within the waters of Kent County, in accordance with the provisions of Chapter 380 of the Acts of the General Assembly of Maryland of 1900, regulating the taking and catching of Oysters. This License does not authorize the taking or catching of Oysters within the waters of any other county than that in which said License is granted, or between the 25th day of April and the 1st day of September.

This License to continue in force from the First day of September until the Twenty-fifth day of April next succeeding.

In Testimony Whereof, the Seal of the Comptroller's Office is hereto affixed.

Cost of License,	$3.50
Clerk's Fee,	.25
	$3.75

TEST: Jas T Dixon

Clerk of the Circuit Court for Kent County.

Issued the 20th day of Sept nineteen hundred & one

This Kent County license, No. 392, was issued to Joseph Hogans on September 20, 1901, to "Catch Oysters with Rakes or Tongs." (Courtesy of H. Edward Beekman Jr.)

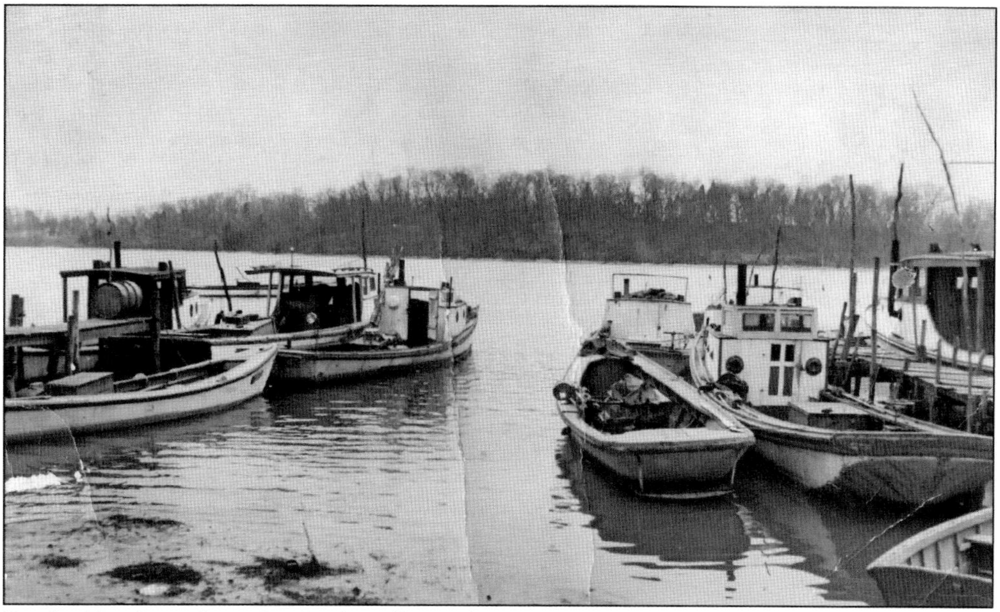

Boatbuilders have thrived in Rock Hall over the years, building both small and large working and pleasure vessels. The names Stevens, Creighton, Bryden, Vansant, White, Deckelman, DuVall, and Coleman are all synonymous with Rock Hall boatbuilding. (Courtesy of Jack Jester.)

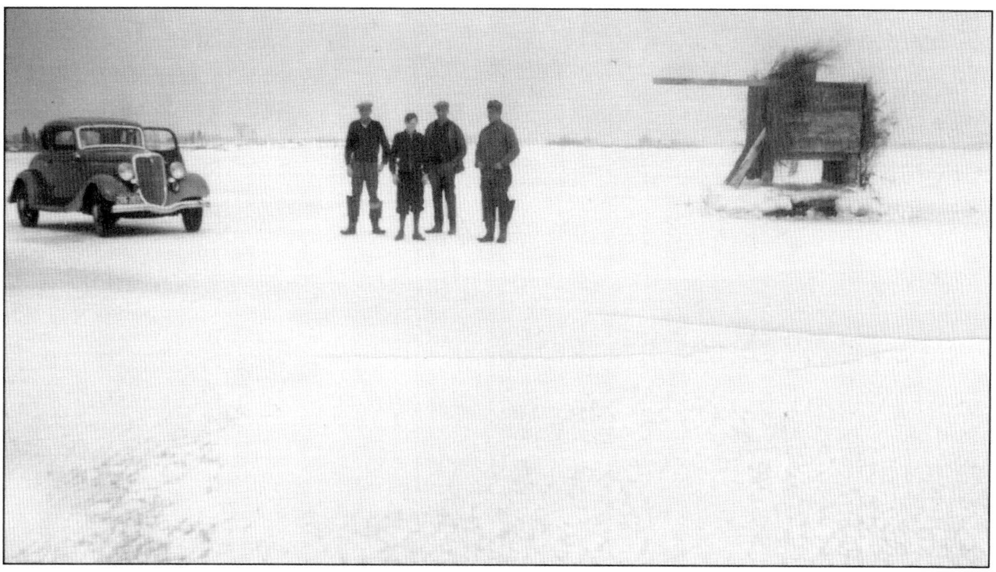

Hunting on the ice was common during big freezes. Some remember the ice being so hard and thick that iceboats, horses, wagons, and cars could be driven on it. The ice also provided an opportunity to enjoy iceboat racing. There are tales of some driving and racing iceboats from Rock Hall, around Eastern Neck Island, and up the Chester River. (Courtesy of Jane and Carroll Thompson.)

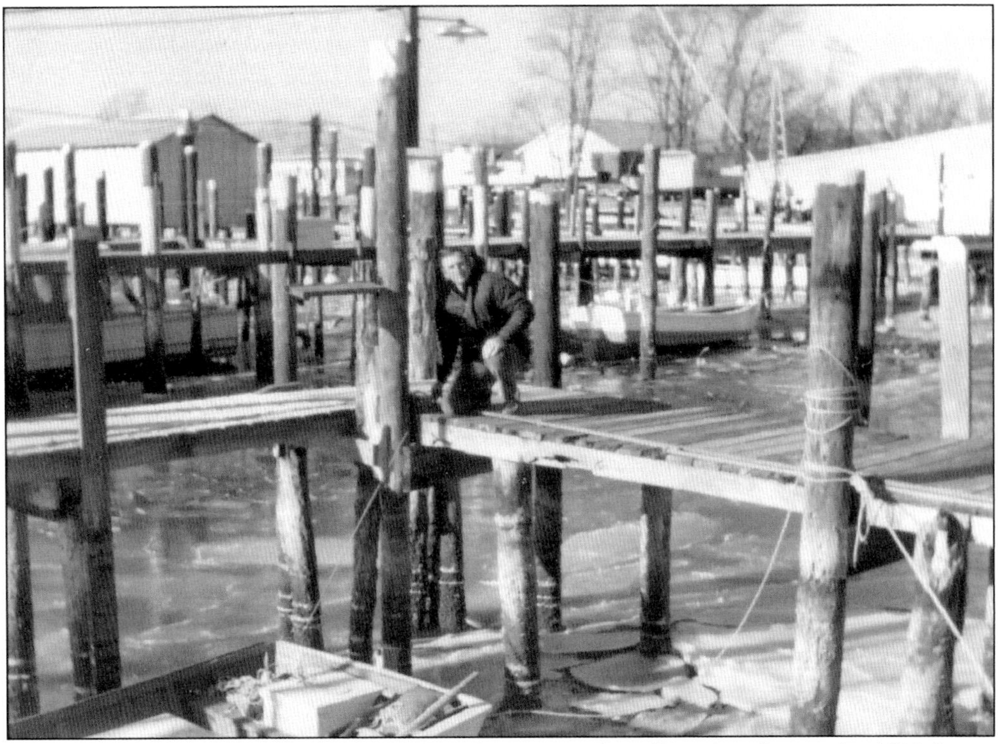

This photograph shows the ice around the pilings at Rock Hall Harbor during the 1982 freeze. (Courtesy of Jerry Creighton.)

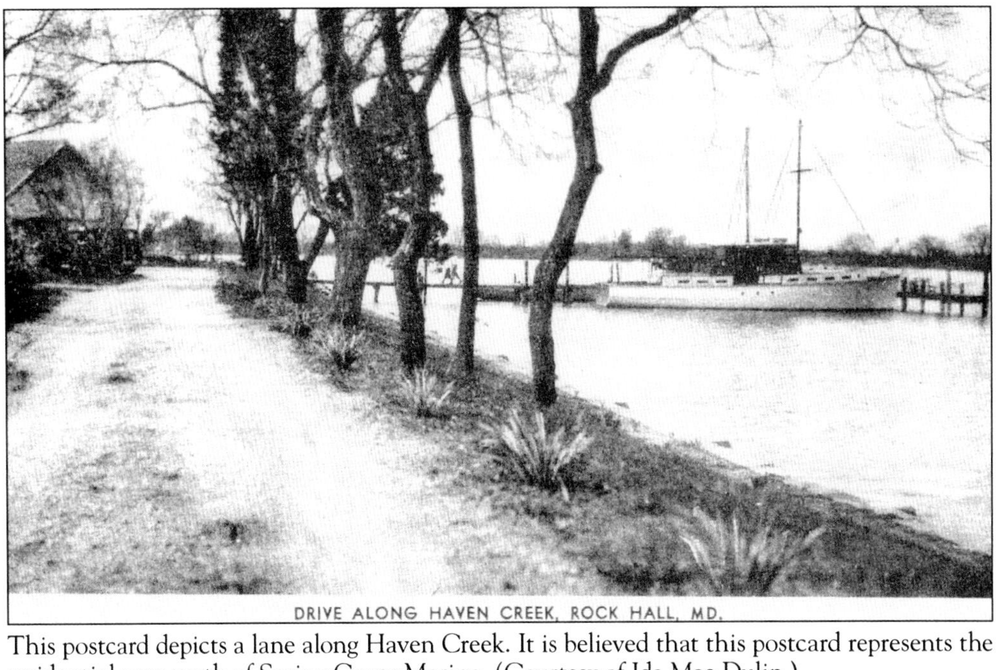

This postcard depicts a lane along Haven Creek. It is believed that this postcard represents the residential area south of Spring Cover Marina. (Courtesy of Ida Mae Dulin.)

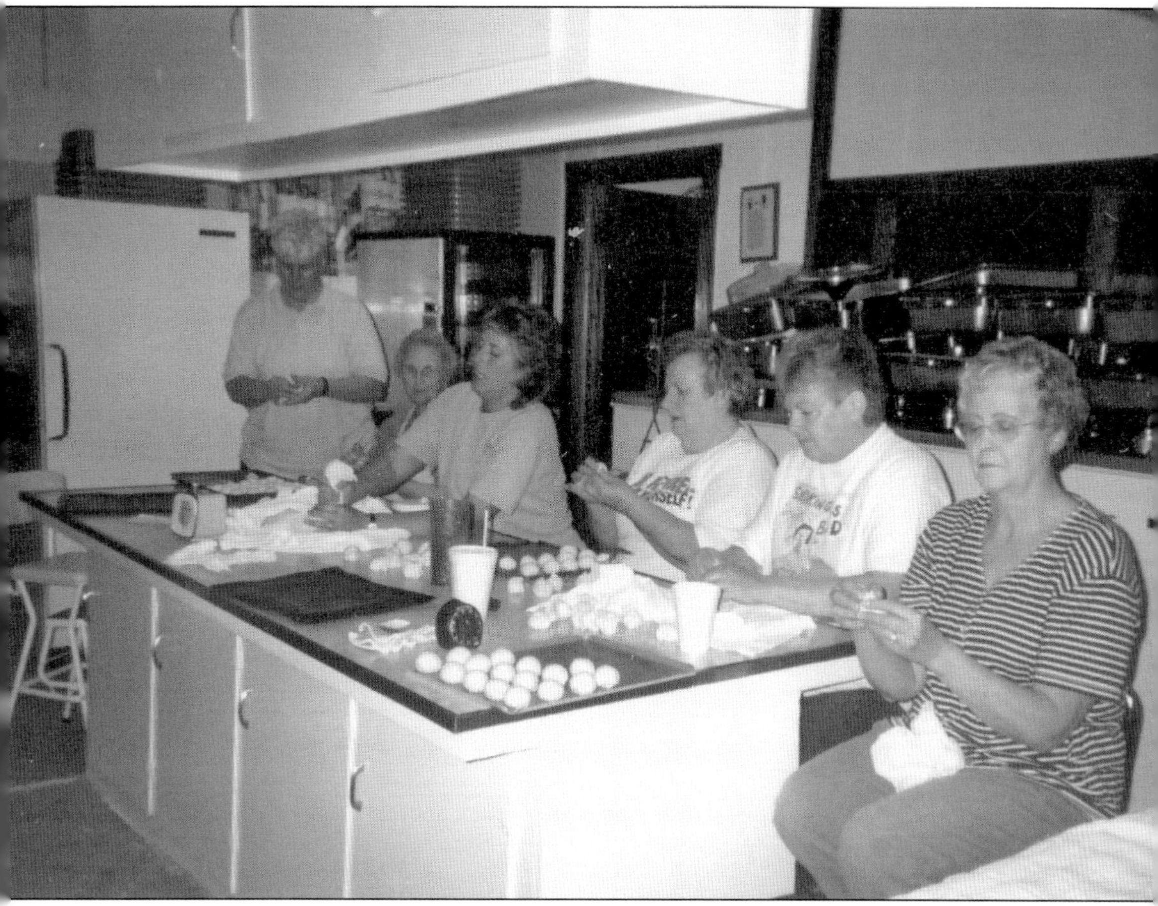

The Ladies Auxiliary of the Rock Hall Volunteer Fire Company (RHVFC) gathers to make their famous Eastern Shore beaten biscuits for a dinner at the old fire hall kitchen on Sharp Street. Shortly after the company was formed in 1927, the auxiliary was created. Many descendants of the original auxiliary are in the present group and serve in the kitchen at the new facility. The RHVFC dates back to 1927, when it was officially incorporated. The first directors included Fred Williams, Harry R. Price, Leonard Rich, William C. Frances, Theodore J. Thompson, G. Cecil Crouch, Joseph B. Davis, Adolph Keller, Max Alexander, Walter R. Rodney, John R. Dowling, J. Robert Lewis, and Thomas A. Tucker. Pictured making the biscuits from left to right are Carolyn Jones, Rose Elma Cornelius, Kelly Ruewer, Ethel Toulson, Madelyn Cornelius, and Jennie Rodney. (Courtesy of Madelyn Cornelius.)

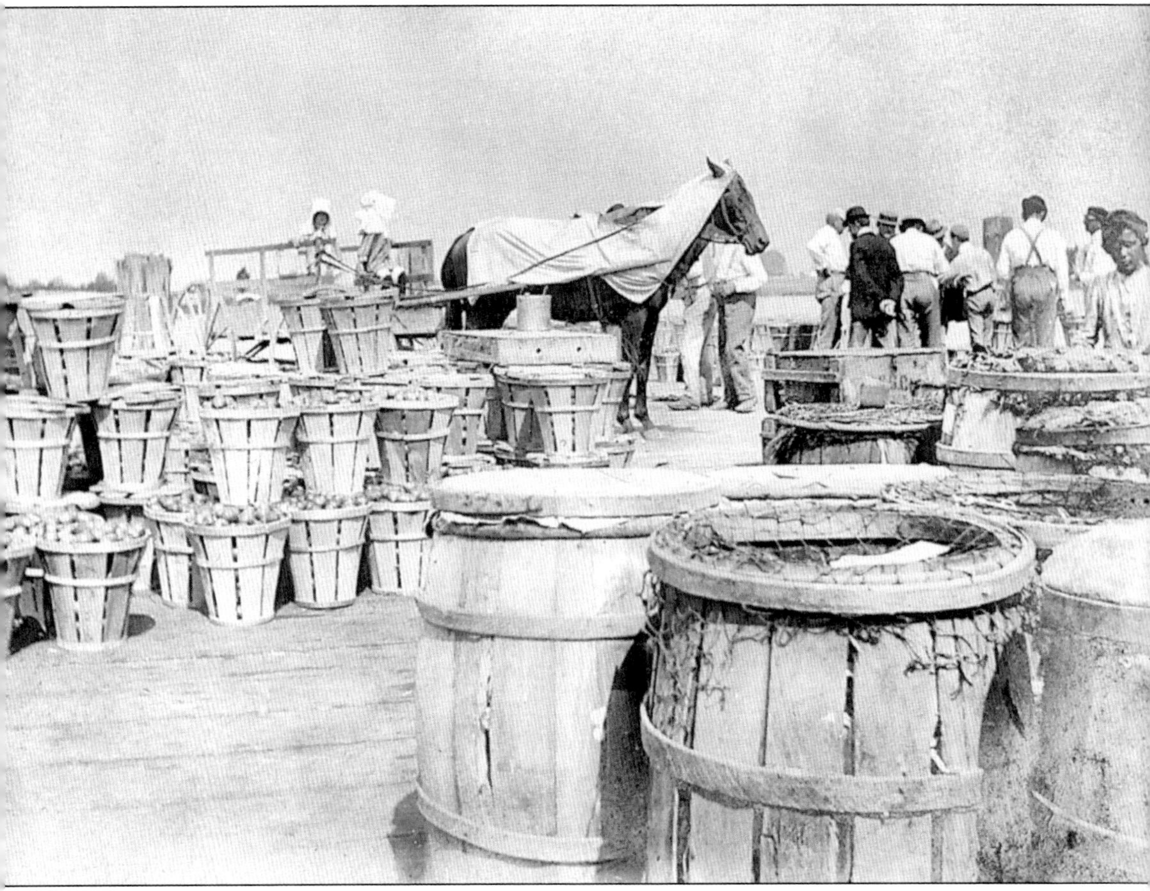

The many granges of Kent County, as well the watermen, depended on the bay to ship their goods to the markets in Baltimore and Philadelphia. The wharf at Rock Hall was the center of shipping for the southern part of Kent County during the 19th and early 20th centuries. Pictured here is a typical day on the wharf at Rock Hall. Note all the tomatoes in the baskets and the seafood, most likely crab, in the barrels. (Courtesy of Patricia Joan O. Horsey.)

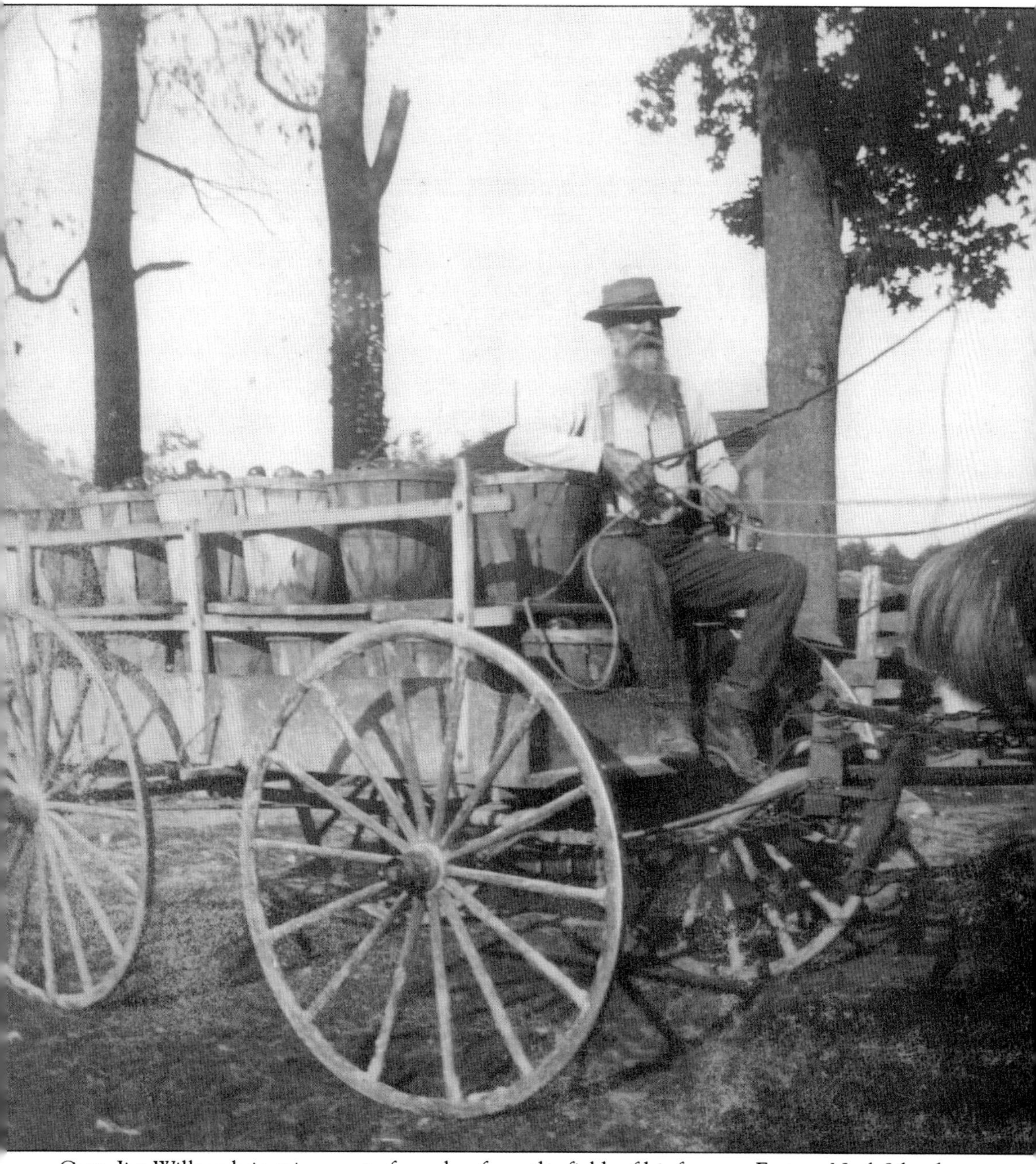

Capt. Jim Willson brings in a cart of peaches from the fields of his farm on Eastern Neck Island. This photograph was taken in the 1800s. The Willson family had 13 children who helped work the farm. Jim's daughter Mary Willson became a schoolteacher on the island and would later marry Franklin Wood. They had a son, Cordray Wood, and they farmed at Spencer Hall, the location of the Wildlife Refuge office on Eastern Neck Island. (Courtesy of Robin Wood Kurowski.)

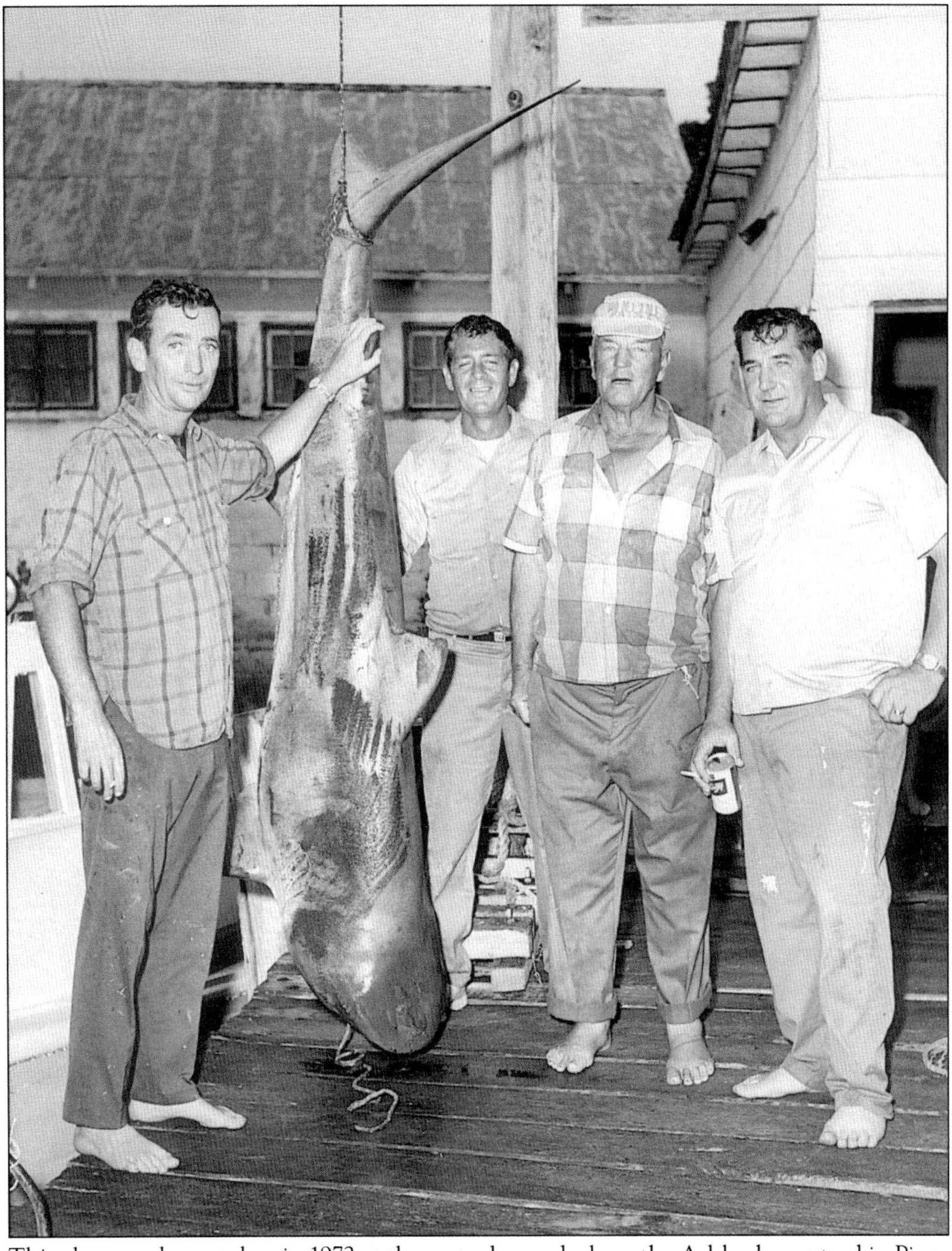

This photograph was taken in 1972 at the oyster house dock on the Ashley homestead in Piney Neck, where the family business, C. H. Ashley and Son Oyster and Crab Packers, was located. Pictured from left to right are Charles "Nails" Ashley Sr., Steven Elburn, Capt. Avery Ashley, and Ernie "Jarbo" Coleman. The shark was reportedly caught in Bluff Hollow on the Chester River. (Courtesy of Maria Ashley Coakley.)

Bibliography

Bourne, Michael Owen. *Historic Houses of Kent County: An Architectural History 1642–1860.* Chestertown, MD: Historical Society of Kent County, Inc., 1998.

Burgess, Robert H., and Graham H. Wood. *Steamboats Out of Baltimore.* Cambridge and Easton: Tidewater Publishers, 1968.

An Illustrated Atlas of Kent and Queen Anne Counties, Maryland. Philadelphia: Lake, Griffing, and Stevenson, 1877.

Johnson, Robert J. *Gravesend, Serene but Still Profound.* Published for the American Revolution Bicentennial Committee of Rock Hall, 1975.

Kent County Bicentennial Committee. *Kent County Guide.* Second printing. Chestertown, MD: Kent County Bicentennial Committee, 1977.

Kent County News. *Tales of Kent County, Volume I.* Chestertown, MD: Kent County News, 2006.

Okonowicz, Ed. *Disappearing Delmarva: Portraits of the Peninsula People.* Elkton, MD: Myst and Lace Publishers, Inc., 1998.

Rock Hall Historical Collection '57. Rock Hall: Rock Hall Commemoration, Inc., 1957.